NEW YORK
IN THE AGE
OF THE
CONSTITUTION

NEW YORK IN THE AGE OF THE CONSTITUTION
1775–1800

Edited by
Paul A. Gilje
and
William Pencak

A New-York Historical Society Book

Rutherford • Madison • Teaneck
Fairleigh Dickinson University Press
London and Toronto: Associated University Presses

© 1992 by Associated University Presses, Inc.

All rights reserved. Authorization to photocopy items for internal or personal use, or the internal or personal use of specific clients, is granted by the copyright owner, provided that a base fee of $10.00, plus eight cents per page, per copy is paid directly to the Copyright Clearance Center, 27 Congress Street, Salem, Massachusetts 01970. [0-8386-3455-9/92 $10.00+8¢ pp, pc.]

Associated University Presses
440 Forsgate Drive
Cranbury, NJ 08512

Associated University Presses
25 Sicilian Avenue
London WC1A 2QH, England

Associated University Presses
P.O. Box 39, Clarkson Pstl. Stn.
Mississauga, Ontario,
L5J 3X9 Canada

The paper used in this publication meets the requirements of the American National Standard for Permanence of Paper for Printed Library Materials Z39.48-1984.

Library of Congress Cataloging-in-Publication Data

New York in the age of the Constitution, 1775–1800 / edited by Paul A. Gilje and William Pencak.
   p. cm.
"A New-York Historical Society book."
Includes bibliographical references and index.
ISBN 0-8386-3455-9
   1. New York (State)—History—1775–1865. I. Gilje, Paul A., 1951– . II. Pencak, William, 1951–
F123.N595   1992
974.7'03—dc20   91-55094
                                                  CIP

PRINTED IN THE UNITED STATES OF AMERICA

Contents

Acknowledgments 7

Editorial Note 9

Introduction: New York in the Age of the Constitution: 1775–1800
PAUL A. GILJE 13

1. Black Revolt in New York City and the Neutral Zone: 1775–83
GRAHAM RUSSELL HODGES 20

2. The Common People and the Constitution: Popular Culture in New York City in the Late Eighteenth Century
PAUL A. GILJE 48

3. The Artisan and the State in the 1790s: A Comparison of New York and London
HOWARD B. ROCK 74

4. Political "Radicalism" in New York City's Revolutionary and Constitutional Eras
ANTHONY GRONOWICZ 98

5. Liberty, Jealousy, and Union: The New York Economy in the 1780s
CATHY MATSON 112

6. Politics of the Middling Sort: The Bourgeois
   Radicalism of Abraham Yates, Melancton Smith, and
   the New York Antifederalists
   SAUL CORNELL 151
7. Education and Politics in Revolutionary Albany
   MARTA WAGNER 176

List of Contributors 197
Index 199

Acknowledgments

We are most grateful to James B. Bell, former Director of The New-York Historical Society, and James E. Mooney, former Librarian, for inspiring us to hold the conference at which these essays were first presented. The staff of The New-York Historical Society, especially Sheryl Jarvis and Marilyn McShane, performed indispensable service in helping us organize the conference and prepare the papers for publication. A special word of thanks, too, must go to Jean Ashton, the Society's present Director of the Library, and Mary L. Nathanson for seeing the volume through to publication. The superb comments at the conference, which enabled the authors to revise their contributions, were provided by Elizabeth Blackmar, Columbia University; Patricia U. Bonomi, New York University; Thomas J. Davis, State University of New York, Buffalo; Douglas Greenberg, American Council of Learned Societies; Peter C. Hoffer, University of Georgia; Sung Bok Kim, State University of New York, Albany; James E. Mooney, the New-York Historical Society; and Carl E. Prince, New York University. Finally, the staff at Associated University Presses, especially Julien Yoseloff, Michael Koy, and the excellent copyeditor Rebecca Woolston, aided us considerably and with good cheer in producing an accurate and attractive book.

Paul A. Gilje
William Pencak

Editorial Note

Lowercase letters for "federalist" and "antifederalist" refer to the struggle over ratification of the Constitution. Uppercase letters describe political factionalism under the post-1789 national government.

NEW YORK
IN THE AGE
OF THE
CONSTITUTION

PAUL A. GILJE

Introduction: New York in the Age of the Constitution: 1775–1800

The War for Independence and its aftermath devastated the city and state of New York. Revolutionaries toppled royal authority in 1776. That summer invading British forces drove the occupying Continental Army into precipitous retreat, and then settled into the city for seven years, turning its churches and public buildings into barracks, barns, and prisons. Fires destroyed whole sections of the city. Half of the population left to be replaced by newcomers loyal to the crown fleeing the discord of civil war. That internecine conflict dominated the countryside as tory raided whig and whig raided tory. A portion of the state seceded to form Vermont. Riots broke out on great landed estates protesting landlord control and proclaiming allegiance to the king. Indians decimated the frontier settlements. An army invaded from the north, while throughout the war another army remained poised to strike up the Hudson or into the surrounding hinterland. Ten thousand sailors rotted and died in prison hulks in New York harbor while the most daring betrayal of the war almost surrendered the Hudson Highlands.

The end of the war brought distress followed by success. Much of New York City's population was again replaced when thousands of loyalists embarked on their journey to exile. In the city, people began the arduous task of rebuilding. Soon, with construction everywhere, the metropolis began to take on its character as a scene of perpetual activity. Trade thrived. Ships searched for new markets in Europe, South America, and even the Orient. Population began to swell, reaching 33,131 by 1790 and 60,489 by 1800. Not even the shock of losing out as the capital of both the state and the nation seemed to affect this growth.

The countryside also was altered. More and more New Englanders streamed into the Hudson valley and the fertile lands beyond. Here, too, communities took on a new character. Washington Irving, who grew up in early national New York, captured much of this change in his classic short story "Rip Van Winkle." When the bedraggled Rip staggered down from the Catskill Mountains after his twenty year sleep, his quiet Hudson River hamlet had been totally transformed. Irving noted that "the very character of the people seemed changed. There was a busy, disputatious tone about it, instead of the accustomed phlegm and drowsy tranquility."

There was good reason for that disputatiousness. Confiscation of loyalist estates led to the exchange of millions of acres in the state. The war had humbled the mighty Iroquois, who now were forced to cede much of their homeland to whites. Yet large sections of the state remained in a jurisdictional limbo. Massachusetts claimed what would be New York's western third, while the Green Mountain Boys still asserted independence. Within a decade of the close of the war, both boundary issues were settled. New York gained sovereignty over the contested area with Massachusetts, ceding its property rights to the territory, while Vermont obtained full and equal status as the fourteenth state in the union. Speculation ran rampant on the frontier; in the wilderness new cities were plotted, but never built. One set of investors replaced another and most of western New York fell into the hands of the Holland Land Company. Fortunes were won and lost, while inextricably settlers moved into the region. New York in the age of the Constitution was a chaotic, yet dynamic, place.

The essays in this collection are a testament to the change and upheaval of New York as it experienced the trauma of the American Revolution and as New Yorkers sought to establish a new political and social order. Originally presented at a conference celebrating the bicentennial of the Constitution at the New-York Historical Society in May 1987, the essays do not represent an all-inclusive coverage of the state at the end of the eighteenth century. Indeed, reflecting the particular interests of the authors, there is a heavy emphasis on the City of New York. The purpose here is not to present a history of the period, or to examine all of the problems then confronted by the state.

INTRODUCTION

Instead, the essays are intended to explore some key issues confronted by historians of New York and the nation in the age of the Constitution.

Taken together, the essays, while fitting into the mainstream of recent trends in the study of history, mark a departure from the usual scholarship spawned by the bicentennial of the Constitution. In nearly all of these essays, with the partial exception of those by Cathy Matson and Saul Cornell, the Constitution takes a back seat to an examination of social and political conditions that were ongoing with or without the meeting of the so-called founding fathers in Philadelphia during the summer of 1787.

Graham Russell Hodges's essay, for example, never mentions the Constitution. Instead, he focuses on black participation in the Revolutionary War. Eschewing a discussion of legal and constitutional changes in the status of blacks, Hodges proclaims that black support for the British, manifested in running away to occupied New York City and in joining the British armed forces, was tantamount to slave rebellion. Indeed, in Hodges's view the members of the Black Brigade that fought for the British participated in the "largest slave revolt in New York and eastern New Jersey during the eighteenth century." It was also the most successful; thousands of area slaves sought and obtained their freedom during the war. Hodges traces the colonial precedents for this revolt and argues that it had a continued impact upon antislavery thought. By examining black runaways and documenting the effective raids of partisans like Colonel Tye, Hodges does much to reveal the social and political turmoil created by the Revolutionary War.

My own essay on popular culture during the late 1780s and early 1790s mentions the Constitution. But the founding fathers are not my concern. Instead I ask how far down support for the Constitution reached. Other scholars have argued that the Grand Federal Procession of July 1788 marked a high point in agreement between New York City's federalist leadership and the majority of the city's adult white male population. My essay questions this thesis and suggests that the procession was an attempt on the part of the elite to invent tradition and that it was taken over by the master mechanics who in turn planned to express their own support for social unity and better economic conditions, as well as to advertise their own trades. Journeymen and apprentices, who participated in the parade, may have had little to do with the intended message of the elite on the Constitution, or the self-promotional message of the masters. While perhaps not conclusive on this issue, the essay at least raises the possibility that the conventional reading of mechanic support for the Constitution could be wrong.

If the common man cared little for the procession organized to support the Constitution in July 1788, what then were the concerns of the people in the street? Where can we discover clues to understanding the popular culture? The answer, I believe, is to be found in much more spontaneous crowd activity in April 1788 and October 1793. On those occasions thousands of New Yorkers, largely from the lower strata, poured into the streets in defense of commonly accepted values. First they rioted against grave robbing to obtain cadavers for use in the medical school. In the second instance, New York crowds destroyed some bawdy houses in reaction to the acquittal of a member of the elite in a rape case. I argue that in both cases the common people expressed ideas representative of a new romantic value system emphasizing personal attachment and egalitarian social relations.

Howard B. Rock also looks at the interaction between political culture and the working class. He provides an interesting comparison between artisans in New York and London in an effort "to gain a clearer insight into the political history of the two nations" and to better understand "why the United States, unlike England never developed a distinct working-class movement." Occupying the same middling rank in society, and barely maintaining their tenuous station above the poor, artisans in London and New York had much in common. Both groups held to a republicanism that included some elements of the classical ideal of virtue, but both also identified more closely with the liberal republicanism of Tom Paine. Each set of artisans organized a political wing—the counterpart of the Mechanics Committee of New York was the London Corresponding Society—to defend and express their interests. Both groups supported the French Revolution. But differences emerged in their relationship with the state.

New York mechanics believed that they had contributed mightily to the Revolution and the new political order. Although suffering from some repression and intimidation during the 1790s, they worked within the political system for change. Their reward was the Jeffersonian revolution of 1800. The London artisans were more divided, and, although they adhered to the English Constitution, they were left out of the political system. For them repression was not a temporary setback; it was the state acting as an enemy. Some London artisans retreated to oblivion. A few declared that they would fight for the French.

Anthony Gronowicz is also concerned with politics in the late eighteenth century. Essentially he questions the radicalism of the revolution in New York and claims that republican politics were an extension of colonial politics. The key to republicanism was the "independent petty producer" who was the "star of the social formation." Gronowicz finds the roots of this idea in seventeenth-century political thinkers and follows it to the 1790s. In Gronowicz's view mechanic efforts to work within the political system in the last decade of the eighteenth century were a continuation of a process started three decades earlier. The Constitution thus becomes little more than a blip on a larger screen of political developments that excluded large segments of the American population—women, blacks, and Indians.

If the first four essays of this volume deal largely with the lower and mechanic elements of society, the last three essays concentrate on the ideas and politics of the highest levels of New York society. Here the writing and the ratification of the United States Constitution plays a more significant, but perhaps not central, role.

Cathy Matson takes as her starting point David Hume's ideas on jealousy and trade. Hume advocated an open competition among nations in the belief that what benefits one nation, benefits all. Many Americans espoused these ideas in the fervor of the Revolution. But during the 1780s there began a retreat from this doctrine. In this process the Constitution appears as one stage in a larger ideological development. In New York State George Clinton and the advocates of state sovereignty pushed for government involvement to guide the economy during the 1780s as they set up a state impost system that enabled New York to retire much of its debt and emerge, by the end of the decade, on a solid fiscal foundation.

Nationalists like Alexander Hamilton, Matson explains, were none too pleased with this rise in state power. They feared that such local interests would not fare well in adversity, a prophecy that an economic downturn in 1785 seemed to bear out. The Constitution thus becomes not so much a repudiation of state power as "the supplanting from the state to the national level of a subtle mixture of powers" to regulate the economy. In the new vision of political economy, articulated by Hamilton in the *Continentalist* and *Federalist* essays, commerce remained the "engine of all great social changes," but it was an engine that was geared to avoid "jealousy" between states and that needed to be tuned and regulated by a strong central government.

While Matson's essay traces the development of a string of ideas on commerce from Hume to Hamilton, and suggests some of the cleavages in New York politics during the 1780s, Saul Cornell and Marta Wagner provide a more detailed analysis of those divisions.

In his "Politics of the Middling Sort" Cornell argues that New York antifederalists like Abraham Yates and Melancton Smith helped to propel American politics into the modern era by presenting a new interpretation of the concept of representation. Federalists viewed the Constitution as a means of choosing the appropriate individual, who stood above the common herd, to represent the true interrests of the commonwealth. Yates and Smith wanted the representative to be of the people, reflective of the common man both socially and politically. Having worked their way up through the ranks, Yates and Smith held a vision of society that emphasized the prominence of men of the "middling sort" and a minimal government involvement in the economy. Although they lost the contest over the Constitution, this bourgeois radical vision remained alive and paved "the way for a distinctly modern middle class ideology."

Marta Wagner's essay pursues the divisions in New York politics further and explores how they permeated many aspects of the New York world, including efforts to establish an academy in Albany during the Revolutionary War. Tracing the Yates faction, and its feud with the Albany elite, back to the 1760s, Wagner shows how both groups organized to influence and to control the academy. Unlike Cornell, who sees elements of interest group politics even during the colonial period, Wagner argues that politics during the Revolutionary War moved from an emphasis on corporate unity to a greater acceptance of political divisions through contests such as the academy controversy. The debate over the Constitution replicated earlier political alignments and contributed to the continuing development of modern politics.

Collectively, these essays portray, in bold strokes, the contours of life, politics, and society of New York in the age of the Constitution. The New York that emerges in this volume, however, is not dominated by the great document that created our nation. Two hundred years distant we might view the writing and ratification of the Constitution as the most significant event for the state and nation in the late eighteenth century. But for many New Yorkers it may not have been the most dramatic. That distinction belongs to the doctors' riots of 1788. Moreover, viewed against the backdrop of the work presented here, certain major developments in American history were in motion regardless of the Philadelphia Convention and New York's ratification at Poughkeepsie in July 1788. Blacks already were gaining their freedom. (Indeed, the Constitution's recognition of slavery may have weakened this trend.) New Yorkers were beginning to espouse new egalitarian and affectional ideals reflective of the age of romanticism.

Politics incorporated more and more individuals, minimizing the potential for social revolution. Government regulation of commerce began under Governor George Clinton in New York State and bourgeois radicals started to compete for office and offered ideas on representation that presaged the politics of the nineteenth century. Indeed, with or without the United States Constitution New York was reconstructing a new order.

GRAHAM RUSSELL HODGES

1

Black Revolt in New York City and the Neutral Zone: 1775–83

> The Year of Jubilee is Time
> Return ye Ransomed Sinners Home.[1]

On 30 November 1783, a few days after the official evacuation day of British forces from New York City, the H.M.S. *L'Abondance* departed from Staten Island on its way to Port Mallton in the province of Nova Scotia. On board was the Black Brigade, the last of the estimated four thousand black refugees leaving behind servitude for a new life of freedom. Unlike the shiploads of escaped slaves and freeborn Afro-Americans who had departed from New York on such voyages since mid-March 1783 accompanied by masters or sponsors, the Black Brigade sailed alone. The brigade was the remnant of the several regiments of escaped slaves and freeborn blacks who fought for the British in Virginia, South Carolina, and around New York City during the American Revolution.[2]

The brigade contained a small community of forty-seven men, thirty-seven women, and sixteen children. It included escaped slaves and freeborn and emancipated blacks from nearly every colony. Several examples illustrate the experience and variety of individuals who composed the Black Brigade. Cato Winslow, a forty-seven-year-old escaped slave from New York City, left his master to fight for Lord Dunmore in mid-1775; his wife, Rose, a "likely wench of forty years," left her master in Boston in the same year along with her son, Toby, aged eleven. The couple's daughter, Hannah, an infant of one year, was "born free within the British lines." From Virginia to New York City in 1779 came Peter Harding, aged twenty-eight. In New York City he married Kate, aged forty. Soon the couple had a daughter Eliza, "born free within the British lines." On board the *L'Abondance* was a group of freeborn women from Newark, New Jersey, including Mary Thompson, aged fifty-four, her daughter May, twenty-five, another daughter, Polly, ten, and two small children, Rachell, three years old, and Sally, one. Another couple, John and Hannah Jackson, left different masters in Morristown, New Jersey, in 1776, "in response to the [Dunmore] Proclamation." One veteran, Toby Castington, aged thirty-three, an escaped slave from Kent County, Virginia, came north with Lord Dunmore when the Governor of Virginia fled the colony in 1776. Accompanying Castington was his wife, Chloe, and daughter Betsy, "born free within the British lines." These members of the Black Brigade arrived in New York City during different periods of the American Revolution. In New York they became a cohesive military force.[3]

The Black Brigade were participants in the largest slave revolt in the New York and Eastern New Jersey area during the eighteenth century. "A desire of obtaining freedom unhappily reigns throughout the generality of slaves at present," complained the *New York Weekly Mercury* on 27 November 1780. Unlike the supressed uprisings of 1712 and 1741, the black revolt that coincided with the American Revolution succeeded for nearly eight years, ending only with the defeat of the British and the subsequent removal of thousands of slaves from North America. Before that event, African Americans established a community in New York City that included elements of religious and secular society. Their example demonstrates how blacks worked within the social fissures created by the American Revolution to develop their own institutions. After their escape to Nova Scotia, black churches, schools, and political organizations emerged from the experiences of the American Revolution in New York.

The black rebellion that accompanied the American Revolution in New York and New Jersey is a major exception to current scholarly theories of slave rebellion. That scholarship emphasizes several factors. There must be an absentee and impersonal master class, economic distress, and famine. Slaveholding units must approach an average of 100 to 200 slaves, far more than in the slave South and infinitely greater than the small masters of New York and New Jersey afforded. Blacks must outnumber whites, with African-born slaves in the majority. The ruling classes must be split, preferably by war. A successful slave revolt required a favorable terrain for escape and formation of maroon colonies. Importantly, the slave-holding regime must permit the emergence of an autonomous black leadership. Finally, true success lay only in political overthrow of slavery. By this standard, revolts before 1792 were "restorationist" or sought escape from slavery into freedom. After the Haitian Revolution, slave revolts with political leaders became truly revolutionary and sought overthrow of the slaveocracy.[4]

Some but not all of these conditions could apply to the urban/small farm slave system operating in colonial New York City and its hinterlands. The lack of these conditions, however, should not undercut the importance of black efforts towards freedom, community, and political power during the American Revolution. The Black Revolt in New York City between 1775–83 was characterized by a conscious choice of alliance with the British who offered personal freedom and the potential for development of a black community. The revolt was fueled by a desire to avenge past wrongs against blacks and to earn new status as soldiers, and even military leaders.

This black slave revolt occurred in New York City and the surrounding "neutral zone," which included Long Island, Staten Island, and Westchester County, New York, and the eastern counties of New Jersey—Bergen, Somerset, Essex, and Monmouth. Several factors besides British support for black resistance made the revolt possible. First was ready access to the city. There were over eighteen thousand slaves within thirty miles of lower Manhattan; mobile, rural slaves were continually filtering into the city on errands, visits, or escapes on foot, by horse, and boat. Second, many of these slaves were skilled and experienced; some were literate, especially those who had learned reading and writing from the Society for the Propagation of the Gospel in Foreign Parts. Those slaves gained visions of equality and freedom through their educations. A third source of resistance was the formative elements of black community. Hampered by the small farm/urban system of slavery in and around New York City during the colonial period, slaves nonetheless created a fluid culture in taverns, at dances, funerals, and executions, along the docks, and in the streets and roads. Extended slave families became the center of African American society. The last and most persistent source was the tradition of violent resistance, collective and individual.

None of these conditions, however, would have activated a black revolt had not the British army occupied New York City for most of the American Revolution. The British were the blacks' most consistent allies. Black Americans, desiring what Boston King described as "the happiness of liberty, of which I knew nothing before,"[5] chose to side with the Crown either for protection from bondage or, frequently, to fight against the Patriots in an effort to end slavery, despite the obstacles of British racism, deception, and support for slavery.

The Patriots recognized the black preferences. Henry M. Muhlenberg realized early in the war that the Negroes "secretly wished the British army might win, for then all Negro slaves will gain their freedom. It is said that this sentiment is universal amongst all the Negroes in America." Muhlenberg complained that "Barbarous Indians & Negroes are being enticed by the so-called Christians with gifts and promises."[6] As the first year of the war unfolded, Patriots worried about a full-scale black revolution. In early 1776, Charles Lee wrote of the need to impose military order over the black population of Virginia. He noted, "dominion over the black is based on opinion, loose that and authority will fall."[7]

Choosing Loyalism did not mean that blacks blindly followed British instruction. Blacks watched the unfolding conflict carefully, choosing sides according to their best interests, and were less pro-British than pro-black. In their guarantees of liberty the British were quite capable of deception and brutal fraud. Nonetheless, the proclamations by Lord Dunmore, Lord William Howe, and Sir Henry Clinton were calls to action received by a highly restive, rebellion-prone black society.[8]

Freedom inside the British lines meant a number of things. Freedom allowed the right to marry and live with one's spouse and to have children, "born free." It allowed blacks to work for wages and to live in integrated housing in previously segregated New York City. During the American Revolution in New York blacks enjoyed the support and membership in a receptive religion, Anglicanism, which offered religious consolation and education. Anglicanism made New York City more than just a hospitable refuge for escaped slaves; it provided them with support to establish a black community.

The choice of Loyalism permitted legal revenge against an American population that not only enslaved blacks but also terrorized them with a patrol system legally enforced by constables, justices of the peace, and minutemen, and a judicial system that employed quick execution for minor crimes. Capital punishment frequently included atrocities such as hanging in chains, burning at the stake, and posting heads after punishments forcibly attended by the area's black population. More blacks were put to death during the colonial period in New York than in any other northern colony. New Jersey was a close second.[9]

Freedom meant becoming a soldier, a prospect more attractive than the whip. Many blacks escaped to become servants of British soldiers. While nominally still enslaved, these blacks did so with the promise of freedom upon British victory, a frequent method of recruitment. Black pilots, guides, and soldiers were aware of the profits of plunder and the potential of rewards for special feats. The Black Brigade, particularly the thirty members from New Jersey, knew the homes of Patriots and could easily raid throughout the neutral zone. For this reason, Patriots feared the Black Brigade more than the regular British army. Henry Muhlenberg warned, "the worst is to be feared from the irregular troops whom the so-called Tories have assembled from various nationalities—for example, a regiment of Catholics, a regiment of Negroes, who are fitted for and inclined towards barbarities, are lacking in human feeling and are familiar with every corner of the country."[10]

The Black Brigade and the Black Pioneers and Guides were invaluable to the British forces. New York City was the most important British holding in North America before and throughout the Revolutionary War. Its protection was fundamental to any British success. Eastern New Jersey, although not always controlled by British forces, was a rich source of agricultural products, cattle, and firewood. The Black Brigade, particularly under the leadership of Colonel Tye, played a key role in protecting vulnerable New York from Patriot incursions. Colonel Tye and the Black Brigade were masters of guerrilla warfare. The Black Brigade, an adjunct force attached first to Banastre Tarleton's regiment, which later worked with General John Graves Simcoe's Queens Rangers, was quite effective in raids on New Jersey and Westchester County. These raids softened up local militias, captured key officers, and acquired valuable livestock and forage for the British forces and loyalists in New York City. They also ushered escaping slaves to their freedom inside British lines, and eventual transportation to new lives in Nova Scotia.[11]

The roots of the revolutionary black experience lie in the context of slave resistance during the colonial period. Blacks historically responded to their enslavement by conspiracy, revolt, and escape. The slave conspiracies of 1712 and 1741 were but the largest of a continuing series of violent confrontations between whites and blacks that spread across the two colonies. In each instance the slaves planned to rise up, burn houses and buildings and, while the whites were distracted, murder and pillage before making their flight. In 1712 the slaves first enacted an African brotherhood ritual before the insurrection in which they succeeded in murdering a number of whites. This incident, coupled with murders in 1708 by slaves in Hallet's Cove, Long Island, worsened white fears and resulted in harsher and more restrictive laws.[12] In 1734 New Jerseyans were shocked by a well-developed conspiracy in Somerset County that endangered the lives of all whites living there. The same decade saw a series of grisly murders by slaves. Using axes and poisons, the bondsmen dispatched their masters despite the grim threat of punishment by burning and hanging. The Slave Conspiracy of 1741 spread terror from Long Island to West Jersey. Each of these revolts included careful planning, a willingness to massacre whites, and a desire to create a black state.[13]

To confront their bondsmen's threats, New York and New Jersey whites instituted the largest and harshest slave system north of the Chesapeake, circumscribing blacks' legal, political, and economic lives. An expanding slave trade managed by New York's most successful merchants was complemented by numerous private transfers by slaveowners. Yet the growth of the slave trade in the 1750s caused some northerners concern. Quaker Anthony Benezet feared that rising percentages of blacks in the North could create a rebellious situation akin to the American South, the West Indies, and Surinam. In a letter to Englishman David Barclay, Benezet, the leading American abolitionist, anxiously requested that certain British antislavery pamphlets not be distributed in America, "as this was thought to be of too tender a nature to be exposed to view, in places where it might fall into the hands of the Negroes."[14] As black percentages of New York and New Jersey populations rose above fourteen percent, reaching a high of 18,000 slaves by 1771, white repression grew more brutal with each threat of slave resistance.

Black resistance to slavery remained an underlying current throughout the colonial period. The proximity of the frontier enabled runaway slaves to join Indians warring on the English, escape to Canada, or form maroon societies on Long Island or the Ramapo Mountains. Some ex-slaves organized tough gangs on the New York City waterfront, mixing freedom with vandalism. Despite heavy penalties and an efficient patrol system, northern slaves continued to flee throughout the colonial period.[15]

Slaves also used religion to question slavery. Under the Dutch there was some ambiguity over the status of Christian blacks. Even during the earliest years of English rule, blacks employed Christianity as an avenue to escape from bondage. During the eighteenth century, the

Anglican church, as a part of its missionary activity, worked to convert blacks and initiated an important alliance. Anglican missionaries, in their efforts to save black souls, taught slaves the important tools of reading and writing, and, in sermon and classroom, espoused doctrines of spiritual and intellectual equality.[16]

Slaveowners regarded Anglican instruction of blacks with suspicion. Not only did such education distract blacks from their labors, and implant dangerous ideas of equality, but it permitted emergence of a literate leadership. Many New Jersey runaway notices mentioned slave literacy. Black preachers, capable of reading and circulating political arguments about liberty, were a natural consequence of "such indulgence." In 1774, for example, Mark Prevost of Bergen County, New Jersey, announced the escape of his slave Mark. Prevost described Mark as "serious, civil, slow of speech, rather low in stature, reads well, is a preacher among the Negroes, about 40 years of age." Accompanying him was his wife, who was "smart, active and handy, rather lusty, has bad teeth and a small cast in one eye; she is likely to look upon, reads and writes well and is about 36 years of age." They were headed for New York City, where during the American Revolution they would be joined by other black religious leaders. There, together, these blacks created an ethos of egalitarianism and salvation, both personal and racial.[17]

New York City was always a magnet for freedom-bound blacks. There were many black females in the city, increasing the possibility of family life. Jobs were available to runaways, either as domestics or as hired hands along the docks. Although colonial law attempted to prohibit sea masters from hiring blacks without proper passes, by the 1770s, New York's docks were filled with black laborers and mariners. The assertive, often skilled, finely dressed, independent, and scarcely deferential New York City blacks appeared as a beacon to their country-cousins, beckoning them to join the ranks of the free, or at least emulate the city black in style and behavior.[18]

It is against this background of long-standing opposition to slavery during the colonial period, and the intensifying disorder created in the mid-1770s, that we must view the black revolt of 1775 to 1783 in New York City and the neutral zone. This revolt took on three related dimensions. First was the continuation of waves of conspiracy spilling over from the colonial era. Second was the large number of runaways who flooded the loyalist lines. Third were those blacks who took up arms to fight for their liberty in the service of King George. Such blacks often formed opportunistic gangs that looted and burned Patriot property for their own gain. These forms of revolt frequently merged.[19]

The years just before the American Revolution were filled with threats of conspiracy from the more than eighteen thousand slaves living either in or close to New York City. In 1772, as Somerset County, New Jersey, slaveowners considered seriously proposals for an African colonization movement, they also fretted over reports of mass meetings of slaves. Owners were shocked by two slaves' retorts that: "it was not necessary to please their masters, for they should not have their masters long." Somerset County slavemasters found themselves unable to keep their bondspeople home after nine o'clock in the evening. Slaves stole liquor, "fowls," and other food. Some stole their masters' horses to ride to late-night meetings. For example, George Van Nest charged his slave Tom with theft and "riding horses three nights after midnight." The bad consciences of Perth Amboy residents in 1774 caused them to beseech the New Jersey Assembly not to consider any more manumission proposals because the "slaves are a very bad and dangerous people."[20] In 1775, as American eyes uneasily considered the unfolding drama of Lord Dunmore's conflict with Virginia planters, a dispute that would result in the governor's famous Proclamation freeing all "indented servants and slaves" willing to fight for the Crown, New Jerseyans and New Yorkers worried about a "wave of revolt." Somerset County was racked by rumors of associations of blacks and disaffected whites, urged on by British soldiers. A report to the Continental Congress asserted that "the story of the Negroes may be depended upon, so far . . . at least to their arming or attempting to form themselves, particularly in Somerset County. Our militia are gone off in such numbers that we hardly have Men in Armes enough left in those parts which are affected to the cause." There were numerous and ominous reports coming from New York as well. In the city, "two Tory Negroes" were hanged for "engaging to murder their masters who were supporters of liberty." On Long Island Patriots burned Dunmore in effigy and worried about slaves "being too fond of the British troops."[21] One prominent Monmouth County Patriot noted with displeasure the union of slaves and refugee whites, pointing out that he had previously employed a number of the Tories and blacks as wheelwrights. These now were "the very fellows who tried to take my Father prisoner and perhaps kill him."[22]

Anguished by reports from near and far in late 1775, the Committee of Safety in Shrewsbury Township, Monmouth County, ordered search parties to stop "meetings of servants Negroes and other disorderly persons as they are attended with great mischief." Reports from Monmouth indicated that blacks were taking advantage of the political splits among whites to engage in practices legally forbidden, particularly night meetings and carousing at taverns. On 11 and 16 October 1775 the committee ordered "Colonel Breeze to secure the Negroes," and cease "Riotous and numerous meetings of Negroes at unlicensed houses." The committee ordered all guns and ammunition taken from blacks "until the present Troubles are setled." Later the committee resolved that all "Slaves, Negroes and Mollattos found off their master's premises shall be arrested."[23] The fears of the slaveholders were more than paranoia; they were a recognition that their bondsmen were preparing for a move.

As in previous decades, escape was the principal means of black revolt. Despite harsh penalties and constant surveillance, black runaways were a persistent and expensive problem.[24] During the American Revolution the number of runaways was nearly four times the amount known in the previous seventy years in New Jersey; in New York City and on Long Island, far more slaves fled their masters than at any previous time. Using newspaper advertisements and the embarkation list of blacks leaving New York City with the British in 1783, it is possible to identify 516 slaves who escaped from their masters in New Jersey and New York Provinces between 1775 and 1783.

The most convenient sources enabling historians to identify runaways are newspaper advertisements. However, New Jersey slaveowners gave notice of only 89 of 308 or 29 percent of runaways during the American Revolution. The remainder may be found in the embarkation list.[25] Runaway notices represented more than an effort to help masters recapture their bondsmen, a method that rarely worked. They also freed the master of any obligations or damages incurred by their slaves. During the war notices acted as warnings to other Patriots of slave intentions, especially "joining the ministerial army," as many planned.[26]

Runaway advertisements provide the clearest available images of individual slaves. Not only do they inform us of the intentions of many to join the British army or of plots by whites, free blacks, and slaves to help free bondsmen, but the notices include detailed information about physical features and clothing. Masters described slaves with limps, severe scars, small-pox scars, and bashful looks. They were "likely, comely, short, tall," in poor health or lusty. Hairstyles were often "bushy," or on occasion, cut in the fashionable "maccaroni" style, indicating the spread of urban fashions into the provinces.[27]

Slaves frequently took not only their own belongings, but an assortment of their master's clothing to keep warm in the harsh winters or to barter in the used clothing markets of New York City. Sam, who ran away from Colonel John Reid in New York City in 1776, took with him "a tight-bodied blue cloth livery coat with red cuffs and a collar and red lining," as well as six pairs of breeches, vests, six pairs of shoes, and numerous stockings. Reverend Smith identified his runaway Michael Hoy as probably wearing "a suit of superfine mixt broad cloth, a red new great coat, white stockings, halfboots, a blue velvet stock and a beaver hat, but littleworn." Hoy also took with him "a dark bay horse . . . a natural trotter."[28] While many slaves stole fine clothes, their own possessions appear to have been more modest. Sixteen wore buckskin breeches; five wore handmade bearskin coats. Beaver hats were very popular as were regimental garb. Women were often dressed in petticoats, jackets, stockings, flat shoes, and bonnets. Although they tried to take extra clothes with them, there is little indication that the women were as successful as males.[29]

Much information about black families is contained in the "Book of Negroes," the ledger kept by the British of departing slaves in 1783. Almost sixty percent of blacks leaving New York City at the end of the war did so in family units. The evidence about New Jersey slaves provides proof of a powerful and opportunistic drive by blacks to take advantage of the war and unite in New York City. Cornelius Van Sayl, thirty years old, escaped from John Lloyd of Monmouth County in 1778; he took with him his wife, Catherine, and his daughter Mary, both of whom formerly belonged to John Vander Veer of Monmouth County. The couple gave birth to Peter in New York City and were joined there by Peter Van Syl, Cornelius's brother from Tom's River. Joseph Collins, aged thirty, escaped from John Kipp of New York City after his master sold him to Dr. Van Buren of Hackensack. In New Jersey he met his wife, Betsy, slave of Nicholas Terhune; together they escaped to New York in 1779. Brothers sometimes escaped together such as Harry and Vaughn Couwenhoven, who formerly belonged to Peter Couwenhoven of Middletown, New Jersey. Some masters lost several slaves. John Sipe of Acquakanonck lost Susan Van Ryper, Polly Richards, Dianah Kingsland, her son, Caesar, and a young daughter, all in 1779. The Van Rypers of Bergen County, New Jersey, lost nine slaves over the course of the revolution. In all, Bergen County masters lost at least 90 slaves, a comparable number probably escaped from Monmouth County slaveowners.[30]

Runaways were not the only Afro-Americans who departed from New York City in 1783. In addition to the 516 fugitive slaves leaving New York City, there were forty-three freeborn blacks from New Jersey and forty-nine from New York. There were also thirty-two blacks from New York and eighteen from New Jersey who were freed by their masters after death through manumission, personal grants, or simple abandonment.³¹ For example, Colonel Stephen Bleuke, later commander of the Black Pioneers and Guides, was freeborn in Barbados; in New York City he met his wife, Margaret, who was "born free in Mr. Coventry's house in New York City." Margaret was probably a black indentured servant because Stephen was forced to purchase her freedom in 1770. The couple also purchased Isabel Gibbon from Coventry's daughter. Isabel, twenty years of age, was probably Margaret Bleuke's daughter. Another slave who purchased his family's freedom was Joseph Paul, thirty years, who bought his freedom from Lawrence Kortwright of New York City. He also paid William Brown of New York City to free his wife, Susannah Paul, aged thirty, and their three children from William Brown of New York.³²

Some former slaves gained their freedom by manumission from religious whites who scrupled at holding slaves. Issac Corlies, twenty-seven, gained his freedom from Will Mott, a Quaker from Great Neck, Long Island. His wife, Hagar Corlies, twenty-two, also became free by manumision from Quaker Joseph Hewlett of Great Neck. Peter Johnson, thirty-five, gained his freedom from a Quaker, Silvestre Brinoly of New Jersey, and moved to New York City in response to General Howe's Proclamation in 1778.³³ The frequent necessity of free blacks to serve some time with white masters may be seen in the case of Charity Morris, twenty-eight, freeborn in Long Island but who completed an apprenticeship with Jonathan Mills at age eighteen. Charity Morris, and her children, Issac, nine, Edward, five, and daughter, Mary Ann, one year, traveled with her husband, Ned Morris, an escaped slave from Fairfield Connecticut.³⁴

Despite the American hope that free blacks and slaves would have little social contact, the case of Prince suggests otherwise. Prince, fifty-three, formerly slave to Abraham Peers of Second River, New Jersey, negotiated a deal with a new master, Joseph Stokes of New Jersey, and purchased his freedom for forty-five pounds. Margaret, his wife, was freeborn in Bergen County, New Jersey, but left with her husband and son, Mintard, for New York City in 1780. There they joined their daughter, Elizabeth, twenty, her small child, and husband, Samuel Van Nostrandt of Acquackanonck, who escaped from his master in 1779.³⁵

Once inside the British lines, blacks became valuable recruits to the English army. As the conflict unfolded, blacks declared their willingness to fight with either side, but met with sharply different reactions from Patriots and Tories. The Whigs were generally negative. Not only was there danger of revolt, but slaves were valuable property, made more so by the absence of white laborers in the army. Further there were ideological problems. American revolutionaries were apprehensive that the British wished to reduce white colonials to the levels of black slaves. Patriots firmly believed that they were engaged in the conflict to avoid English enslavement of the colonies. Such talk of liberty was dangerous if heard by America's true slaves.[36]

Throughout the war, however, blacks served in military roles for the revolutionaries. Some Patriots used their slaves as replacement substitutes for their own military service. In smaller states such as Rhode Island and Connecticut blacks made up significant portions of the regiments. Even though most Americans rejected Henry Laurens's proposal that the Continental Congress purchase slaves from their masters and then draft them, blacks continued to filter into the American forces.[37]

In contrast, the British openly enlisted blacks in their army. Blacks aided the British cause around New York in several ways. One hundred and twenty blacks worked as laborers in the Quarter Master General's Department, for the Wagonmaster, or in the Forage and Provision Departments of the Army around New York City. While the British paid these laborers less than white Loyalists, several occupations filled by Loyalist blacks such as cartman, wagon driver, and carpenter had been rigidly segregated in New York City before the war. Now the black Loyalists were given an opportunity to work at whole new occupations. As the labor shortage worsened, blacks were able to command the same inflationary wages as whites.[38] Tory blacks served as personal servants. For an escaped slave, offering one's services to a British officer was a good way to avoid detection. Unskilled labor and personal service have customarily been viewed as the sum of black activity in the American Revolution. Except for the few who filled the ranks in a handful of cases, most blacks were, according to historians, the "men behind the men with the guns."[39]

Recently, however, scholars are uncovering not just individual black participation in the Revolution, but whole units of black soldiers fighting for the British. The Black Guides and Pioneers in North Carolina and Pennsylvania, the Ethiopian Regiment fighting in Virginia, New York, and South Carolina, and the Black Brigade of New York City were not exceptions but were parts of an important, sustained black participation in the British and Loyalist efforts.[40]

General Sir Henry Clinton commissioned the first Black Pioneer company on 2 April 1776 in New York. Similar companies existed in the Carolinas, Virginia, and Pennsylvania. Each had two white officers, a lieutenant and an ensign. The rest of the company usually consisted of sixty to seventy black recruits including three sergeants, three corporals, and thirty-two privates. Pay was the same as for white infantrymen, a shilling a day for a sergeant, eightpence for a corporal, and sixpence for a private.[41]

The British swore blacks into the pioneer company with a simple oath. The oath briefly noted that volunteers entered the Black Pioneer company without compulsion and that applicants would faithfully serve the British army. Thomas Peters recalled being sworn in on 14 November 1776 by Alderman William Waddell in New York City. His captain, George Martin, was, like other officers commanding the Black Pioneers, a member of the Queen's Rangers. Peters remembered promises from the officers that after the war, he would be "at our own liberty to do & provide for ourselves."[42]

The British quickly put black fugitives to work in paramilitary ways. The "Black Pioneers" performed paramilitary services as guards, pilots, spies, interpreters with Indians, performed executions, and were able horsemen, hunters, and drummers. The British richly rewarded one black guide for informing them of a prospective Patriot attack on New York City in 1779.[43]

The British frequently used Black Pioneers as spies. The roster of "Capt. Martin's Company" gave the names of blacks, their geographic origin, and their knowledge of specific areas. One example was Benjamin Whitecuff, freeborn on Long Island. At the beginning of the war, Whitecuff first joined the Americans to become a sergeant. Whitecuff joined the British forces on Staten Island in 1776 and worked for General Sir Henry Clinton as a spy for two years, earning over fifteen guineas in that time. Caught by the Patriots near Cranbury, New Jersey, Whitecuff was hanged. The Americans left him dangling and a few minutes later he was rescued by an English regiment. Whitecuff proceeded to Staten Island then went to Virginia. Captured by the Americans, Whitecuff was again condemned to be hanged in Boston. Fortunately for him the British recaptured him a second time and brought him to England for refuge. Later he served in the Siege of Gibraltar as a regular British soldier.[44]

The Black Pioneers were officially part of the British army from the earliest years of the war. Less recognized, but equally valuable, were the many blacks termed loosely "followers of the Army and Flag." These were escaped slaves and free blacks expert in guerilla warfare and very useful for softening up Patriot militias with nightime raids or securing valuable livestock for the English garrison in New York City. At first the British used "followers of the Army and Flag" opportunistically. By the close of the war, however, the British recognized the importance of their service by formally organizing them into the Black Brigade.⁴⁵

The Black Brigade resembled several historic British formations of slaves. First were "Black Shot" organizations of whole units of slaves, armed for military action. Used in Jamaica in the 1740s and again in the 1780s, the Black Shot was usually a one-time temporary military system. A second type were "Black Corps," which were special military units of free blacks, mulattos, and recently freed slaves. "Black Corps" could be auxiliaries to other fighting units added to the militia or created as units of black rangers that could be transferred between colonies to meet special crises.⁴⁶

Volunteers for these units came largely from fugitive slaves attracted by British proclamations offering freedom to those willing to serve in the King's Army. For example, in 1779 General Sir Henry Clinton issued a proclamation promising to "every Negro who shall desert the Rebell Standdard full security to follow within these lines any Occupation which he shall think Proper."⁴⁷ The American reaction to this invitation was racist ridicule. A New Jersey poet wrote:

> A proclamation oft of late he sends
> To thieves and rogues who are only his friends
> Those he invites; all colours he attacks
> But deference pays to *Ethiopian Blacks*.⁴⁸

Clinton's promise of sanctuary, widely circulated in Loyalist newspapers, set off a rush of black enlistments as buglers, drummers, and common soldiers. According to their own testimony inscribed in the "Book of Negroes" in 1783, hundreds heard Clinton's proclamation and left their masters for freedom in Philadelphia and New York City. There they joined with family and friends and formed their own communities.

Blacks in New York City lived in "Negro barracks" at 18 Broadway, 10 Church Street, and other locations. The quality of such housing may be inferred from the grousing of Thomas A. Jones, the Loyalist historian, that excellent housing was being wasted upon refugee blacks that could have been rented to deserving white Loyalists with the profits to be used to support the war effort. Jones's attitude was not uncommon among American Tories, many of whom felt the British commanders were unduly concerned about the former slaves. New York was the scene of "Ethiopian Balls" in which Afro-Americans and British officers and soldiers freely mingled to the music of black fiddlers and banjo players. Black tavern life, no longer restricted by law, flourished. Afro-Americans joined British soldiers, if comments about their fraternization may be credited, in various sports, especially horse racing, which enlivened occupied New York life.[49] The size of this community at times frightened the British and they attempted to limit its further growth. The British asked the ferrymen along the Hudson River to refuse passage to escaping blacks desirous of entering New York. However, the British ambivalence could not stem the tide of freedom-seeking blacks. In this light Clinton's proclamation not only allowed the general to fill important manpower needs, a problem for both sides as the war wore on, but offered a positive method of dealing with the hundreds of young blacks, eager to fight against the Americans and who could have easily become rebellious if not allowed to fulfill their desires. The British were able to channel the black revolt for their own purposes, yet in return for military service had to recognize black demands.

One of the most important "followers of the Army and Flag" was Colonel Tye, who escaped from John Corlies, a prosperous Quaker farmer from Colt's Neck, New Jersey. Corlies's farm was located along the Navesink River, which stretched along sandy beaches and wooded inlets until it emptied into the Atlantic Ocean. On the Navesink Tye mastered river piloting and learned about Corlies's property as well as that of his neighbors.[50] Fearful Patriots knew that Tye could provide the British with information on their homes, wealth in livestock, plate, and other valuable commodities. Monmouth's Patriots were especially vulnerable. Located directly across a narrow strip of water from Staten Island, the headquarters of British regular and irregular forces, Monmouth was an easy and profitable prey. In the nearby Bay of New York, British warships offered protection for periodic raids on Patriot towns. To add to Patriot difficulties, Monmouth was not only geographically impossible to defend, but many residents were sympathetic to the English cause. Part of the militia was suspected of working openly with the British; others engaged in lucrative smuggling along the coast. Much of Monmouth's population was disaffected, many by religious conviction. Anglicans were openly Tory while Quakers, who constituted twenty percent of Monmouth's population, remained at least neutral, and in the eyes of many Patriots, hostile to their efforts. A few Friends were willing to sign loyalty oaths to the new government, but as the war progressed, the Shrewsbury Meeting expelled members with any contact with either army. Worse, there was the continual problem of Tye and other refugee blacks.[51]

Tye's first known military venture was during the Battle of Monmouth in 1777. Elisha Shepard, a captain in the Monmouth Militia, recalled his capture and transfer by "Captain Tye" to the Sugar House in New York City. That Tye should assume first the title of captain and later of colonel, was, if unusual, not without precedent, as the British army often granted such titles out of respect, particularly in Jamaica and other West Indian islands. Tye not only commanded blacks but directed whites as well.[52]

Tye's next recorded appearance came in the summer of 1779. During a period of intense racial anxiety in New Jersey aggravated by reports of an anticipated massacre of whites by blacks in Elizabethtown, Tye and his men, accompanied by the fierce Loyalist John Moody, began a series of raids against Monmouth's Patriots. On 15 July 1779, "about fifty negroes and refugees landed at Shrewsbury and plundered the inhabitants of near 80 head of horned cattle, about 20 horses and a quantity of wearing apparel and household furniture. They also took off William Brindley and Elisha Cook, two of the inhabitants."[53]

This combined force of black and white Loyalists was the military arm of a plan sponsored by the erstwhile New Jersey governor, William Franklin, to employ the bitter anger of Loyalists against Monmouth's Patriots. For the first years of the war, British commanders chose the cream of New Jersey's Loyalists as officers, enlisted a few others, but largely ignored the common Loyalist. Made unhappy by Patriot sales of their confiscated property, New Jersey's pro-British citizens were infuriated by the revolutionaries' summary executions of Loyalists. Whigs hanged several captured Loyalists under the vigilante law that governed Monmouth after early 1779. "A Loyal Refugee," demanded immediate retaliation in the *Royal Gazette* of 5 June 1779.[54]

Tye's July 1779 raid established a pattern that continued for over a year. These raids were a combination of banditry, marronage, and commissioned assistance to the British army. All three aspects, moreover, were conscious methods of rebellion, often aimed directly at former masters and their friends. Tye and his men, at times aided by white refugees known as "cow-boys," would surprise Patriots in their homes, kidnap soldiers and officers, carry off plate, clothing, and other valuables, and secure badly needed cattle for British troops in Staten Island and New York City. For these accomplishments, Tye and his men were paid handsomely. Tye's deep knowledge of Monmouth's swamps, rivers, and inlets made his presence undetectable until it was too late. After a raid, Tye and his "motley crew" would return to Refugeetown at Sandy Hook, headquarters for maroon activity, or hide in nearby swamps.

The fall and winter of 1779–80 were filled with raids from Sandy Hook and Staten Island. The planting season of 1779 was "unfavorable to crops" and although farmers preferred selling food to the British for gold than to Americans for paper money, food, hay, and firewood were scarce. One Loyalist in New York City contented himself with green twigs for firewood. That winter was unusually harsh, and the ice-bound Hudson River made the British apprehensive about protecting New York City. The combined forces of the Queen's Rangers and the Black Brigade enabled the British to both protect the city and send out exploratory raids to secure food and fuel.[55]

On 30 March 1780 Tye and his men captured a Captain Warner, who purchased his freedom; less lucky were Captain James Green and Ensign John Morris, whom Tye took to Refugeetown at Sandy Hook enroute to imprisonment in the Sugar House in New York City. In the same raid Tye and his men looted and burned the home of John Russell, a fierce Patriot associated with raids on Staten Island, before killing him and wounding his young son. Three weeks later a band of refugees and blacks captured Matthias Halsted at his home near Newark and plundered the house of "bed, bedding, family wearing apparel and 7–8 head of creature [cattle]."[56]

These attacks came during a period of rising concern about Patriot prospects in New Jersey. Governor William Livingston, who two years before on the advice of Samuel Allinson, had attempted to abolish slavery in New Jersey, now wrote fearfully of Lord Dunmore's effect upon local blacks. The borders between New York and New Jersey were flooded with black refugees bound for sanctuary with the British. Loyalists in New York, eager to organize against Livingston's government, were encouraged by reports that George Washington's army was down to 1,600 men. As part of the concern over black runaways to New York City, New Jersey slaveholders were urged to remove their slaves "to some more remote or interior parts of the state."[57]

On 9 June 1780 Colonel Tye and his men murdered Private Joseph Murray of the Monmouth County militia at his home in Colt's Neck. Murray was a nemesis of local Tories and had been personally responsible for several executions.[58] This was the first of several such retaliatory assaults in the month of June 1780. On 12 June Colonel Tye commanded a large band of slaves and refugee whites in a daring attack on the home of Barnes Smock of the Monmouth militia while the main body of British troops attacked Washington's forces. Smock, a horse trader and a promoter of local thoroughbred races, was the leader of Patriot resistance in Monmouth County. Using a six-pound cannon to warn residents of the raid, Smock summoned a number of men around his house to fight Tye. After a stiff battle, Tye and his men captured Smock and twelve other Patriots, disabling much of the leadership of Monmouth's militia and preventing them from aiding Washington's troops. The victors captured valuable livestock and looted Smock's home. Tye spiked Smock's cannon, a symbolically disheartening action. Tye and his men then spirited their prisoners back to the Loyalist stronghold at Refugeetown before sending them on to imprisonment at the Sugar House in New York City. Immediately local Patriots wrote anguished letters to Governor William Livingston, begging for help against the ravages of Colonel Tye. In response to Tye's attacks of 8, 9, and 12 June 1780, Governor William Livingston ordered martial law effective in Monmouth County. But many farmers ordinarily warm to the Patriot cause were in the middle of the planting season and Livingston openly despaired of supplying Washington with a full complement of troops from Monmouth County because of the farmers' needs. While the New Jersey Patriots were distracted by Tye and his men, other blacks took advantage. The *New Jersey Journal* noted that "twenty-nine Negroes of both sexes deserted from Bergen County in early June, 1780."[59]

Tye's June incursions caused great fear among New Jerseyans. In one week Tye carried off much of the officer corps of the Monmouth militia, destroyed their cannon, and demonstrated his ability to strike at will against a weakened Patriot population. If before he was a banditti in service to the British, he now became an important military force. There were more attacks to come. On 22 June 1780 "Tye with thirty blacks, thirty-six Queen's Rangers and thirty refugees landed at Conascung, New Jersey." The invaders slipped undetected past Patriot scouts and captured James Mott, Second Major of the Second Regiment of the Monmouth militia. Tye's men sacked and destroyed Mott's and "several Neighbor's" homes. Tye's troops also captured Captain James Johnson of the Hunterdon militia, and six privates.[60]

It was a stunning blow to the Patriot side. Tye captured eight men, plundered their homes, and then took the captives to New York. Despite the martial law and the presence of several militias, Tye and his men escaped without any reported casualties. Although the notorious Tory John G. Simcoe, commander of the Queen's Rangers, was present, Tye received credit for the raid in newspapers. Throughout the summer of 1780 Tye led his "motley band" on raids into Monmouth County burning barns and looting farms. On one such raid in late August, Tye and his men captured Hendrick and John Smock, brothers of Barnes, and sent them to join the latter in prison in New York City.[61]

On 1 September 1780 Tye attempted his greatest feat. For years Loyalists had tried to capture Captain Josiah Huddy who was famed for his leadership in raids on British positions in Staten Island and Sandy Hook and much hated for his quick executions of captured Loyalists. Colonel Tye led a small army of blacks, refugees, and Queen's Rangers against Huddy's home in Tom's River. Normally the center of Patriot activity in the area, Huddy's house was occupied only by its owner and a female friend, Lucretia Emmons. As Tye's men attacked, Huddy ran from room to room, firing muskets, which Miss Emmons quickly reloaded, creating an illusion that Patriots filled the house. After a two-hour battle Tye set fire to the house and flushed out Huddy. During the battle, Tye was shot in the wrist. The fighting attracted the attention of other Patriots and, as Tye was leading Huddy back to Refugeetown, the militia intercepted his band. During the ensuing skirmish, Huddy escaped by jumping overboard and swimming to his rescuers, shouting, "I am Huddy."[62]

Tye's wound proved more serious than originally thought. Within days lockjaw set in and, without proper medical attention, shortly killed him. Though Tye's exploits ended in this savage encounter, his memory was avenged when Huddy, captured nearly two years later, was snatched by Loyalists from a British prison ship on a pretext and hanged on the shore of Monmouth County. A black man performed Huddy's execution. This arbitrary justice, occurring after Cornwallis's surrender at Yorktown and as peace negotiations were underway, caused an international furor and threatened to affect peace terms between the Americans and the British. Its effect was to deepen local animosities between Patriots and Loyalists.[63]

Colonel Stephen Bleuke of the Black Pioneers replaced Tye as the leader of black raiders in the New York area, but Tye's memory lived on. Patriots remembered Tye's revolutionary activities with admiration in contrast to their hatred of white Loyalists. Even during the angry dispute over Huddy's execution, Americans recalled Tye as a "brave and courageous man whose generous actions placed him well above his white counterparts." Despite his opposition to the American side, Patriots admired his military skill and argued that had Tye been enlisted in the American forces the war would have been won much sooner. Such sentiment remained common in New Jersey through the antebellum period.[64]

As the war continued in the early 1780s, Bleuke and the Black Pioneers and the Black Brigade propped up the fading hopes of local Loyalists. Despite Cornwallis's defeat in 1781, Loyalists refused to accept the inevitable, and raided Long Island and New Jersey constantly. On 5 June 1782 forty whites and forty blacks landed at Forked River, New Jersey, plundered Patriot homes, and burned a number of salt works, to the great anger of New Jersey's Patriots.[65] Such actions, combined with the constant runaway problems, indicate that despite the British defeat at Yorktown, slaves continued their revolt by any means possible.

The close of the war in November 1783 found racial relations between whites and blacks in New York and New Jersey permanently altered. The slave populations of Monmouth and Bergen Counties in New Jersey and Westchester County and Long Island in New York were significantly reduced. Both states began a long-drawn out debate over the abolition of slavery. The debate's tenor was far less egalitarian than in Pennsylvania or New England. Rather, the two largest slave states north of the Chesapeake desired to acquire more white immigrants, which they hoped would be a more loyal and less contentious labor force.[66]

One institution remained open to blacks. Trinity Church, composed of many conservative Whigs and leaders of the New York City government, opened its doors to blacks. Within a few years Anglicans held an average of forty black marriages a year in Trinity, including many between slaves and the free. Trinity Church members were prominent in the New York Manumission Society, founded in 1785 to combat the institution of slavery and, most immediately, to confront slavecatchers who attempted to re-enslave the free blacks living in the city. In 1787 Trinity reopened its African Free School after a hiatus of four years.[67]

The 4,000 blacks who sailed to Nova Scotia in 1783 faced an uncertain future. Colonel Stephen Bleuke led his regiment of Pioneers and Guides to a remote area where they founded Birchtown, named after the commanding general in New York City who had given them their passport to freedom. Bleuke thrived in his new environment and over the years became a school teacher, politician, and wealthy landowner. Others such as Thomas Peters found the British to be deceptive and soon sought to leave. By 1790 Peters negotiated with John Clarkson of the English Manumission Society for over one thousand refugee blacks to leave for Sierra Leone where Peters, along with becoming a landowner, ran into his own father after a thirty-year absence. Still other blacks went to London where they became impoverished; eventually a few declared their intention to return to America.[68]

The overall effect of the American Revolution upon Afro-Americans has yet to be written. In the nineteenth century many black scholars and citizens concentrated on the achievements of Patriots such as Crispus Attucks in an effort to insure that black contributions to the War for Independence were not completely disregarded by white scholars and citizens. At the same time, an underground perception of the revolution emerged. David Walker in his profoundly revolutionary *Appeal*, written in 1829, sought to rouse his fellow blacks into open rebellion against their slavemasters. As part of that effort he reminded his black readers that during the American Revolution the British were "our real friends and benefactors."[69]

Notes

1. From a hymn sung by black loyalists as quoted in Wallace Brown and Hereward Senior, *Victorious in Defeat: The American Loyalist in Exile* (New York, 1984), 170.

2. For the roster of black loyalists on *L'Abondance* see "Book of Negroes Inspected on the 30th of November . . . on Board the fleet laying near Statten Island"; *Papers of the Continental Congress, 1774–1789*, National Archives microcopy 247, reel 66, item 53 (hereafter NAM 247 r 66 i 53). See also Esther Clark Wright," The Evacuation of the Loyalists from New York in 1783," *Nova Scotia Historical Quarterly* 4 (1984): 5–27; and *Loyalists of New Brunswick* (Frederickton, N.B., Canada, 1955), 249.

3. Wright, *Loyalists of New Brunswick*, 290–93.

4. See Eugene Genovese, *From Rebellion to Revolution: Afro-American Slave Revolts in the Making of the Modern World* (Baton Rouge, 1979), 11–12; David Barry Gaspar, *Bondsmen and Rebels: A Study of Master-Slave Relations in Antigua with Implications for Colonial British America* (Baltimore, 1985) and Philip Morgan, "Black Society in the Lowcountry, 1760–1810," in Ira Berlin and Ronald Hoffman, eds., *Slavery and Freedom in the Age of the American Revolution* (Charlottesville, Va., 1983), 83–143. See also Michael Craton, *Testing the Chains: Resistance to Slavery in the British West Indies* (Ithaca, N.Y., 1982) and the classic and most sympathetic studies of C. L. R. James, *The Black Jacobins: Toussaint L'Overture and the San Domingo Revolution*, 2d ed. (New York, 1963) and Herbert Aptheker, *American Negro Slave Revolts* (New York, 1944).

5. Quoted in Phyllis Blakely, "Boston King: A Black Loyalist," in *Eleven Exiles: Accounts of Loyalists in the American Revolution* (Toronto, 1982), 266.

6. See William H. Nelson, *The American Tory* (Oxford, 1961), 111–12 and Theodore G. Tappaert and John W. Doberstein, eds., *The Journals of Henry Melchior Muhlenberg*, 3 vols. (Philadelphia, 1942–58), 3:53, 105.

7. "Lee Papers," 4 vols., *Collections of the New-York Historical Society* (New York, 1871–74), 1:379, 410.

8. James W. St G. Walker, "Blacks as American Loyalists: The Slaves' War for Independence," in *Historical Reflections/Reflections Historiques* 2 (1975): 53–54; Peter Wood, "The Dream Deferred: Black Freedom Struggles on the Eve of White Independence," in Gary Okihiro, ed. *In Resistance: Studies in African, Caribbean and Afro-American History* (Amherst, Mass., 1986), 167–87.

9. For laws regulating behavior of blacks in New York see *Colonial Laws of New York from 1664 to the Revolution*, 5 vols. (Albany, N.Y., 1894), 1:158, 519, 588, 1073; and for New Jersey see Bernard Bush, ed., "Laws of Royal Colony of New Jersey, 1703–1769," *Documents Relating to the Colonial History of the State of New Jersey* (hereafter *New Jersey Archives*), 3d ser., vols. 2–4 (Trenton, N.J., 1900–82), 2:27–30, 138–40, 163–64, 496; and John C. Pomfret, *The Province of East New-Jersey, 1609–1702, The Rebellious Proprietary* (Princeton, 1962), 292, 297. For a discussion of rigor and cruelty of laws see T. J. Davis, "Slavery in Colonial New York City" (Ph.D. diss., Columbia University, 1974), 20; Edgar J. McManus, *Black Bondage in the North* (Syracuse, N.Y., 1976), 73–88.

10. See Tappert and Doberstein, *Journals of Henry Melchior Muhlenberg*, 3:105.

11. See Robert D. Bass, *The Green Dragon: The Lives of Banastre Tarleton and Mary Robinson* (New York, 1957), 40–58; J. W. Fortescue, *History of the British Army*, 13 vols. (London, 1910–30), 3:259.

12. For coverage of the 1712 revolt see Davis, "Slavery" (Ph.D., diss., Columbia University, 1974), 99–113; Kenneth Scott, "The Slave Insurrection in New York of 1712," *New-York Historical Society Quarterly* 45 (1961): 43–74; Aptheker, *American Negro Slave Revolts*, 172; McManus, *Black Bondage*, 127–32.

13. The 1741 conspiracy is receiving new attention from scholars who emphasize its potential rather than its failure. For coverage of the 1741 conspiracy see T. J. Davis, ed., *The New York Conspiracy by Thomas J. Horsmanden* (Boston, 1971); Davis, *A Rumor of Revolt* (New York, 1985); Davis "These Enemies of Their Own Household: A Note on the Troublesome Slave Population in Eighteenth Century New York City," *Journal of the Afro-American Historical and Genealogical Society* 5 (1984): 133–47; and Marcus Rediker and Peter Linebaugh, "The Many-Headed Hydra: Sailors, Slaves and the Atlantic Working Class in the Eighteenth Century," *Journal of Historical Sociology* 3 (1990): 225–52. For a discussion of the 1734 plot see *The New-York Gazette*, 25 Mar. 1734; *The American Weekly Mercury* (Philadelphia), 5 Mar. 1734; *The Weekly Rehearsal* (Boston), 8 Apr. 1734. For murders see *American Weekly Mercury*, 14–20 Jan. 1729; *New York Gazette*, 1–8 June 1730; *Pennsylvania Gazette* (Philadelphia), 28 Feb.–7 Mar. 1737; *Boston Weekly News-Letter*, 18–25 Jan. 1739.

14. Anthony Benezet to David Barclay, 29 Apr. 1767, as quoted in Betty Fladeland, *Men and Brothers: Anglo-American Antislavery Cooperation* (Urbana, Ill., 1972), 15–16.

15. For black conspiracies with the Indians see Alexander M. Flick, *The Papers of Sir William Johnson*, 13 vols. (Albany, N.Y., 1931), 2:165–66, 174–75, 201; 4:424, 431, 439–40, 495–97, 500; *New-York Weekly Post-Boy*, 18 July 1765. For gangs in Westchester County see *New-York Weekly Post-Boy*, 29 Dec. 1746. For Bergen County see *Boston Weekly Post-Boy*, 4 June 1744 and *Pennsylvania Gazette* (Philadelphia), 10 Mar. 1754.

16. The work of the Anglican church and its missionary arm, the Society

for the Propagation of the Gospel, has recently renewed attention after decades of neglect. See Patricia Bonomi, *Under the Cope of Heaven: Religion, Society and Politics in Colonial America* (New York, 1986), 119–22; John C. Van Horne, *Religious Philanthropy and Colonial Slavery; The American Correspondence of Dr. Bray, 1717–1777* (Urbana, Ill., 1985), 22, 34–36, passim. For older and still very useful studies see Nelson R. Burr, *The Anglican Church in New Jersey* (Philadelphia, 1954), 24–28; Frank Klingberg, *Anglican Humanitarianism in Colonial New York* (Philadelphia, 1940), 124–39; William W. Kemp, *The Support of Schools in Colonial New York by the Society of the Propagation of the Gospel* (New York, 1913), 234–61; Charles Briggs, "Elias Neau, the Confessor and Catechist of Negro and Indian Slaves," *Proceedings of the Huguenot Society of America* 3 (1903): 103–16.

17. See *New York Journal or General Advertiser*, 13 Oct. 1774. For the importance of black preachers see Albert J. Raboteau, "The Slave Church in the Era of the American Revolution," in Berlin and Hoffman, *Slavery and Freedom*, 193–217.

18. For this point see Gary B. Nash, "Forging Freedom: The Emancipation Experience in the Northern Seaports, 1750–1820," in his *Race, Class and Politics: Essays in American Colonial and Revolutionary Society* (Urbana, Ill., 1986), 284–88.

19. Here I am employing the models for slave revolts developed by Marion D. deB. Kilson, "Towards Freedom: An Analysis of Slave Revolts in the United States," *Phylon* 25 (1964): 175–87 and extended by Genovese, *From Rebellion to Revolution*, 1–51.

20. See Clement A. Price, *Freedom Not Far Distant: A Documentary History of Afro-Americans in New Jersey* (Trenton, N.J., 1980), 56–60. For Somerset County troubles see the many citations in "Docket of Jacob Van Noorstrat, J.P., Somerset County," *Genealogical Magazine of New Jersey* 43 (1968): 65–67. For early colonization plans see Eli Seifman, "A History of the New-York State Colonization Society" (Ph.D. diss., New York University, 1965), 17.

21. See "New Jersey Provincial Congress to John Hancock, NAM 247 r 82, i 68, 169, 173. For the hanging of blacks see *New England Chronicle* (Cambridge, Mass.), 1 June 1775. For incidents in northern New York see Jeptha R. Simms, *The Frontiersmen of New York*, 2 vols. (Albany, N.Y., 1882–83), 2:176; James Sullivan, ed. *Minutes of the Albany Committee of Correspondence, 1775–1778*, 3 vols. (Albany, N.Y., 1907), 1:24, 649–50. For rebellious conditions on Long Island see Richard Shannon Moss, "Slavery on Long Island: Its Rise and Decline during the Seventeenth through Nineteenth Centuries" (Ph.D. diss., St. John's University, 1985), 232–52.

22. See Samuel S. Forman, "Memoirs," 3 vols. 1765–1867, 1:16, New-York Historical Society Manuscript Collection.

23. See Larry R. Gerlach, *New Jersey in the American Revolution, 1763–1783: A Documentary History* (Trenton, N.J., 1975), 147–50.; Colonel Breeze could not have done that good a job because a year later his slave, Samuel Smith, left him to join the British army. See NAM 332, roll 7, book 2, p. 17.

24. For a computation of New Jersey colonial runaways see Harry B. Weiss, *The Personal Estates of Early Farmers and Tradesmen of Colonial New Jersey, 1670–1750* (Trenton, N.J., 1970), 17.

25. This is based upon comparison of the slave notices in *New Jersey Archives*, 1st ser., vol. 31, 2d. ser., 1–5 and the New Jersey slaves leaving with the

British in 1783 listed in the embarcation lists in NAM 332 r 7 and NAM 247 r 66 i 53. Thus it is a conservative estimate.

26. Historians of the southern provinces have noted that only about one of every four runaways was advertised and argue that costs, distances to newspapers, and the belief that slaves could be captured quickly and locally cut down on the number of notices. See Margaret Washington Creel, *A Peculiar People: Slave Religion Among the Gullah* (New York, 1988); Philip Morgan, "Black Life in Eighteenth Century Charleston," *Perspectives in American History*, n.s. 1 (1984): 187–232 and Betty Wood, *Slavery in Colonial Georgia, 1730–1775* (Athens, Ga., 1984), 147–50, 168–87.

27. See, for example, *Pennsylvania Gazette* (Philadelphia), 14 Sept. 1774; *Pennsylvania Packett* (Philadelphia), 25 Aug. 1778 for extended discussion of maccaroni hairstyle. For a discussion of the used-clothing markets of New York City see Shane White, "A Question of Style: Blacks in and Around New York City in the late Eighteenth Century," *Journal of American Folklore* 102 (Jan. 1990): 23–44.

28. See *New Jersey Archives*, 2d ser., 1:17 and 4:419.

29. For buckskin breeches see *New Jersey Archives*, 2d ser., 1:209, 335–36, 2:78–79; 3:14, 73–74, 225, 235, 273; 4:169, 267; 5:116, 183, 196. For beaver hats see 1:134, 498–99; 2:78–79, 364–66 (This description of Harry includes a two-page discusson of the "maccaroni" style), 4:197, 419; 5:326. For women see 2:511, 612; 3:14, 400; 4:176, 180, 193, 255, 272.

30. For the Van Sayls see NAM 332 r 7 book 1, p. 26; for the Couwenhoven brothers book 1, p. 42; for John Sipe's losses book 1, p. 33. That the five were traveling together suggests a relationship. For the Collins see NAM 247 r 66 i 290. For a discussion of the extended nature of black family during revolutionary era see Mary Beth Norton, Herbert G. Gutman and Ira Berlin," The Afro-American Family in the Age of Revolution," in Berlin and Hoffman, *Slavery and Freedom*, 175–93; for an important study of the black family in New York City see Vivien Kruger, "Born to Run: The Slave Family in Early New York, 1626–1827" (Ph.D., diss., Columbia University, 1985). For additional information on blacks in the American Revolution in these two counties see Graham Hodges, "Black Resistance in Colonial and Revolutionary Bergen County, New Jersey," *Bergen County Historical Society Occasional Papers* (River Edge, N.J., 1989) and Hodges, *African-Americans in Monmouth County During the Age of the American Revolution* (Lincroft, N.J., 1990).

31. See Kenneth Scott, ed., *Rivington's New York Newspaper* (New York, 1973); NAM 247 r 6, i 66 and NAM 332 r 7, p. 40.

32. For Stephen and Margaret Bleuke see NAM 332 r7, book 1, 28; for Joseph Paul and family see book 1, p. 40.

33. See NAM 332, r 7, book 1, p. 32 for both.

34. See NAM 332 r 7, book 1, p. 24.

35. See NAM 332 r 7, book 1, p. 36.

36. Donald L. Robinson, *Slavery in the Structure of American Politics, 1765–1820* (New York, 1971), 54–98; F. Nwabueze Okoye, "Chattel Slavery as the Nightmare of the American Revolutionaries," *William and Mary Quarterly*, 3d ser., 37 (1980): 3–28.

37. The best review of American use of blacks remains Benjamin Quarles, *Negro in American Revolution* (Chapel Hill, N.C., 1960), 68–111. For a discussion of the Laurens' proposal see Peter Maslowski, "National Policy towards

the Use of Black Troops in the Revolution," *South Carolina Historical Magazine* 72 (1972): 1–17.

38. See William Kelby, ed., "Orderly Book of Three Battalions of Loyalists," in *Collections of New-York Historical Society* (New York, 1916), 6; "Lee Papers," 1:369, 372, 379, 410, 425; 2:104–05. See also Quarles, *Negro in American Revolution*, 94–110, 156 and black reminiscences in Jon C. Dann, *The Revolution Remembered: Eyewitness Accounts of the War for Independence* (Chicago, 1980), 46–48, 390–99.

39. The phrase is Quarles's in his *Negro in American Revolution*, 94–111.

40. See Jeffrey J. Crow, *The Black Experience in Revolutionary North Carolina* (Raleigh, N.C., 1977); Gary B.; Nash, *Forging Freedom: The Formation of Philadelphia's Black Community* (Cambridge, Mass., 1988); Wood, "Dream Deferred," in Okihiro, ed., *In Resistance*, 167–87. For Black Pioneers arriving in Canada see Robert S. Allen, ed., *The Loyal American: The Military Role of the Loyalist Provincial Corps and their Settlement in British North America, 1775–1784* (Ottawa, 1983), 12, 14, 71, 83. For a good portrait of the slave-soldier see Gary B. Nash, "Thomas Peters: Millwright, Soldier and Deliverer," in his *Race, Class and Politics*, 269–83. See also James W. St. G. Walker, *The Black Loyalists: The Search for a Promised Land in Nova Scotia and Sierra Leone, 1783–1870* (New York, 1976), 1–17 and Ellen Wilson, *The Loyal Blacks* (New York, 1976), 1–41.

41. For company organization see the many pay vouchers for the Black Pioneers in the British Headquarters Papers, Public Record Office (hereafter PRO)/55/57 fol. 6492; PRO 30/55/57 fol. 6480; PRO 30/55/79, fol. 8918; "Return of Strength and Distribution of His Majesty's Provincial Troops, 1779," Cortlandt Skinner Papers, Library of Congress. Further evidence of Black Pioneer presence in New York from August 1779 until June 1780 comes from the account book of William D. Faulkner, brewer. Faulkner supplied beer to the British troops and sold more than 260 gallons to the Black Pioneers in that time. See William D. Faulkner Account Book, 1773–1790, Faulkner Manuscripts, New-York Historical Society, 76, 110, 112–19, 130, 139–46. For organization in New York City see Allen, *Loyal Americans*, 71, Walker, *Black Loyalists*, 22, and using his evidence with different emphasis, Philip Ranlet, *The New York Loyalists* (Nashville, Tenn., 1986), 116–17.

42. "Return of Troops in the North Fit For Duty, April 2, 1776," Clinton Papers, 19:40; "The State of the Black Company of Pioneers as Given up by Captain Martin to Capt. Stewart, July 13, 1777," Clinton Papers, 41:29, Clements Library; Mackensie Papers, 10 May 1776, 19 Aug. 1776, Clements Library; "Muster Roll of Butler's Rangers," *New York Genealogical and Biographical Record* 31 (1900): 13, 16; Wilson, *Loyal Blacks*, 34.

43. Quarles, *Negro in the American Revolution*, 92–97, 134–54; Peter Michael Voeltz, "Slave and Soldier: The Military Impact of Blacks in the Colonial Americas" (Ph.D. diss., University of Michigan, 1978), 57–67, 92, 126–31, 178–81. For black executions of Hessian soldiers see "Intelligence," Green Manuscripts, 5 Nov. 1782, Clements Library, Ann Arbor, Mich., and Rodney Atwood, *The Hessians: Mercenaries from Hessen-Kassel in the American Revolution* (New York, 1980), 193. For discovery of conspiracy see Thomas H. Edsall, ed., *Journal of John Charles Phillip Von Kraft, 1776–1784* (New York, 1888), 104.

44. "List of the Names of Negroes belonging to Capt. Martin's Company, whom they Belonged to, and the Respective Places They Lived At," Gold Star Manuscripts, no. 30, Clements Library; PRO Audit Office Records, "Transcript for Benjamin Whitecuff," 41:223; Hugh Edward Egerton, *The Royal*

Commission on the Losses and Service of American Loyalists, 1783–1785 (New York, 1971 reprint), 132; Robert Ernst, "A Long Island Black Tory," *Long Island Forum* 41 (1978): 18–19; For other spies see John Bakeless, *Turncoats, Traitors and Heroes* (Philadelphia, 1959), 100, 148, 260.

45. "Extract of General Orders Given by His Excellency General Sir Henry Clinton, Commander in Chief of the Army in America," Mackensie Letter Book E., Clements Library.

46. Voeltz, "Slave and Soldier" (Ph.D. diss., University of Michigan, 1978), 8, 19, 35–41, 640–48.

47. For Howe's proclamation see Wilson, *Loyal Blacks*, 29. Clinton's proclamation ran for several months in the *Royal Gazette* (New York), 3 July 1779–25 Sept. 1779.

48. See *New Jersey Journal* (Chatham), 20 July 1779. As with Patriot commanders, British officers were sometimes inconsistent about offering places in their armies to blacks. Oliver DeLancey, for example, a Loyalist given a key position in the British army, declared in 1777 that "all Negroes Mullattoes and other Improper Persons who have been admitted to the Corps be immediately discharged." See Kelby, ed., "Orderly Book of Three Battalions of Loyalists," *Collections of the New-York Historical Society* (1916), 6. Also E. Alfred Jones, "A Letter Regarding the Queens' Rangers," *Virginia Magazine of History and Biography* 30 (1922): 369–70.

49. For black housing see Thomas A. Jones, *History of New York during the Revolutionary War*, 2 vols. (New York, 1879–80), 2:76; William A. Stone, *History of New York City from Discovery to the Present Day* (New York, 1872), 232; Kruger, "Born to Run," 674.

50. For descriptions of Corlies's land see George H. Moss, *Nauvoo to the Hook* (Trenton, N.J., 1964), i and "Conveyance Records," vol. G–2: 331–34, New Jersey State Archives, Trenton.

51. For good coverage of Monmouth's problems and the doubtful loyalty of its citizens see Dennis Ryan, "Six Towns: Continuity and Change in Revolutionary New Jersey, 1770–1792" (Ph.D. diss., New York University, 1974), 127–28, 178, 181–83; Francis Lundlin, *New Jersey; Cockpit of the Revolution* (New Brunswick, N.J., 1960), 291. For George Washington's doubts about Monmouth see John C. Fitzpatrick, ed., *Writings of Washington*, 30 vols. (Washington, D.C., 1932), 5:226–27.

52. For this incident see John Stillwell, *Historical Genealogical Miscellany of New York and New Jersey*, 5 vols. (New York, 1903), 5:290. For the British custom of informally awarding titles see Craton, *Testing the Chains*, 52–99.

53. See *New Jersey Archives*, 2d ser., 4:504. For Moody's participation see *Lieutenant James Moody's Narrative of His Exertions and Suffering in the Cause of Government since the Year 1776*, 2d ed., (London, 1783), 11–12; for the fear of uprising in Elizabethtown see *Gaine's Weekly Mercury* (New York), 23 June 1780 and Edward F. Hatfield, *History of Elizabeth Town, N.J.* (New York, 1868), 476 and Aptheker, *Negro Slave Revolts*, 89.

54. For Loyalist plots and anger see Edward H. Tebbehoff, "The Associated Loyalists: An Aspect of Militant Loyalism," *New-York Historical Society Quarterly* 63 (1979): 115–44. See also *Royal Gazette* (New York), 5, 23 June 1779.

55. For weather and crops in New York City see David Ramsay, *The History of the American Revolution*, 2 vols. (London, 1789), 2:181–84, 191.

56. *Pennsylvania Evening Post* (Philadelphia), 12 Apr. 1780.

57. For removal of blacks to interior regions see *New Jersey Gazette* (Burlington), 5 June 1780. For mass exodus of blacks see *New Jersey Journal* (Chatham), 13 June 1780, *Pennsylvania Post* (Philadelphia), 23 June 1780. For Loyalist confidence see William Smith, *Historical Memoirs* (New York, 1971), 261, 286, 289, 314–17. For Livingston see Carl Prince et al. eds., *Papers of William Livingston,* 5 vols. (New Brunswick, N.J., 1979–89), 1:427.

58. For account of Murray's death Franklin Ellis, *The History of Monmouth County, New Jersey* (Philadelphia, 1885), 209.

59. For the attack on Smock see Ellis, *Monmouth County,* 209. For the British attack see *Pennsylvania Packett* (Philadelphia), 13 June 1780. For cannon see *New Jersey Archives,* 2d ser., 4:434–35. For the importance of spiking cannon see Ernest Mandeville, *The Story of Middletown, New Jersey* (Freehold, N.J., 1927), 63. For Smock's damage claims see "An Account of Captain Barnes Smock for Loss of Arms," Miscellaneous Manuscripts, nos. 1059, 1077, 1092, New Jersey State Archives, Trenton. See also "David Forman to William Livingston," 9 June 1780, in *Livingston,* 3:423, and Asher Holmes to William Livingston," 12 June 1780, Monmouth County Historical Association. For martial law see "Acts of Assembly of the State of New Jersey," 29 Oct. 1779–19 July 1780), (Trenton, 1780), 243 and "William Livingston to the Assembly," 7 June 1780 in *Livingston* 3:421; for a nice description of Tye's attack see Sidney Kaplan, *The Black Presence in the Era of the American Revolution* (New York, 1973), 66–67.

60. *Pennsylvania Evening Post* (Philadelphia), 30 June 1780.

61. *New Jersey Archives,* 2d ser., 4:603.

62. For accounts of this famous battle see "Nathaniel Scudder to Joseph Scudder," 11 Sept. 1780, New-Jersey Historical Society Manuscript Collection, Newark, N.J.; *Gaines Weekly Mercury* (New York City), 25 Sept. 1780; *Pennsylvania Packett* (Philadelphia), 3 Oct. 1780.

63. For first reports on Huddy's capture see *New Jersey Gazette* (Burlington), 24 Apr. 1782 in which Tye's death in 1780 is prominently mentioned. The article describes Tye as "justly to be more feared and respected than any of his breathern of a fairer complexion." For part of the voluminous literature on the Huddy-Asquill case see Charles Forman, *Three Revolutionary Soldiers* (Cincinnati, Ohio 1902), 12–15 and Allan J. Donor, "The Melancholy Case of Captain Asquill," *American Heritage* 31 (1970): 81–92.

64. See, for example, John H. Barber, *Historical Collections of New Jersey; Past and Present* (New Haven, 1865), 365; Ellis, *Monmouth County,* 88.

65. See *New Jersey Archives,* 2d ser., 5:446.

66. For damage to slavery in New York see Kruger," Born to Run," 640–41, 650–53, 690–91; for New Jersey see Arthur Zilversmit, "Liberty and Prosperity: New Jersey and the Abolition of Slavery," *New Jersey History* 88 (1970): 215–27; for the region see McManus, *Black Bondage,* 159; for racial attitudes see Shane White, "Impious Prayers: Elite and Popular Attitudes towards Black and Slavery in the Middle Atlantic States, 1783–1810," *New York History* 67 (1986): 261–85. For the tenor of abolition in these areas see Robert Fogel and Stanley Engerman, "Philanthropy at Bargain Prices: Notes on the Economics of Gradual Emancipation," *Journal of Legal Studies* 3 (1974): 377–401 and Claudia Goldin, "The Economics of Emancipation," *Journal of Economic History* 33 (1973): 66–86, esp. 68–71.

67. See "Register of Marriages in Trinity Church," 1:149–53, passim;

"New York City Manumission Society Standing Committee Reports," 1785–95, New-York Historical Society; Carleton Mabee, *Black Education in New York State* (Syracuse, N.Y., 1979), 20–21.

68. See especially, James W. St. G. Walker, "The Establishment of a Free Black Community in Nova Scotia," in Martin Kilson and Robert J. Rotberg, eds., *The African Disapora* (Cambridge, Mass., 1976) and for Bleuke see Wilson, *The Loyal Blacks* 70, 85, 202–19 and Wilson, *John Clarkson and the African Adventure* (New York, 1980).

69. Herbert Aptheker, ed., *One Continual Cry: David Walker's Appeal to the Colored Citizens of the World* (New York, 1965), 114.

PAUL A. GILJE

2

The Common People and the Constitution: Popular Culture in New York City in the Late Eighteenth Century

Displayed in the halls of the New-York Historical Society is a very attractive banner from 1788. It is the standard of the Society of Pewterers paraded in the Grand Federal Procession celebrating the ratification of the Constitution. Just one of many such banners in evidence on that day two hundred years ago, the Pewterers' flag gives us a sense of the dimensions and detail of that momentous event. As an artifact of the past, the insignia and inscription appear to document artisanal support for the new government. The pewterers proudly proclaim:

> The Federal Plan Most Solid & Secure
> Americans Their Freedom will Endure
> All Arts Shall Flourish in Columbia's Land
> And All her Sons Join as One Social
> Band

This procession, and similar demonstrations in Philadelphia and elsewhere, has attracted the historians' attention. The old line of interpretation was that the Grand Federal Procession, with its wide participation and column after column of master, journeyman, and apprentice, marked the triumph of the new Constitution and its near unanimous acceptance.[1] More recently scholars have gotten beyond these whiggish notions and have begun to look at the procession from different angles. Sean Wilentz uses the procession as a vehicle to examine craft organization and as a counterpoint to the development of class conflict in the early nineteenth century. Wilentz argues that if artisans temporarily united to demonstrate their support for the Constitution in 1788, that unanimity lasted only a few decades. By the early nineteenth century, when other processions were organized for somewhat different purposes, master and journeyman found it more difficult to march under the same banner. After 1825 whatever cracks that may have existed in the social order, evident in the external and internal hierarchy of the trades, had turned into gaping class chasms.[2]

Susan Davis, in her analysis of Philadelphia parades, views processions as an important medium of communication and associates them with the exercise of power. She therefore emphasizes that it was the Philadelphia elite and the affluent master mechanics who planned Philadelphia's federal procession on 4 July 1788, and that the parade excluded large numbers of powerless workers like blacks, laborers, most sailors, and women. Davis believes that the Grand Federal Procession was an important "ceremonial resource and precedent" for later nineteenth-century craft ceremonies. She also admits, however, that few of these later ceremonies copied the extensive representation of craft organization and artisan work structure.[3]

In his discussion of all of the federal processions in 1788, which is in an essay on the English roots of American popular radicalism, Alfred Young focuses more on the antecedents of craft processions. He argues that similar practices had existed in England before 1700, and faded in the eighteenth century, only to revive briefly after 1760. Young thus suggests that although a few mechanics might have been aware of these traditions, most probably were not. Therefore he sees these processions largely as innovations created by the mechanics themselves.[4]

For this essay the Grand Federal Procession is one of three incidents to be analyzed in the hope of gaining some insight into popular culture in New York City in the late eighteenth century. Although the Grand Federal Procession has been frequently seen as offering insight into popular attitudes, the other two incidents to be examined here—the Doctors' Riot of April 1788 and the Bawdy House Riot of October

1793—tell us more about the culture of the common man. In particular, a close examination of the procession allows us to begin to address two crucial questions: What did common New Yorkers think about the United States Constitution and how important was the document to the popular consciousness?

At first the Grand Federal Procession seems to answer these questions. If all those craftsmen paraded in front of throngs of people, certainly the Constitution must have been important. Certainly New Yorkers must have thought about the Constitution a great deal. But does the procession prove this? To make an ahistorical comparison, we might think for a moment about the current bicentennial. There are millions of dollars being spent on the celebration. There continue to be birthday parties for the Constitution, parades, fireworks, even symposia. The celebration of the bicentennial is very much on the minds of Americans. But the celebration is not the same thing as the document. How many Americans will read the Constitution, think about it, and decide that it is or is not the best form of government for America based on a rational analysis of its provisions?

By extrapolation, we may wonder how many of the artisans in the Grand Federal Procession had read the Constitution or even the famous, high-sounding *Federalist Papers* that first appeared in New York newspapers in the fall of 1787? Did they really know very much about this government that they were celebrating? Did they really care? Why did so many artisans join in the procession? Why, for instance, were the apprentices there? Were they there simply to experience the celebration? These questions cannot be answered in any definitive manner. Few, if any, of the participants have left us documents recording their thoughts on these issues. Yet we can begin to gain some insight into the relationship between the people and the Constitution by placing the Grand Federal Procession into the larger context of street theater, represented here by the procession and the Doctors' and Bawdy House Riots, and the popular culture of the period.

Popular Culture and Street Theater

Popular culture is an ambiguous concept. Simply, it is the culture of the common man. Regardless of the term's connotations today, for the eighteenth century popular culture refers to those bits of evidence which reveal the mental universe of ordinary people. This definition follows the lead of several European scholars in the past two decades.

Historians like Emmanual Le Roy Ladurie, E. P. Thompson, Robert Darnton, Carlo Ginsburg, Eric Hobsbawm, and Peter Burke have studied carnivals, riots, charivari, ritual processions, folk tales, as well as specific incidents such as a great cat massacre by printer journeymen and apprentices, and the Inquisition's examination of the cosmos of a Friulan miller. Taken together this work utilizes a variety of approaches and sources to make the inarticulate speak to us and to allow us to view the popular culture of the early modern period.[5]

Perhaps one of the most successful approaches to popular culture has been an intensive examination of public or street theater ranging from the unorganized riot to the stylized procession. Thus E. P. Thompson surveys the eighteenth-century bread riot to unravel the complexities of popular concepts of an economy dictated by local morality rather than a national market.[6] Likewise Emmanuel Le Roy Ladurie dissects the carnival in Romans at the end of the seventeenth century to reveal the inner tensions of that society, while Robert Darnton uses a bourgeois description of a local religious procession to demonstrate eighteenth-century perceptions of the ordering of society.[7] Public or street theater offers a similar opportunity to understand the eighteenth-century American world as is evident in the work of Rhys Isaac and Greg Roeber on court day and the application of ritual by Virginia gentry to reinforce their hegemonic rule.[8]

Isaac's work is particularly instructive because of his discussion of methodology. Isaac argues that in the agrarian society of eighteenth-century Virginia the written word was less important than the oral gesture. Relying heavily upon anthropology, Isaac asserts that in the pre-industrial world the oral dramaturgical process was crucial in defining the parameters of social custom. The ritual on court day, with the gentry gathered to decide upon the community's welfare, as well as the ritual of the Anglican church, down to the timed and ordered entry and departure of the local leadership, all contributed to the way participants in that society defined social relationships.[9]

Although the two locations were different, what was true for eighteenth-century Virginia held for eighteenth-century New York as well. Public or street theater was an extremely important part of the mental universe of all its participants, be they patrician—lawyers, merchants, landowners—or plebeian—mechanics and laborers. Throughout the eighteenth century the public spectacle had a special role for New York society. In the colonial period processions were organized to celebrate the king's birthday, the arrival of a new governor, a victory on the battlefield, or some other special occasion.[10] In Revolutionary New York effigy processions, popular demonstrations, and celebrations were very important and the Grand Federal Procession in 1788 demonstrates their significance in the postwar period.[11]

Of course, the procession was but one form of street theater. Of equal importance, as several European scholars have written, were moments of less decorum.[12] These varied from repeated plebeian celebrations of carnival-like holidays such as Pope Day and New Year's, to less regular occasions of disorder and riot. Both types occurred with frequency in eighteenth-century New York City. Pope Day celebrations began in the city in 1748 and probably continued until the mid 1760s, while rowdy New Year's antics persisted well into the nineteenth century. Riots broke out in the colonial period for a variety of reasons ranging from impressment to the valuation of pennies. Both forms of plebeian disorder merged in the 1760s and 1770s in the street theater used to oppose British imperial measures and to propel New York into the Revolution in 1775 and 1776.[13]

Street theater relies heavily upon ritual or "ritualization" to convey its meaning. "Ritualization," according to anthropologist Max Gluckman, is "a stylized ceremonial" in which individuals "perform prescribed actions" that "express and amend social relations so as to secure genial blessing, purification, protection, and prosperity for the persons involved in some mystical manner which is out of sensory control."[14] The key here is that there is a formula for behavior that dictates the dramaturgical activity, that has a function within the society, and that has some extrasensory content. For example, the standard way to celebrate a national holiday during the colonial period—such as the king's birthday or a military victory—was for the city magistrates to organize a procession and march from City Hall, at the corner of Wall and Broad Street, to Fort George at the tip of Manhattan Island. Joining them would be some military company, either militia or regulars. They would hold a dinner of their own, drink to the health of the king, while supplying a public treat of liquor or food for the people. Cannon would fire salutes and at night bonfires were lit and city windows were illuminated with candles. The formula of behavior in this example is the repeated procession, dinner, treat, salutes, and illuminations. Its function was to reassert loyalty to the king. Like court day in Virginia, it also reassured the local elite of their dominance. The mystical or extrasensory component is less apparent. But the whole process had a mystical air to it. The pageantry of the procession accentuated the mythical identity of the elite with the person of the king. Less logical was the connection between the fires and the king. But through custom, long practice, and a bit of hocus pocus illuminated candles and bonfires had come mysteriously to represent a united community loyal to its monarch.[15]

Ritual, however, was neither frozen nor static. It could be adjusted or altered to meet the circumstance. At times its very meaning could be inverted. Certainly this happened during the 1760s and 1770s in New York City and elsewhere, when, through a process that may never be fully understood, many of the rituals of loyalty to the king were taken over by the resistance movement and wielded in opposition to the king. Much of this process was unconscious, piecemeal, and unintended. Some of this transition, however, was planned and orchestrated.[16]

Eric Hobsbawm refers to practices that are intentionally borrowed from the past and then repeated as "invented tradition." He defines this term as "a set of practices, normally governed by overtly or tacitly accepted rules and of a ritual or symbolic nature, which seek to inculcate certain values and norms of behaviour by repetition, which automatically implies continuity with the past." He contrasts it with custom, which he sees as more adaptable, less rigid, and better connected to previous practices. Hobsbawm also implies that custom tends to have common roots while invented tradition is created from above to symbolize cohesion, legitimize institutions and leadership, and inculcate values.[17]

Exactly how much of the street theater of the revolutionary movement can be seen as unplanned adjustment of crowd ritual undertaken by common folk, what Hobsbawm might call custom, or how much as intended adaptation dictated from above, invented tradition, is not the issue to be addressed here. (Indeed there may be no clear way of demarcating such a distinction for the crowd activity of the 1760s and 1770s). But it is important to distinguish between the two as a preliminary caution to a discussion of popular culture and street theater in the years immediately around 1788. Both customary ritual and invented tradition might be part of a popular culture, but the source of a particular practice is important for our reading of it. Any examination of street theater must be done carefully. We must ask what it tells us about popular attitudes and what it might tell us about attitudes towards the populace.

The Grand Federal Procession

The distinction between custom and invented tradition, as described above, has some relevance for an understanding of the Grand Federal Procession of July 1788. Certain questions need to be addressed: who is running the show? what is the purpose of this street theater? where did the idea for the procession come from? and what does it say about popular culture? Had the procession been an ad hoc adaptation of customary street theater, with strong plebeian roots, then the link between the Grand Federal Procession and the popular culture would have been direct and the conclusion that the common people of New York supported the Constitution justifiable. The situation, however, was more complex. The intricate plan—it is important here to distinguish between the plan and the event—did not reflect a custom derived from those on the bottom of society. Instead, it revealed an attempt to create or "invent" tradition by the city's elite. In this effort the federalist patricians were only partially successful. The city's leading mechanics also hoped to utilize the procession to demonstrate certain ideas of their own. The master mechanics, after decades of struggle, asserted their republican identity in the procession (the event) by intermingling self-created craft symbols with support for a new prosperous and industrious United States. They also organized their craft displays to emphasize social cohesion within the craft work structure. Although these efforts represented an expression of ideas closer to the common man, they had little resonance with the people in the street.

The New York City procession was very well planned. Every minute was organized and every participant had his set place. The pre-parade itinerary set a starting time of 8:00 a.m.. The procession was to form in the fields and was to march down Broadway to Great Dock Street, through Hanover Square, Queen, Chatham, and Arundel Streets, and end on Bullock Street at Bayard's Tavern. Everything was to be regulated. Thirteen cannon were to signal the start. Adjutants were appointed to help the marchers find their places. These men were to be identified by their blue coats, red sashes, and white feathers tipped in black. On a level above this group were the assistants who were to wear a uniform of a white coat with blue cape and sash and a white feather tipped in blue. The assistants carried speaking trumpets. The order of the procession was elaborate breaking down the various categories of participants into some very small groups.

> Two Horsemen with Trumpets.
> 1 piece of Artillery.
> FIRST DIVISION.
> Foresters in frocks, carrying axes,
> Columbus in his ancient dress, on horseback.
> 6 Foresters, &c.
> A Plough.
> A Harrow.
> Farmers.

United States Arms, borne by Col. White, supported by the Society of the Cincinnati.
Gardners.
A Band of Music.
Taylors.
Measurers of Grain.
Millers.
Inspectors of Flour.
Bakers.
Brewers.
Distillers.
SECOND DIVISION.
Coopers.
Butchers.
Tanners and Curriers.
Leather Dressers.
THIRD DIVISION.
Cordwainers.
FOURTH DIVISION.
Carpenters.
Farriers.
Hatters.
Peruke makers and Hair dressers.
FIFTH DIVISION.
White Smiths.
Cutlers.
Stone Masons.
Painters and Glaziers.
Cabinet Makers.
Windsor Chair Makers, Ivory Turners and Musical Instrument-Makers.
Upholsters.
Fringe Makers.
Paper Stainers.
Civil Engineers.
SIXTH DIVISION.
Ship Wrights.
Black Smiths.
Ship Joiners.
Boat Builders.
Block and Pump Makers.
Sail Makers.
Riggers.
SEVENTH DIVISION.
Ship and Crew.
Pilot Boat and Barges.

Pilots.
Marine Society.
Printers, Bookbinders and Stationers.
EIGHTH DIVISION.
Cartmen.
Mathematical Instrument Makers.
Carvers and Engineers.
Coach Makers.
Coach painters.
Copper Smiths and Brass Founders.
Tin Plate Makers.
Pewterers.
Gold and Silver Smiths.
Potters.
Chocolate Makers.
Tobacconists.
Dyers.
Brush Makers.
Tallow Chandlers.
Sadlers, Harness and Whip Makers.
NINTH DIVISION.
Gentlemen of the Bar.
Philological Society.
President and Students of the College.
Merchants and Traders.
TENTH DIVISION.
Clergy.
Physicians.
Strangers.
Militia Officers.
1 Piece of Artillery.

At the end of the parade, the participants were to close ranks and be reviewed by division by the Committee of Arrangements, followed by Congress, foreigners of distinction, and "the Gentlemen on horseback." At the firing of some more cannon, the marchers were to proceed to tables set up outside the tavern and around a pavilion designed by Pierre L'Enfant. Banners, like that of the Pewterers, were to indicate where the various participant groups were to sit. Finally, as the plan indicated "At five o'clock P.M. two guns will fire as a signal retiring from the table by the left."[18]

The procession plan, although following a pattern set by other Federal festivities, most resembled the rituals of rule in the colonial period when the city's magistrates might parade in the streets to the accompaniment of the local militia. Here the magistrates were to be replaced by various members of the elite in the Order of Cincinnati in the First Division and the various patrician occupations represented in divisions nine and ten.[19] In between came the city's mechanics arranged in divisions. The whole procession was to be regimented in an almost military manner with cannon firing signals and uniformed marshals (assistants and adjutants) overseeing the show. Indeed, the patrician effort to dominate the festivities was evident in the selection of the assistants. The thirteen men listed as assistants included six militia officers, three Livingstons, five lawyers, at least two members of the Order of Cincinnati, and several merchants. Only one of the thirteen, Captain Stagg, may have been a mechanic.[20]

Like many rituals of rule in the eighteenth century, the procession's organizers hoped to reinforce the legitimacy of the social hierarchy. The mechanics were to obey instructions from aristocratic New Yorkers bellowed out from speaking trumpets. They also had to march between divisions of the elite, allowing the patricians to dominate the last sections of the parade, and thereby occupy the most dramatic position upon the stage of this form of street theater. Finally, the corps of mechanics had to undergo a review by various sections of the elite. During this latter process the social distance between most of those in the parade and their reviewers was strengthened by that crucial distinction between those who rode upon horseback and those who traveled upon foot.

What did the mechanics get for their efforts? Of course they got a meal (although spirituous liquors were not allowed). But the city patricians also made a significant concession. The procession signaled an important step in the recognition of the mechanics as an interest group. Only a few years earlier the state assembly had snubbed efforts by the mechanics to incorporate their society.[21] Exclusion of mechanics had also marked previous rituals of rule. On 4 July 1787, for example, the city's leadership rehearsed a ritual borrowed directly from the colonial period. In the morning the city militia were reviewed and put through maneuvers. At noon the Society of Cincinnati assembled at City Hall to hear some speeches (among others, two Livingstons spoke), after which the society moved in procession to the fort (the same route of colonial processions), where tents had been erected "under which they partook of a cold collation" and drank thirteen toasts.[22] A year later the situation had changed. As the federalists wrestled with the antis in the state convention at Poughkeepsie, the mechanics' support was needed for the new Constitution.[23] The mechanics were to be recognized as mechanics and included not only in the procession, but by implication, in the power structure as well. The mechanics had struggled for this acceptance since the 1760s.[24]

There were limitations to this recognition of the mechanic interest besides the intended domination of the festivities by the elite. In their announcement of the order of the parade, the organizers reminded New Yorkers that decorum must "prevail on the day of the Procession." The caution continued "Any person who is interested in the event . . . will doubtless consider that much of the honor of the day depends upon the harmony which subsists among the different orders of citizens, who compose the Procession—Every man should esteem each other as a Brother, engaged in testifying their joy on the commencement of the 'EPOCHA OF LIBERTY AND JUSTICE'."[25] If the procession recognized distinctions within the ranks of society, indeed sometimes drawing very subtle distinctions among the trades, the idea behind the parade was to submerge those differences and join in the new brotherhood to be created by the Constitution.

The aims of the federalist leadership in sponsoring the Grand Federal Procession were almost all met despite a rain that caused delays. The procession began at 10:00 a.m. instead of 8:00 a.m.. A few of the trades did not participate. But the vast majority of mechanics did join in, even in those trades in which there were only a dozen or so practitioners. Support for the Constitution was exhibited. Reinforcement for the hierarchy was offered. Decorum was maintained and social cohesion was manifested.[26]

But the procession did not quite meet up to the federalist expectations. Federalist newspapers afterwards gushed with excitement over its success. Five thousand men and boys participated with elaborate floats and insignias attesting loyalty to the Constitution. But the official description of the day makes it evident that the elite did not quite dominate the event as they intended. Indeed, column after column of newspaper coverage reveals a different outcome: the mechanics took the procession and made it their own.[27]

Dwarfing all the other displays in the parade, and having the greatest dramatic impact, was the "Federal Ship Hamilton," which headed the seventh division of the procession. In all likelihood the merchant elite had contributed money to construct this scaled down thirty-two-gun frigate. But by doing so they had guaranteed that when most of them marched after it, they would hardly be noticed. The *Hamilton* was twenty-seven feet in keel and ten feet in beam and was manned by about thirty seamen and marines. It was the cannon of the

THE COMMON PEOPLE AND THE CONSTITUTION 59

Hamilton that fired the starting signal for the procession. The *Hamilton* also participated in the most overt performances of street theater of the day: the taking on of a pilot to guide the ship from the "Old Constitution" to the new in front of the Confederation Congress and president, and the exchange of salutes with the French packet. Although modeled after similar ships in other processions of that year, and built to represent the ship of state, the *Hamilton* may have had some hidden meanings. Following close upon the heels of the sixth division of the procession, which included most of the trades that would have been active in its construction—shipwrights, ship joiners, boat builders, block and pump makers, sailmakers, and riggers—and in front of the pilots and ship captains who were not that far removed from the lower class, the *Hamilton* belonged to the plebeians.[28]

It may also have represented one of those forms of popular culture retained in the collective consciousness only to be revived at an appropriate moment. Processions using ships as a focal point had occurred in Germany in the seventeenth and eighteenth centuries and this may well be a logical adaptation of those earlier practices. (Philadelphia, which had a ship in its federal procession before New York, was heavily influenced by German culture.)[29]

Borrowing insignias from London guilds and improvising some of their own, mechanics went beyond an expression of support for a stronger central government and used their banners, floats, and participation to express the uniqueness, industry, and virtue of their own trades.[30] In some instances there was hardly a reference to the official purpose of the procession. The cabinet makers, for example, marched with three masters in the lead, followed by an arms bearer. Thirty apprentices then marched four abreast, trailed by twenty journeymen in the same order. Then came the cabinet makers' float; a stage drawn by horses upon which a cradle and a table were completed during the march. Also on the stage was a banner with a representation of a furniture warehouse displaying different aspects of their craft. The cabinet makers' motto only obliquely referred to the Constitution; it declared "Unity with Fortitude." Sixteen master workmen, marching four by four, closed up the order. The onlooker certainly got a sense of what cabinet makers did, and could see that their trade adhered to a strict craft structure, but learned little about their support for the new form of government.[31]

Some trades presented a greater mixture of symbols that demonstrated confidence in the Constitution as well as revealing the intricacies of the trade. The description of the upholsterers' section was incredibly detailed and reads almost like a fashion interior design report. Clearly the upholsterers saw an opportunity to exhibit their command of the finer points of their trade. Their float consisted of

> A four wheel'd carriage on which was erected a handsome oblong square stage, railed round and painted light blue, the railing adorned with light blue and white fringe, the lower part ornamented with a deep festoon border . . . the floor covered with an elegant wilton carpet; on the rear of the stage stood the Federal Chair of State, seven feet high and four wide, exclusive of decorations, covered with rich light blue sattin; down the back on each side hung a piece of drapery, drawn in festoons; a rich white fringe with Circasian tassels decorated the drapery. The wood part that appeared was carved and whitened to be in uniformity with the fringe, and in contrast with the sattin; on the outer edges of the chair back hung oak and laurel: the oak emblematical of strength of mind, the laurel of proof against vice, being ever green.

The float, however, contained more than this example of the upholsterers' art. On either side of the chair stood a boy, "dressed in true characters, with mantles, girdles, sandles &" to represent "Liberty" and "Justice." "Liberty" held the staff and liberty cap in his right hand and a roll of parchment with the words "Federal Constitution, 1788" in his left hand. "Justice" had a sword in one hand, scales in the other. The upholsterers were sticklers for symbolic detail and loaded their float with other emblems, including "a most superb canopy" with ten stars emblazoned upon it to represent the ten ratifying states. The various insignias attached to the canopy included, among others, two watchful tigers, and a map of North America, topped by a bald eagle that reached nineteen feet above the ground. "A tall comely young man in the character of America, dressed in the real Indian style, with elegant plumage, belt, &c." stood upon the float with a banner that declared "May the Federal Constitution be supported as is the canopy and chair of state," by liberty and justice.[32]

All of this display had been produced by the thirteen city upholsterers who marched six on either side with the last trailing the float. These men, too, carried banners that advertised the trade; upon each was "an emblematical figure representing the different articles of their business, such as marquees, tents, sofas, beds, &c." Thus the upholsterers jumbled their support for the Constitution with their identity as mechanics.[33]

Many of the banners and insignias of the other trades carried similar messages. One side of the bakers' banner depicted their trade flourishing and two ovens. The motto declared

THE COMMON PEOPLE AND THE CONSTITUTION

> We are all built both sound and tight,
> We hope to serve the ships in sight
> With the best bread, bak'd of good flour
> When Congress have the Federal power.

The butchers' flag had "three bullocks' heads, two axes crossways, a boar's head, and two garbs, supported by an ox and a lamb" and proclaimed

> Skin me well, dress me neat,
> And send me aboard the federal fleet

The windsor and rush chair makers had a standard borne by two men, depicting workmen in a large manufacturing shop, in front of which there was a view of a river with boys carrying chairs down to the wharves. The chair makers called for free trade and lyricized:

> The federal states in union bound
> O'er all the world our chairs are found.

The repeated use of the nautical metaphor only strengthened the mechanic identity with the ship *Hamilton*. A few trades made the connection explicit. The ship joiners for instance, who had no doubt a special claim to the *Hamilton*, crested their flag with the motto

> Our merchants may venture to ship without fear,
> For pilots of skill shall Hamilton steer.
> This federal ship will our commerce revive.
> And merchants and shipwrights and joiners shall thrive,
> On the ocean of time she's about to set sail,
> Fair freedom her compass and concord the gale.

The 300 cartmen, who followed shortly after the *Hamilton*, also took up this theme, depicting the Federal ship *Hamilton* on their banner and offering the following lines.

> Behold the federal ship of fame,
> The Hamilton we call her name;
> To every craft she gives employ,
> Sure cartmen have their share of joy.

Alexander Hamilton was raised to dizzying heights through the persona of the ship. Only Washington was similarly deified. In both cases, it was almost as if there was a need to glorify the individual, identify him with the nation, and, like the colonial procession in support of monarchy, assert a regal identity with a head of state. Thus the tallow chandlers displayed figures of both Washington and Hamilton with the words "The illustrious WASHINGTON, may he be the first president of the United States." The boat builders also had a print of Washington. The picture showed him standing over the construction of a boat and various boat building tools.

> Accept great Chief that share of honor's praise,
> A grateful people to your merit pays,
> Verse is too mean your virtue to display,
> And words too weak our meaning to convey.

The cordwainers' flag showed Washington leaving the Philadelphia Convention and handing a copy of the Constitution to an allegory of fame.[34]

The Grand Federal Procession, then, is full of twisted and sometimes contradictory meanings. But one thing is clear. In all of the banners, displays, and pageantry there was little about the content of the Constitution. The mechanics agreed upon the need for a stronger central government and believed that somehow, perhaps through the being of a monarch-like president, it would create greater economic prosperity. But exactly how this was to work remained vague.[35]

The message of all of this symbolism also had a more fundamental meaning. The Constitution was perceived as being good because it included a call for unity. This message is certainly evident in the pewterers' banner when it declared that all of Columbia's sons shall "Join as one Social Band." This theme was implicit in most of the mechanic mottos. On the one hand it seems as if the banners are talking about the union of the thirteen states; on the other, as is evident on the pewterers' banner, this talk might have been a metaphor for a social bond.

To explore this last idea further it would help to identify the people who created these symbols and models—the mechanics. But which mechanics? As appears in the order of march among the cabinet makers, most of the trades represented in the procession were hierarchical and organized on the craft master-journeyman-apprentice work structure. Indeed the master upholsterers did not even have their apprentices and journeymen participate unless they agreed to wear an Indian costume or ancient toga. Given the structure of the trades, the banners, stages, and floats were probably the product of the minds, if not the hands, of the masters. If that is true, then maybe they, too, like the elite, were using the federal procession to "invent tradition" to solidify their own dominance of their trade.[36]

The Grand Federal Procession, then, presents us with the odd spectacle of two layers of invented tradition; one patrician and the other master mechanic. This conclusion suggests that this procession did not fully represent the popular culture of the lower orders and was not really a product of the people.

However, the July 1788 procession does tell us some things about popular culture. First, it demonstrates the significance of street theater in late eighteenth-century New York. The federalist leadership recognized its importance and planned to use it for their own purposes. The master mechanics also understood how meaningful a well-orchestrated procession could be. They, too, approached it with a degree of utilitarianism. For the masters, the Constitution represented a means to a more prosperous future and a way to express some basic notions of social unity. For the journeymen, apprentices, and the crowd, the Constitution and, one suspects, the Grand Federal Procession were less important. They would not argue with the call for greater prosperity or with the message of social unity. And, of course, everyone loved a parade and a picnic. Street theater was a very important way for eighteenth-century Americans to express themselves and their notions of society. But if we really want to get a better idea of what the lower orders—the rest of the crowd—thought in the 1780s and 1790s, we need to turn to other more extemporaneous types of street theater.

Death, Love, and Money in New York City

Any discussion of popular culture must return to the basic concerns of the common people. In this, although attitudes may vary, there is some universality. Emmanuel Le Roy Ladurie's innovative analysis of the Abbé Fabre's short novel, *Jean-l'ont-pris,* focuses on three related themes—Love, Death, and Money—and connects the eighteenth-century tale to folklore and to the very real problems of the peasant in Pays d'Oc. New York's popular culture in the late eighteenth century may not have shared the same odd configuration explored by Ladurie, but the issues of love, death, and money were evident in popular manifestations of street theater.[37]

These ideas can be seen in the Doctors' Riot of 1788 and the Bawdy House Riot of 1793. Both were unprecedented disturbances in New York City. During the 1760s and 1770s hundreds and even thousands of New Yorkers had joined in the popular demonstrations and mobs. But although a mixture of motives drove these people into the street, their cause was overtly political. In the colonial period before 1765 there were several major riots in New York City, but nothing on the scale of what took place in April 1788 and October 1793. An older customary form of street theater was therefore being extended into new areas in the closing decades of the century. But this was not invented tradition. Instead, these riots struck to the very core of New York popular culture and derived from widely shared ideas about death, love, and money.

The Doctors' Riot began, so the story goes, when a young boy peered into a window of the New York Hospital and a cynical medical student lifted the arm of a cadaver and taunted that it was the boy's mother. Unfortunately, the boy's mother had just died and had been buried. The boy ran to his father, a mason who was working nearby. Outraged, the mason led a mob in an attack on the hospital. The mob gutted the building, roughed up a few doctors, and captured several medical students who were later surrendered to the authorities. The next day, rioting continued as a mob searched for cadavers in the homes of the city's doctors. Later that day, rioters attacked the jail in an effort to retake the medical students held there. Officials called out the militia. The few men who actually mustered obeyed the order to fire into the crowd, killing three rioters. Soon thereafter the disturbance subsided.[38]

Like many riots in the eighteenth century, the Doctors' Riot was an example of street theater in which the common people wrote the script. Although not nearly as stylized as more formal ritual processions, the rioters did follow a pattern of behavior typical of other riots in the eighteenth century. The question here, however, revolves not so much around what the rioters did, but why they did it. In other words, what does the Doctors' Riot tell us about popular attitudes?

One thing the Doctors' Riot made glaringly evident: the people in the street retained a firm belief that they continued to have a right to riot. Throughout the eighteenth century, and reinforced by the experience of revolutionary mobs, riots occurred to protect perceived community interests. The robbing of graves, and the use of the dead as cadavers, violated popular sensibilities and appeared to run counter to the community interests. Even the magistrates recognized this point. The Common Council had passed laws against grave robbing in the months before the riot, officials tolerated the first day and one half of the disturbance, and even after the riot the court recognized the legitimacy of the popular complaint.[39] But perhaps even more important than this belief in the right to riot for the purposes of our understanding of late eighteenth-century popular culture is what the riot says about attitudes toward death.

Death is a historical certitude often overlooked by scholars. In part that neglect is a product of twentieth-century perceptions and practices that separate death from everyday life by removing it from view and placing it in the hospital. Philippe Ariès, however, argues that attitudes toward death have undergone several transitions. Only within the context of these changes can the sensibilities of the New York mob be understood.[40]

By the late eighteenth and early nineteenth centuries, Ariès suggests, a new phenomenon had emerged; people became less concerned with their own death than with, as Ariès put it, "la mort de toi" (the death of the other person). This development led to a new emphasis on graveyards and tombs, as well as "the romantic, rhetorical treatment of death." Previously, except in places like Puritan New England, the remains of the deceased were of little consequence.[41] In New York, for instance, laws had to be passed in the late seventeenth century to ensure that some sort of proper burial took place.[42] However, with intensifying emotional ties marking the rise of romanticism, a new and greater concern for the dead appeared. The little boy who peered into the hospital window, and who believed he saw his mother being dissected, then, partook of this new phenomenon and reacted to the supposed violation of his mother's grave. That so many New Yorkers joined with the father in the subsequent riot only suggests that this attitude toward death had become very pervasive indeed.

Popular motivation, which often has to be surmised, was probably more complex. Ariès cautions that although we can delineate major patterns of change in attitudes toward death over long periods of time, these patterns often overlapped and intermingled.[43] Peter Linebaugh's discussion of the Tyburn Riots in England protecting the corpses of hanged criminals from dissection by surgeons confirms this observation. Linebaugh argues that the common people's "attitude to death . . . was a compound of Christian and quasi-pagan beliefs" that can never be entirely disentangled. He examines several of these beliefs as they refer to hanged criminals. Of special interest for the analysis here, however, is his discussion of the popular concern for the proper burial of the deceased. Linebaugh asserts that the rioters were worried about more than the need for a correct Christian burial; the common people also believed that the dead had the power "to come again" and would do so "to be troublesome," or haunt, those who failed "to perform some last kindness."[44] Such beliefs, when placed in the framework offered by Ariès, hark back to ancient and even prehistoric notions of death.[45] Thus a combination of beliefs probably lay behind the action of the Doctors' Riot. On one hand the disturbance reflected a popular culture influenced by the rising tide of romanticism and affection, on the other, it reflected some basic and primitive ideas on the nature of death.

The Doctors' Riot also represented a fundamental distrust of science and can be viewed as a popular reaction to the Enlightenment. During the eighteenth century medicine as a field of enquiry became increasingly scientific and professionalized. The creation of medical schools in Great Britain and then in America were important steps in this development. The teachers and students of these medical schools saw themselves on the cutting edge of science and of the Enlightenment. Young doctors believed that the only way for them scientifically to understand human anatomy was through dissection and viewed popular attitudes toward the sanctity of the dead as mere remnants of a bygone and unscientific age.[43] There can be little doubt, therefore, that cadavers were obtained surreptitiously in New York in the months before April 1788. The repeated reports in newspapers and even action taken by the Common Council both point to the existence of this practice.[47] Although many New Yorkers were angry in 1788 because the doctors really were robbing graves, those New Yorkers were also rejecting the new science represented by that practice. The rioters, when they broke into the hospital, not only buried all of the dead bodies they found, they also gutted the place, destroying scientific instruments and stealing scientific samples—such as a piece of mica taken by one apprentice.[48]

As a guide to understanding New York popular culture at the end of the eighteenth century, the Doctors' Riot has limitations. There is no question that the practice of grave robbing and using stolen corpses for dissection irritated sensibilities and triggered some of the most extensive urban rioting of the period. But much of the analysis of motivation has to be derived from other contexts. Be that as it may, the Doctors' Riot demonstrated a popular concern and interest with death—and treatment of the dead. It thereby provides greater insight into popular culture than the examination of the Grand Federal Procession.

Popular attitudes toward love and money appeared in a large New York riot five years later when irate New York crowds tore down several bawdy houses. Animosity toward prostitution was not the cause of these disturbances. Instead, the hundreds of New Yorkers, most of whom were artisans and laborers, who joined in the riot acted from anger and disappointment over the outcome of a well-publicized rape case.[49]

The case of Lanah Sawyer versus Henry Bedlow was the talk of the town in late September and early October in 1793. Bedlow was a well-known rake and even his defense attorneys admitted that Bedlow was not above a little deception with a lady if he believed it would help him to have "his wishes" with her. From an affluent family, well dressed and smooth talking, Bedlow cut an imposing figure for any girl. Lanah, from a poor background and just seventeen, thus became in the minds of many New Yorkers an easy mark for the "gallant" Bedlow. One day in late August, Lanah found herself being insulted in the street by some Frenchman visiting the city. Bedlow came to the rescue and escorted her home. He introduced himself as "lawyer Smith"—a name that indicates the social distance between the two. Sawyer either did not want to believe otherwise, or else was so entranced that a real gentleman expressed interest in her, that when a neighbor told her that she had a fine "Beau" of a fellow and that his name was really Harry Bedlow, she continued to insist on calling him "lawyer Smith." After a few proper refusals she accepted a date with him. Most of that evening must have been glorious for Sawyer. They stopped at Corre's Hotel to have ice cream and promenaded twice around the Battery. When they started to head home it was very late. Bedlow, according to Sawyer's story, then forced her to go to an infamous house of assignation, Mother Carey's, and, locking her in a room with him, tore off her clothes and raped her.[50]

Whatever the real facts of the case—Bedlow claimed he had only seduced Lanah—the common people of the city were outraged. The ensuing trial only exacerbated that anger. Bedlow's lawyers attacked not only Sawyer's reputation, but also the reputation of girls of her social strata by arguing that what these young women might view as "discretion and prudence" might be "termed the highest indiscretion and highest imprudence" by those "people of more mature judgement." This portrait of Lanah and her friends stood in marked contrast to the prosecution attorney who described Sawyer as "an artless simple girl" and grated public sensibilities because much of the defense of Bedlow centered on testimony by Mother Carey and her tenants. The prosecution characterized these witnesses, accurately as all New Yorkers knew, as "women of the most infamous occupations, employed in the destruction of the innocent, or in support of themselves by prostitution."[51] Bedlow's acquittal, in light of popular attitudes, triggered a mob attack not on the affluent Bedlow, but on Mother Carey's and a few similar houses of ill repute.

What does this riot tell us about popular culture? Christine Stansell, who has analyzed this case, argues that Lanah Sawyer's situation demonstrated both the vulnerability and the opportunities for girls of her class and social station in this period. Sawyer enjoyed a degree of independence permitted young girls from the lower class; they could walk the streets alone, maybe even flirt with strangers. But the open world of the street was also a harsh world. If they were not careful, young women might find themselves in an awkward situation from which they could not escape. Such was the plight of Lanah Sawyer. No doubt thrilled by the attentions of "lawyer Smith," she misread the intentions of Harry Bedlow. Stansell points out that Bedlow's lawyers capitalized on Sawyer's mistake and argued a typical late eighteenth-century position: given the base passion found in all women and the relative social position of Sawyer and Bedlow, she could not possibly have misunderstood his signals. "Considering the difference of their situations, to what motive could she attribute his assiduities? Could she imagine that a man of his situation would pay her any attention . . . unless with a view of promoting illicit commerce? Was it possible that Lawyer Smith had any honorable designs in his connection with a sewing girl?"[52]

If the New York court accepted this argument, the people in the street did not. Herein lies our entree into the popular culture of the day. For most New Yorkers Lanah Sawyer's behavior was not lascivious. It was not an open invitation to sexual connection with "lawyer Smith." As improbable as it seemed to Bedlow and his cronies, the people in the street did not think it impossible, however unlikely, for a gentleman to express sincere interest in this young seamstress. A certain amount of interaction between young men and young women was accepted by New Yorkers, even if that meant, as Bedlow's defense attorneys claimed, young women "accustomed to levity" allowed "male friends liberties."[53] Popular attitudes toward sex were at this time somewhere between the bawdy world of Defoe and Hogarth and the high morality of Victorianism. Romantic notions of love and a rejection of social boundaries were just beginning to take hold. Bedlow's treatment of Sawyer, and the attacks of his lawyers upon all girls of her social standing, flew in the face of these notions.

The driving force behind the mob busy demolishing "Mother Carey's nest of chickens" on the night of 13 October 1793 was the popular attitude toward both love and money. The social distance between the rakish Bedlow and the "simple" Sawyer was highlighted in the popular mind by the association of these houses of ill-repute with the leaders in society. Bedlow's defense attorneys admitted that because of his previous exploits he knew and patronized Mother Carey. After the riot, one irate commentator, "Justitia," who identified herself as a woman, even declared that these houses of ill-fame were not closed down because many of the city's leading male citizens patronized them. "Justitia" asserted that the magistrates had "not corrected one single house of ill fame, nor shewn their disapprobation," but instead "some of these honorable gentlemen (aye and married ones too) are pretty liberal contributors to the support of these nunneries." Resentment that wealth influenced the courts and the law, and the belief that aristocrats violated popular ideas of love, combined to drive hundreds of New Yorkers to demonstrate their anger in a violent manifestation of street theater.[54]

When viewed against the backdrop of these popular expressions of cultural values the Grand Federal Procession appears as a more limited avenue for understanding the common people of New York in the late eighteenth century. The Grand Federal Procession was an attempt to garner support for the new Constitution and to invent tradition. The city's elite hoped to utilize the procession to order their society and maintain their own dominance. Instead, the city's master mechanics took over the procession, celebrating their crafts and their own views of social unity while expressing an oblique support for the Constitution. For those further down in society the procession was, no doubt, a grand occasion. It was a day off from work and a day when they could participate in a demonstration both of their craft and of ideals that they partially shared. But, except for an expression of hope for a new prosperity, the Grand Federal Procession did not touch the core of popular concerns.

For an insight into the world of the common man in the age of the Constitution we need to turn to other expressions of the popular culture. The Doctors' and Bawdy House Riots offer us a brief view of those values. We see here a continued interest in the fundamental problems of love, death, and money. We also see that popular ideas on those subjects remained mixed. Ideas about death reached back toward a more primitive past as well as forward toward romanticism and individualism. Love and money provoked similar contradictions. The common people allowed that a young woman like Lanah Sawyer might be out on the street alone, talk with a stranger, and even make a date with him, while maintaining her chastity and overcoming obvious social boundaries. Here, too, popular attitudes looked to both past and future. In other words, New York popular culture at the end of the eighteenth century was caught between older traditional notions and the modern era.

Notes

1. See for example Carl Van Doren, *The Great Rehearsal: The Story of the Making and Ratifying of the Constitution of the United States* (New York, 1948), 239–251. For descriptions of the Federal Procession see Whitfield J. Bell, Jr., "The Federal Processions of 1788," *New-York Historical Society Quarterly* 46 (1962): 5–39; Sarah H. J. Simpson, "The Federal Procession in the City of New York," *New-York Historical Society Bulletin* 7 (1925): 39–57.

2. Sean Wilentz, "Artisan Republican Festivals and the Rise of Class Conflict in New York City, 1788–1837," in Michael H. Frisch and Daniel J. Walkowitz, eds., *Working-Class America: Essays on Labor, Community, and American Society* (Urbana, Ill., 1983), 37–77; Wilentz, *Chants Democratic: New York City and the Rise of the American Working Class, 1788–1850* (New York, 1984), 87–97.

3. Susan G. Davis, *Parades and Power: Street Theatre in Nineteenth-Century Philadelphia* (Philadelphia, 1986), 117–32.

4. Alfred F. Young, "English Plebeian Culture and Eighteenth-Century American Radicalism," in Margaret Jacob and James Jacob, eds., *The Origins of Anglo-American Radicalism* (London, 1984), 185–89, 200–206.

5. Emmanuel Le Roy Ladurie, *Carnival in Romans*, trans. Mary Feeny (New York, 1979); Ladurie, *Love, Death and Money in the Pays D'oc*, trans. Alan Sheridan (New York, 1982); E. P. Thompson, *The Making of the English Working Class* (New York, 1963); Thompson, "The Moral Economy of the English Crowd in the Eighteenth Century," *Past and Present* 50 (1971): 76–136; Thompson, "Time, Work-Discipline, and Industrial Capitalism," *Past and Present* 38 (1967): 56–97; Thompson, "'Rough Music': Le Charivari anglais," *Annales* 27 (1972): 285–312; Thompson, "Patrician Society, Plebeian Culture," *Journal of Social History* 7 (1974): 382–405; Thompson, "Eighteenth-Century English Society: Class Struggle Without Class?" *Social History* 3 (1978): 133–65; Robert Darnton, *The Great Cat Massacre and Other Episodes in French Cultural History* (London, 1984); Carlo Ginsburg, *The Cheese and the Worms: The Cosmos of a Sixteenth-Century Miller,* trans. John and Anne Tedeschi (Baltimore, 1980); Eric Hobsbawm and Terence Ranger, eds., *The Invention of Tradition* (Cambridge, 1983); Peter Burke, *Popular Culture in Early Modern Europe* (New York, 1978).

6. Thompson, "Moral Economy of the English Crowd," *Past and Present* 50 (1971): 76–136.

7. Ladurie, *Carnival in Romans;* Darnton, *The Great Cat Massacre,* 107–43.

8. Rhys Isaac, "Dramatizing the Ideology of Revolution: Popular Mobilization in Virginia, 1774 to 1776," *William and Mary Quarterly* 3d ser., 33 (1976): 357–85; Isaac, *The Transformation of Virginia, 1740–1790* (Chapel Hill, N.C., 1982), 58–138, 322–357; A. G. Roeber, "Authority, Law, and Custom:

The Rituals of Court Day in Tidewater Virginia, 1720 to 1750," *William and Mary Quarterly* 3d ser., 37 (1980): 29–53.

9. Isaac, "Dramatizing the Ideology," *William and Mary Quarterly*, 3d ser., 33 (1976): 357–85; Isaac, *Transformation of Virginia*, 58–138, 322–357.

10. For typical colonial processions see I. N. Phelps Stokes, *The Iconography of Manhattan Island*, 6 vols. (New York, 1922), 4:533, 535, 539, 541, 543, 554, 585.

11. Paul A. Gilje, *The Road to Mobocracy: Popular Disorder in New York City, 1763–1834* (Chapel Hill, 1987), 39–68; Gilje, "Republican Rioting" in William Pencak and Conrad Edick Wright, ed., *Authority and Resistance in Early New York* (New York, 1988), 202–25.

12. Gilje, *Road to Mobocracy*, 16–30; Thompson, "'Rough Music'," *Annales* 27 (1972): 285–312; Violet Alford, "Rough Music or Charivari," *Folklore* 70 (1959): 505–18; Natalie Zemon Davis, "The Reasons of Misrule," in Davis, *Society and Culture in Early Modern France: Eight Essays* (Stanford, Calif., 1975), 97–123; Davis, "Charivari, Honor, and Community in Seventeenth-Century Lyon and Geneva," in John J. MacAloon, ed., *Rite, Drama, Festival, Spectacle: Rehearsals Toward a Theory of Cultural Performance* (Philadelphia, 1984), 42–57; Ladurie, *Carnival in Romans*; Burke, *Popular Culture*, 178–204; Martin Ingram, "Ridings, Rough Music, and the 'Reform of Popular Culture' in Early Modern England," *Past and Present* 105 (1984): 79–113; Bryan D. Palmer, "Discordant Music: Charivaris and Whitecapping in Nineteenth-Century North America," *Labour/Le travailleur* 3 (1978): 5–62; Young, "English Plebian Culture," in Jacob and Jacob, eds., *Origins of Anglo-American Radicalism*, 185–206.

13. Gilje, *Road to Mobocracy*, 9–68.

14. Max Gluckman, ed., *Essays on the Ritual of Social Relations by Daryll Forde, Meyer Fortes, Max Gluckman, Victor W. Turner* (Manchester, 1962), 24–25.

15. Stokes, *Iconography*, 4:533, 535, 537, 539, 541, 543, 554, 585.

16. For examples see Gilje, *Road to Mobocracy*, 39–68.

17. Hobsbawm and Ranger, eds., *The Invention of Tradition*, 1–14.

18. *Independent Journal* (New York), 23 July 1788.

19. Even the farmers of the first division were later referred to as "gentlemen farmers" in ibid., 2 Aug. 1788.

20. David C. Franks, *The New-York Directory* (New York, 1787); *The New York Directory and Register For the Year 1789* (New York, 1789).

21. New York (State) General Assembly *Journal of the Assembly of the State of New York* (New York, 1785), 13; Edward Countryman, *A People in Revolution: The American Revolution and Political Society in New York, 1760–1790* (Baltimore, 1981), 233, 242–44.

22. *Daily Advertiser* (New York), 5 July 1787.

23. For the story of New York's ratification of the Constitution see Linda Grant De Pauw, *The Eleventh Pillar: New York State and the Federal Constitution* (Ithaca, N.Y., 1966).

24. On the mechanics' struggle to gain recognition see Carl Lotus Becker, *The History of Political Parties in the Province of New York, 1760–1776* (Madison, Wis., 1909); Staughton Lynd and Alfred Young, "After Carl Becker: The Mechanic and New York City Politics, 1774–1801," *Labor History* 5 (1964): 215–24; Lynd, "The Mechanics in New York Politics, 1774–1788," ibid., 225–46; Young, "The Mechanics and the Jeffersonians: New York, 1789–1801,"

ibid., 247–76; Young, *The Democratic Republicans of New York: The Origins, 1763–1797* (Chapel Hill, N.C., 1967); Countryman, *A People in Revolution.*
25. *Independent Journal* (New York), 23 July 1788.
26. A full report is in ibid., 2, 6 Aug. 1788. For an anti-federalist account see *New-York Journal*, 23, 24 July 1788.
27. *Independent Journal* (New York), 2, 6 Aug. 1788.
28. Ibid., 6 Aug. 1788.
29. Alfred Young provides an inciteful analysis of how plebeian culture was transmitted across the Atlantic in "English Plebeian Culture," in Jacob and Jacob, eds., *Origins of Anglo-American Radicalism*, 185–206. For the Philadelphia ships see Davis, *Parades and Power*, 120–21. See also Bell, "The Federal Processions," *New-York Historical Society Quarterly* 46 (1962): 5–39.
30. On the source of the insignias see Young, "English Plebeian Culture," in Jacob and Jacob, eds., *Origins of Anglo-American Radicalism*, 201–3.
31. *Independent Journal* (New York), 6 Aug. 1788.
32. Ibid.
33. Ibid.
34. All of the above can be found in several newspapers. I used ibid., 2, 6 Aug. 1788.
35. Lynd, "The Mechanic in New York Politics, 1774–1788," *Labor History* 5 (1964): 225–46.
36. Davis emphasizes the role of master craftsmen in organizing the Philadelphia procession. *Parades and Power*, 117–25.
37. Ladurie, *Love, Death and Money.*
38. Discussion of Doctors' Riot based on the following sources: William Alexander Duer, *New-York as It Was during the Latter Part of the Last Century: An Anniversary Address Delivered before the St. Nicholas Society of the City of New York, December First, 1848* (New York, 1849), 20–22; *New-York Journal*, 15–17, 19 Apr. 1788; *Packet* (New York), 15, 18, 25 Apr., 13 May, 1788; *Daily Advertiser* (New York), 23, 26 Apr., 10 May 1788; *Boston Gazette*, 28 Apr., 5 May 1788; Alexander Anderson, "Diarium," 28 Jan. 1793, microfilm, Columbia University. For secondary accounts, see Joel Tyler Headley, *The Great Riots of New York, 1712–1873* . . . (Indianapolis, Ind., 1970 [orig. publ. New York, 1873]), 55–65; Jules Calvin Ladenheim, "'The Doctor's Mob' of 1788," *Journal of the History of Medicine and Allied Sciences* 5 (1950): 23–43; Sidney I. Pomerantz, *New York, an American City, 1783–1803: A Study of Urban Life*, 2d ed. (Port Washington, N.Y., 1965), 401–2; Isaac Q. Leake, *Memoir of the Life and Times of General John Lamb, an Officer of the Revolution, Who Commanded the Post at West Point at the Time of Arnold's Defection* . . . (Albany, 1850), 332–36.
39. Gilje, *Road to Mobocracy*, 78–83.
40. Philippe Ariès, *Western Attitudes Toward Death: From the Middle Ages to the Present*, trans. Patricia M. Ranum (Baltimore, 1974); Ariès, *The Hour of Our Death*, trans. Helen Weaver (New York, 1981).
41. Ariès, *Western Attitudes Toward Death*, 55–82; David E. Stannard, *The Puritan Way of Death: A Study in Religion, Culture, and Social Change* (New York, 1977), 96–134.
42. Stannard, *Puritan Way of Death*, 129.
43. Ariès, *Western Attitudes Toward Death*, 1–2, 27.
44. Peter Linebaugh, "The Tyburn Riot Against the Surgeons," in Douglas

Hay, et al., eds., *Albion's Fatal Tree: Crime and Society in Eighteenth-Century England* (New York, 1975), 65–117. Quotations from 102 and 106.

45. Stannard, *Puritan Way of Death*, 3–28.

46. Linebaugh, "The Tyburn Riot," in Hay, et al., eds., *Albion's Fatal Tree*, 69–78; Peter Gay, *The Enlightenment: An Interpretation,* 2 vols. (New York, 1969), 2:12–23; Richard Harrison Shryock, *Medicine and Society in America, 1660–1860* (New York, 1960), esp. 28–29, 58–62; Brooke Hindle, *The Pursuit of Science in Revolutionary America, 1735–1789* (Chapel Hill, 1956), 36–58, 280–301.

47. *Daily Advertiser* (New York), 28, 29 Feb. 1788; New York City, Common Council, *Minutes of the Common Council of the City of New York, 1787–1831* (New York, 1917–30), 1:363–64.

48. Anderson, "Diarium," 28 Jan. 1793; *Packet* (New York), 10 May 1788.

49. For a more complete discussion of the riot and the participants see Gilje, *Road to Mobocracy,* 85–92. For sources on the riot see *Daily Advertiser* (New York), 16, 17 Oct. 1793; *Diary,* 15, 16, 18, 23–25 Oct. 1793; *New-York Journal,* 16, 19 Oct. 1793; Moreau de St. Méry, *Moreau de St. Méry's American Journey* (1793–98), trans. and ed. Kenneth Roberts and Anna M. Roberts (Garden City, N.Y., 1947), 312; *People v. Clawson,* New York City General Sessions, 8 Nov. 1793, Municipal Archives and Record Center, New York City; *People v. Burr* et al., New York City General Sessions, 7 Nov. 1793, Municipal Archives and Record Center, New York City; Anderson, "Diarium," 14 Oct. 1793.

50. William Wyche, *Report of the Trial of Henry Bedlow, for Committing a Rape on Lanah Sawyer, and Arguments of the Counsel on Each Side, at the Court of Oyer and Terminer, and Gaol Delivery for the City and County of New-York, Oct. 8, 1793* (New York, 1793).

51. Ibid., 22, 30, 36–37, 44, 48.

52. Christine Stansell, *City of Women: Sex and Class in New York, 1789–1860* (New York, 1986), 23–26, 86, 88. Quotation is in Wyche, *Report of the Trial of Henry Bedlow,* 40.

53. Wyche, *Report of the Trial of Henry Bedlow,* 44.

54. *Diary* (New York), 18 Oct. 1793.

HOWARD B. ROCK

3

The Artisan and the State in the 1790s: A Comparison of New York and London

For both Great Britain and the United States, the 1790s represented a turbulent and a critical era. For America, the issue was nothing less than the future destiny of the newly launched republic, with a Constitution but a few years old. Would its example lead the rest of the Western world to an "age of democratic revolution" or would it fail as had Athens and Rome before? It was a decade of momentous events: the Hamiltonian financial system created a national bank, national debt, and strong federal fiscal engine. The French Revolution met with a mixed reception. War with Britain or France loomed. National political parties emerged and Federalists attempted to squelch opposition through the Alien and Sedition Laws. For the mother country these years were equally ominous. They marked the emergence of a serious popular reform movement and of new revolutionary ideologies given enhanced strength by the American and then the French Revolutions. The war with France that began in 1793 and continued with only a few interruptions until 1815 also imposed hardship on the population and stress on the political structure.

New York and London were the entrepreneurial centers of the two nations. With a population of 45,000 in 1790 and 60,000 in 1800, New

York was about to overtake Philadelphia as the country's largest metropolis. Similar in size to a British port town such as Bristol, it boasted a growing and prosperous hinterland, an excellent deep water harbor, good port facilities, and a local merchant and artisan community of exceptional skill and ambition. London, with nearly a million inhabitants, dwarfed New York and all other American towns. It was the seat of an impressive empire, containing within its boundaries the City of London, the hub of British banking and mercantile interests; Westminster, home of Parliament, the court, and some of the city's most splendid homes; and other sprawling districts such as Spitalfields with its famous weaving community. It also included such rural areas as the outparish of Middlesex and suburban regions such as Chelsea and Marylebone.[1]

Artisans dominated New York occupations. They worked in a variety of trades, ranging from goldsmithing, silversmithing, and cabinetmaking to butchering and baking to carpentry and ship construction. While there were considerable variations in income, craftsmen occupied a middling level in New York society. They were well below the merchant and professional elite, but higher in position than the unskilled laborers and slaves common in the city. Tradesmen tended to live in the outer wards. For instance the cartmen congregated in what would become the sixth ward and the tanners in the future fourth ward. Most crafts were housed in small shops in which a master worked and employed a few journeymen and apprentices. The ratio of journeymen to masters was increasing, though in the 1790s a journeymen still hoped with some reason to become a master. Above all, New York's artisans remained highly conscious of their position above the poor: they believed that their skills and business independence allowed them a respectable position in society.[2]

The artisans of London, too, were a varied lot. Like their New York counterparts they occupied the middle of society. Over one hundred thousand journeymen worked at the various trades along with apprentices and masters. Some areas, such as Southwark where many hatters lived, were known for housing specific trades. Like New York, the small-scale establishment in which the proprietor hired a few journeymen and took on a few apprentices predominated. Outwork also existed with journeymen laboring in their homes, taking in raw material and returning it in finished form to a master or merchant. Many of these journeymen were artisans of exquisite skill, responsible for the cabinetware, silverware, musical instruments, and other fine craftware of the era. London, as well, housed many able craftsmen preparing the necessities of daily urban life, from shoemakers to tailors and bakers. These artisans remained several notches above the large number of poor struggling to get by in this cold and anonymous city such as the unskilled laborers, beggars, vagrants, and children who clogged the streets in search of food and shelter. Still, except for the artisan "aristocracy" of masters at the top of their trades, most craftsmen did not enjoy economic security. Steady employment was uncommon. Construction workers seldom labored in winter. Coopers could be idle in spring and brushmakers had little work after Christmas. Mechanics who failed to mind their accounts or who had a propensity to drink could and often did find themselves in considerable debt or in Newgate.[3]

In both cities the term *artisan* or *mechanic* was somewhat ambiguous. The boundaries between master craftsman and merchant and the distinction between the poorest journeymen and the unskilled remained indistinct. Indeed, tailors who took on mercantile functions often became known as "merchant-taylors." Within the artisan community there were diverse interests and outlooks. For example, the attitude toward the state among the regulated and/or licensed mechanics for whom government stood as employer or regulator was often different from artisans who had little contact with municipal supervision.

Yet the strong sense of occupational identity current in the eighteenth and early nineteenth centuries makes it necessary to discuss mechanics as a separate community. Men with skills acquired through long apprenticeships, who formed and mingled in their own friendly societies, congregated in common taverns, wore leather aprons, and who often lived in common residential areas and in similar housing quite naturally shared a sense of commonality. Thus, even though the outer limits of artisanship were not clearly demarcated, the sense of common identity remained strong.[4]

In the late eighteenth century, artisans in both New York City and London began to build upon their common identity, sought out a republican form of government, and attempted to redefine their relationship with the state. Because of the new forms of government in the United States, mechanics of all political persuasions were allowed to participate in the decision-making process. The situation in London, however, was quite different. Artisans had a muted political voice; organized political parties did not yet exist. The London Corresponding Society (LCS), which enrolled thousands of artisans on its membership list during its seven years of existence, had limited impact on the politics of the day. Considering the tens of thousands of craftsmen and laborers who never joined, it constituted a distinct minority. Yet it laid the foundations for the British working-class movement and was a forerunner of democratic change that would be obtained some generations later. By comparing the political role of mechanics in New York City and London and by examining their respective relationships to the state, we will gain a clearer insight into the political history of the two nations and, in particular, why the United States, unlike England, never developed a distinct working-class political movement.[5]

* * *

The mechanics of New York were actively involved citizens. During the late colonial era in New York, most master craftsmen, including the cartmen, had obtained the freedom of the city and were thus entitled to cast ballots in municipal and assembly elections. Political leaders actively courted them. Moreover, they possessed enough political savvy to gain elective office. Sixty percent of local offices and an amazing thirty percent of aldermanic seats on the Common Council went to craftsmen. Elections were periods of intense attention to this constituency. Yet artisans did not shape the issues or become leaders of contending factions. Prominent merchants and attorneys still expected and usually received deference.[6]

In the revolutionary era artisans extended their influence. While early protests against British policy were often led by the mercantile community, craftsmen composed the heart of the crowds that forced the repeal of the Stamp Act. When protests continued in response to new enactments of Parliament, mechanics moved into leadership roles. Most politically active artisans differed with the more conservative merchants. For example, the merchants were willing to resume trade after the Townshend Acts had been repealed except for the impost on tea, while mechanic spokesmen within the Sons of Liberty protested. Strains existed between importers and many local craft producers and between merchants and mechanics over the refusal of the craftsmen to follow the merchants' lead. Trust between the two communities crumbled.[7]

As war with Britain neared, New York artisans moved into greater prominence. While conservative whigs tried to guide resistance with their own ad hoc organization, artisans organized a Mechanics Committee that espoused a radical egalitarian outlook, influenced by the thought of Thomas Paine. By early 1776 the Mechanics Committee demanded immediate independence as well as the right to pass judgment on the new constitution being drafted for the State of New York.[8]

The political involvement of London artisans was more limited. In Westminster and Middlesex householders voted while in the City of London the famed livery companies such as the Goldsmiths Company and the Taylors Company formed the Court of Common Hall, responsible for the nomination of the mayor and the election of the city's two members of Parliament. For the vast majority of London craftsmen, however, there was no entry to politics other than the street. For example, during the "Wilkes and Liberty" demonstrations of the 1760s thousands of journeymen became briefly involved in reformist politics. While this event represented "something new in the nation's political life," such ritualized mass participation also displayed an "ideological immaturity." Artisans soon abandoned politics and were subject to manipulation during their brief involvement. This was evident in June of 1780 when many of these same craftsmen participated in the Gordon Riots against legislation that reduced Catholic political disabilities. Finally, even for the artisan householders who could cast ballots, there was little chance of ever seeing their brethren on the ballot or even in local office. Government was remote, the force of deference immense. Many prominent masters were politically aware and informed, but still far from the center of power—even when that power resided close to their neighborhoods.[9]

* * *

A comparison of the artisans' relation to the state and politics in London and New York requires discussion of the meaning of republicanism within the two mechanic communities. The debate over the meaning of republicanism in the late eighteenth century—whether or not it was grounded in the civic humanism reaching back to Machiavelli's Florentine state or the relation between individuals and the state put forward by Locke in the late seventeenth century—has reached into artisan studies. Artisan public discourse in the 1790s included both commonwealth ideals based on public virtue, the sacrifice of particular interests, and a common sense of purpose as well as Lockean contractual relations. The issue is the extent of that influence.[10]

In New York, on the whole, a liberal Lockean ideology had the greatest appeal and influence among mechanics. Former staymaker Paine's advocacy of a limited republican state based upon a compact among all citizens, each of whom retained natural rights and was capable of rational political judgment, influenced many mechanics. In 1776 this impact was evident in the Mechanics Committee's demand that all inhabitants be allowed to take part in the ratification of the new state constitution. In the 1790s and into the early 1800s the artisan view of the marketplace, in harmony with the Jeffersonians, also reflected a liberal, non-classical view of republicanism. Like the ambitious Paine who was forever trying to sell his idea of an iron bridge, most artisans saw American republicanism as creating a state in which they could succeed as entrepreneurs. Bakers deeply resented the traditional restriction (assize) on their profit and waged a campaign against it that briefly succeeded in 1800. The anxiety of mechanics to obtain banking privileges and even to have their own bank, the growth of newspaper advertisements and business cards, the expanding number of mortgages, and increasing real estate investments all point to the importance of capitalist freedom as part of the republican tradition.[11]

Artisans did adhere to some aspects of commonwealth ideology in this era. The many attacks on men of wealth, particularly those speculators amassing riches without pursuing a productive trade, became part of artisan politics and ideology. This was in harmony with their sense that they were part of a corporate society, in which artisans contributed their share to the welfare of the community through productive labor carried on in the small shop. This limited but autonomous enterprise represented the embodiment of republican simplicity. Allusions to civic humanism were present in patriotic sermons on the Fourth of July as orators recalled unselfish sacrifices during and after the War of Independence, denounced the unwarranted power of the well-to-do, and lauded the central contribution of the artisan shopkeeper and journeymen to the well-being of the state.[12]

The thrust of artisan politics and ideology, however, was egalitarian and populist. As Joyce Appleby has pointed out, the artisan rejection of the Federalist party in the 1790s detached "republican" from its classical deferential context and made it synonymous with democratic and popular government. They spurned the idea that liberty rested on the ability of the better educated and affluent to rise above the ambition, selfish interest, and mindless enthusiasm of the common man. Rather, Jeffersonian artisans welcomed and endorsed informal political associations and raucous local political meetings at the ward level in which they had a chance to participate actively and take on leadership roles. Thus, if Fourth of July speakers often recalled the collective efforts made in gaining independence, the artisan audience did not believe that these sacrifices were offered to install a government of the elite. The ever-widening split between Federalists and Democratic-Republicans, between the old-school merchants and the struggling, ambitious mechanic entrepreneurs seeking entry into the marketplace, represented a rejection of traditional ideals. Instead, artisans espoused an open meritocratic political society not tied to past practices and institutions but based on equal representation and a trust in the reason and intelligence of the people.[13]

The republicanism of radical London artisans was largely expressed by the British counterpart to the Mechanics Committee, the London Corresponding Society (LCS). Founded by Thomas Hardy, a master shoemaker heavily influenced by the American Revolution and by dissenter Richard Price, and composed largely but not exclusively of craftsmen, the LCS was very much in the swirl of radical ideas circulating in the 1790s. In various militantly democratic division meetings, the craftsmen met weekly for intensive debate and discussion of books, ideas, and political programs. Also, the General Committee, composed of division delegates, printed addresses, and reprinted important texts.[14]

The intent of the society was not revolution; instead the LCS sought fundamental political reform. Its major platform, the basis of its republicanism, focused on three uncompromising demands: annual elections, universal manhood suffrage, and equal representation. To a large extent New York's artisans had achieved these basic political reforms and were continuing to develop their ideas with the growth of the new state. For London's artisans, however, republicanism remained a speculative subject. They lacked the revolutionary experience of the Americans: the submersion in the processes of governing and the continued participation in the mainstream of politics.

The intellectual fathers of the LCS's program were well-known reform advocates, particularly Thomas Hollis, James Burgh, and John Cartwright. The most important contemporary theorist was Tom Paine whose *Rights of Man* especially *Part II*, was one of the key texts in English working-class history. The political tenets of these figures, while including expressions of classical ideals, largely stressed the concept of natural rights; the state as a voluntary, contractual agreement among equals; an emphasis on reason rather than the weight of tradition; and the advocacy of popular participation and the sovereign authority of the people.[15]

These ideas, as well as the general history and publications of the London Corresponding Society, show little of the republican promise of capitalist opportunity and of the meaning of the expanding marketplace so important in New York. Late eighteenth-century Britain was developing a strong consumer culture reaching well into the middling levels of society, and craftsmen were clearly part of this movement.[16] However, the LCS was active during wartime conditions when consumer goods were particularly scarce and expensive. The sense of capitalist opportunity may have been overcome by such conditions as well as by the exigencies and anxieties of war. Ninety percent of London craftsmen were not independent tradesmen and may not have shared the entrepreneurial hopes still strong in New York.[17] Finding it difficult or impossible to advance in the marketplace, and in constant fear of falling into poverty or crime, artisans became disaffected and alienated; the LCS represented an alternate avenue of hope.

With this exception, Republicanism among New York's mechanics did not differ greatly from that advocated by the radical craftsmen active in the LCS. That classical republicanism may be found in both of their writings is not surprising considering that commonwealth ideology was the mainstay of opposition thought for the past century. What is the more significant is that Tom Paine's brand of republicanism should be so influential among both artisan constituencies. This itinerant radical became the ideological mentor for both craftsmen communities.

* * *

Among the specific issues that tied or divided the two artisan communities to or from the state, the concept of a constitution was prominent. The United States, of course, had a new written national charter, and there is little question that most New York craftsmen stood behind it. For them this recently ratified document represented both economic salvation and an affirmation of the new nation for which many had fought. Burdened by the flood of British imports into New York following the Peace Treaty of 1783, a strong government willing to enact protective tariff legislation was most attractive. A powerful national state could also thwart Britain's attempts to destroy American liberty by dumping manufactures such as hats and shoes on the market, and by keeping American ships out of the British West Indies. Such moves threatened to create a state of national dependency that for craftsmen resembled second-class citizenship in a deferential society. The newly founded United States offered a sense of personal and economic independence, including the hope of competing fairly in the marketplace, which was deeply tied to artisans' understanding of the republic.[18]

Evidence of New York mechanics' support of the Constitution—or at least of the master craftsmen—was apparent in the famous parade of 23 July 1788 in which the various trades built displays and marched by craft. The bakers hoisted a ten-foot loaf with the slogan, "Americans, encourage your manufactures," while the blacksmiths' salutation was "Forge me strong, finish me neat, I soon shall moor a federal fleet." To these craftsmen, the federal constitution was no retreat from the spirit of '76. Under it they could still vote for their representatives, and also for their assemblymen who would select presidential electors. The seat of government was New York. The constitution represented the permanent enactment of popular revolutionary and republican ideals.[19]

There was, of course, no single written document called the British Constitution. The venerable British Constitution generally was distinguished as the powers, traditions, and balance of responsibilities shared by the monarchy, Commons, and Lords. In large measure commonwealth opposition in the eighteenth century argued that the various problems and evils that beset the country were caused by an undue influence of the crown through corrupt ministers. There was nothing wrong with the constitution; what was required was the resurgence of the gentry, the backbone of British liberty.[20]

This was an unsatisfactory solution for London artisans. Perhaps traditionally the country gentry had a prominent place in governing, but most urban tradesmen did not. The archaic British electoral structure excluded them from formal politics. Thus it is not surprising that they admired the American convention process for writing state and national constitutions, well described by Burgh, Cartwright, and others. The question was how to incorporate the idea of an American-like charter into the British experience. Unfortunately no legal channel existed that would allow most craftsmen to work for this goal within the existing political process.[21]

While American artisans were quite content to be rid of the British system of government, and to reject openly nonelective bodies or executives, and while the ideal of popular sovereignty that the Americans had worked out was not unknown or unappreciated in radical circles, publicly the LCS chose not to embrace fully Thomas Paine's condemnation of the monarchy and lords. Rather, the society sought to use the past to support its concept of republicanism. "We are told," it declared, by those "interested in supporting the Corruption List and the innumerable Host of sincere Placemen" that the English Constitution was "the perfection of human wisdom. That our laws (we should say, THEIR laws) are the perfection of justice." But the truth was that of the Magna Charta and Bill of Rights, indeed, "of the venerable Constitution hardly a vestige remains." These references clearly showed respect for a tradition of British liberty. At one of its large public gatherings in 1795, the society's speaker asked the assembled crowd:

> Are we men, and shall we not speak? Are we BRITONS, and is not LIBERTY OUR BIRTHRIGHT?

Members of the LCS equated the British Constitution with a heritage of liberty. Artisans did not want to return to balanced government as envisioned by the commonwealthmen; instead they envisioned a reassertion of popular government supposedly exercised at certain times in the past.[22]

The American experience with constitution making influenced the London Society's efforts at major political reform. In 1793, at a time when the war with France was going badly, spokesman Joseph Gerrald issued a noted pamphlet, *A Convention the only means of saving us from Ruin*. In it he argued that the salvation of the nation depended upon the creation of a new and truly representative assembly. Gerrald noted that the American patriots, having used such means in resisting the "arms of England," now possessed a new state where "God and Man have concurred to render the blissful habitation of abundance and peace." This was the time for British citizens to reclaim their rights. With public credit plunging and hunger facing much of the population, it was both just and necessary for the "interposition of the great body of the people themselves, electing deputies in whom they can confide, and imparting instructions which they must enjoin to be executed." Englishmen had acted in a similar vein as recently as 1688 when the aldermen and MPs assembled for the urgent cause of overthrowing a tyrannical king. In all periods of crisis, he declared, "THE SAFETY OF THE PEOPLE IS THE SOVEREIGN LAW."[23]

The LCS attempted to put these words into practice in 1794 when Gerrald and Maurice Margarot, two of the society's leading spokesmen, were chosen as delegates to a reform convention in Scotland. There they were arrested, tried, and convicted of sedition and then given harsh sentences of fourteen years at Botany Bay. In shock and anger, the LCS issued a nationwide call for a general convention should either *habeas corpus* be suspended or foreign troops be brought into Britain.[24] Secretary Hardy explained that the only reason for such an assembly was for the redress of grievances and for finding a means to obtain "a full representation of the people." The LCS did not dare to suggest that the convention attempt to restructure the British government or write a new constitution. If radical reform in representation and suffrage could be achieved, the present structure of government, the presence of aristocracy and monarchy as found in the existing "British constitution," would be acceptable. Consequently, the LCS's call for a convention was less radical than the new state and federal constitutions advocated by New York City artisans that, theoretically, were created out of a "state of nature." Even so, this action led to the arrest of the leadership of the LCS for high treason.[25]

If the public position of the LCS and most of its members was cautious, some artisans held far more extreme ideas about government than the New York craftsmen. During a prolonged debate over the writing of a new constitution for the society, a number of divisions argued that all rules, laws, and constitutions would be unnecessary once knowledge was diffused among the people and social harmony secured. Moreover, while disputes might still arise, no two situations or crises would be alike. Therefore no general laws or procedures could be prescribed for a particular future problem. Rather, "all law ought to be made extempore." More common was the position that despite education, perfection was unattainable; that laws and constitutions were necessary to secure and maintain moral ideals and prudential action; and that, despite differences in cases (less likely in criminal law), general laws would inhibit partisan and selfish actions. Still, the presence of anarchist writings is significant. The remoteness of these artisans from power and from the political process gave rise not only to moderate, but to some very radical ideas as well.[26]

In general, republican-minded London artisans regarded the ideal of a constitution favorably. While admiring the written American charter most members of the LCS were willing to accede to British tradition if at the least the House of Commons was made to operate within an egalitarian republican context. Barred from the political process like the American colonists a generation earlier, they turned to out-of-doors gatherings and supported the idea of a convention. Their fate, however, was different from that of their American brethren, who had not only advocated but actually participated in such conventions in the 1770s and then in 1787.

* * *

Another issue of great importance that deeply touched both artisan communities was the French Revolution. Although Federalists and Jeffersonians divided over several questions in the 1790s, artisan enthusiasm for the French Revolution helped to drive the mechanics away from the Federalists and into the Republican camp. The London response was more ambiguous. The LCS endorsed many of the principles of the French Revolution but had to tread a careful line; the war that broke out in 1793 left the LCS vulnerable to charges of treason.[27]

The events of Paris were carefully reported in New York, and support among mechanics for the French ran high. Artisans believed that the flame that they had ignited in America was now burning in the old world. There was even a sense among New Yorkers in 1792 that the fate of the French Revolution would be influential in the success or failure of their new federal state. Many New Yorkers, including craftsmen, began adopting the French address of "Citizen." Toasts to the Rights of Man, the Fall of the Bastille, and Tom Paine were common. Columbia College suspended classes in honor of Bastille Day. Bells were rung and the guns of the Battery fired at news of the French recapture of the Port of Toulon. When the French fleet entered New York harbor it was greeted with great celebration, while "Citizen Genet" found welcome from a large retinue of "sailors and mechanics." Peter Livingston observed that the laboring classes were "almost to a Man . . . Frenchmen."[28]

Even the Reign of Terror and subsequent death of Robespierre were not sufficient to turn most New Yorkers from their support of the Revolution. Indeed, a number of creative Francophile artisans constructed a model guillotine that was displayed at Tammany Hall; thousands of New Yorkers turned out to watch the wax heads of dummy aristocrats fall to the ax of justice. Even more important, a New York Democratic-Republican Society was founded, modeled after the Jacobin societies of Paris. With entry open to all, large numbers of craftsmen joined, forming the heart of the organization's membership. Solidly behind the new French government, the society openly defended the Revolution and its consequences, declaring that "he who is an enemy to the French Revolution cannot be a good republican."[29]

The Federalists soon became critics and opponents of the French Revolution. Few wealthy merchants or prominent attorneys could take kindly to the crowd's delight at the city's model guillotine. Once the Revolution turned against the monarchy and attempted to restructure the French social order, it could not but be opposed by Federalists who admired British constitutional government based on tradition, hierarchy, and deference. It played upon Federalist fears of reform and democratization. As one writer stated, to give more power to "every good democrat" by extending suffrage would provide the opportunity for those American Jacobins, who "if the proper time should ever arrive will with equal readiness bawl out for the erection of a guillotine in the park and endeavour practically to shew the possibility of perpetual motion in the action of its bloody knife."[30]

Unfortunately for the Federalists' political fortunes, most artisans found that party's position unacceptable. The *Rights of Man,* Paine's spirited defense of the Revolution, was a best seller in New York, particularly among the mechanics. Artisans identified with the French and celebrated a new age of revolution and a new set of political institutions that promised dramatic political and economic mobility to all men of talent. The Revolution made Federalist arrogance toward the common man, such as Mayor Varick's high-handed and brutal treatment of ferrymen in the Keteltas Affair or attempts at economic coercion of votes, all the harder to accept. Moreover, many of the political events of the 1790s like the controversy over the Jay Treaty, Washington's criticism of the Democratic-Republican societies, and the Alien and Sedition Acts, were connected to the French Revolution. Federalists invariably supported the British side while Jeffersonians generally took up the French position. Consequently, mechanic allegiance to the Federalists was all the more difficult to justify while alliance with the Democratic-Republicans made perfect sense.[31]

The relationship of republican British artisans to the French Revolution was more complex than that of their American counterparts. First, France was only a day's journey away. Events in one nation could immediately affect the other. A message from the LCS to the French National Convention, for example, was read and approved in the Convention only a week after its dispatch. Second, relations between the two countries were precarious. While there was general British approval of the earliest events in France after 1789, relations soured quickly following the publication of Burke's *Reflections* and the onset of the war in Europe against the Revolution. On 1 February 1793, ten days after the execution of Louis XVI, France declared war on Britain.[32]

There is little evidence of the same kind of general rejoicing in the streets of London over the fall of the Bastille as there was in New York. Britain was not, after all, a country born of a recent revolution. Britain had been at war with France intermittently for over a century deciding the question of which nation was to be Europe's preeminent imperial power. Many English soldiers and sailors had died in these conflicts.

The ideal of church and king remained strong among patriotic London artisans. France was an enemy. France was Catholic. No group of citizens despised "popishness" more than the craftsmen.

This position was a contrast to the attitude of New York's mechanics. For New Yorkers the French had been a trusted and valiant ally in the War of Independence. Catholicism—which appeared weakened by the Revolution—was of less importance given the liberal American spirit of tolerance. There was no conflict: France's revolution was an affirmation of their revolution, of similar nationalistic and republican aims.

The consequences of these differences were profound. After the first few years London artisans who continued to support the French Revolution had to do so knowing they were supporting a nation that threatened to invade their shores. Furthermore, the English government was solidly against the new Parisian regime—far different from America where the state's attitude was less certain. In Britain advocacy of the French Revolution was seen as directly threatening the survival of the government and social structure. Consequently support for France bordered on and in some cases, the Pitt administration charged, constituted high treason.

Because of their advocacy of the French cause the republican artisans of the LCS became more isolated from the general artisan community. They had to contend with an active recruitment and propaganda campaign by government supporters who brought in many tradesmen to local loyalist associations. By far the major problem was overcoming patriotic instinct and popular prejudice. Francis Place, the radical though not revolutionary tailor, complained that even in 1795 in the midst of severe hardship, many craftsmen and laborers supported the notorious Two Acts that harshly limited freedom of expression and assembly:[33]

> Working people may be said to have approved them without understanding them. Such was the terror of the French regicides and democrats, such the fear that the throne and altar would be destroyed.

Yet many of the ideals of the French and American Revolutions remained popular among mechanics. The *Rights of Man* sold upwards of two hundred thousand copies in inexpensive editions. Paine's description of the new French republic's willingness to open the political process, in contrast to the moribund British state, and especially his proposals for tax reductions, pensions, child support, and assistance to the poor, found many receptive readers and listeners. The LCS, as the most significant organization of craftsmen in Great Britain, was the leader and often the spokesman for these ideas.[34]

The society's task was to find a way to support the ideals of the

Revolution and even the French government itself while remaining loyal Britons. This quandary was less significant in the early days of the LCS's existence, prior to the outbreak of war. It then sent an *Address* to the National Convention in Paris (also signed by four other British societies and used as a model by eleven more) that proclaimed "an inviolable friendship with the French" who were "our Fellow Citizens of the World and Brethren by the same heavenly father." The common enemy was the "all consuming aristocracy" that was to blame for the "oppressive system of government" nearly enslaving Britain.[35]

The society never forsook its friendship with the French cause—at least until the rise of Bonaparte—but after the commencement of war it could no longer communicate directly with the state. Rather its public pronouncements criticized hostilities as cruel and wrongheaded, and declared the society to be "Friends of Peace." The war was part of a plan to destroy the liberties of Britain and "annihilate those of France." In *Convention the Only Means of Saving us from Ruin*, Gerrald praised the French for overthrowing the "feudal tyranny of the nobles and the supercilious imposture of the priesthood." Arguing that Louis XVI was executed only after receiving a "fair trial" for attempting to subvert the liberties of his people, he stated that France only desired peace, that all war was evil, and that the current conflict was justifiable as self-defense.[36]

In general the LCS remained cautious in its public statements. While never retracting its support for the French Revolution, its pronouncements centered on the need for parliamentary reform and the waste of manpower and wealth caused by a needless war. There was less need for caution within the various divisions, and sentiments emerged there even more radical than could be found in New York. Henry Yorke, for example, announced at a meeting that he would be leaving for Belgium to join the French army. He planned to return to London at the head of that army, at which time he expected to see the heads of Pitt and other ministers "upon the Temple-Bar." Praising the work of the *sans-culottes* of Paris, Yorke trusted that when the same opportunity presented itself—as, he predicted, it soon would—that LCS members would be ready. Unfortunately, "it was impossible to do anything without some bloodshed." Even so, artisans would "not shrink from what they pretended to be." In another division, a member of similar persuasion offered the spirited toast of a "Speedy Guillotine to the King."[37]

Because of their support of the French, the craftsmen of the LCS had to watch for spies within their organization. The work of various government informers led to the arrest of Secretary Thomas Hardy and other members for treason. But the society had been careful, and the government's accusation that the organization had plotted with the French Convention was not proved to the satisfaction of the jury during the subsequent trial. The LCS successfully defended itself by stating that it had never communicated with the French Jacobins and that its earlier *Address* merely expressed an attitude that "the whole nation held at that time."[38]

But there is little question of the unwavering support of the LCS for the French cause. Shortly after its defense of Hardy, a spy reported that the General Committee was heartily cheered by news of French naval victories and that it was carefully studying Robespierre's Address to the National Convention. These artisans were much closer to the historic events of Paris than the New York craftsmen. The LCS leadership did have to be much more cautious with their words than did their American brethren. France was the enemy of the state. But France was the symbol of a new egalitarian society, and a number of society members, including some key figures, did wind up in Paris. The LCS faced a difficult predicament, more dangerous and more troubling than that of New York's mechanics.[39]

* * *

The reaction of New York and London artisans to the French Revolution was closely connected to their reaction to state repression. Attempts at repression were made by the national government in both cities in the 1790s. The success and the intensity of these efforts varied as did the response of the craftsmen who were the targets of persecution and prosecution.

In New York City the target of the state was not specifically the mechanics but the Jeffersonian party, which, along with artisans, included in its ranks former antifederalists, ambitious merchants, and allies of Governor George Clinton. The local Democratic Society, closely connected to this emerging party, was attacked, together with its counterparts in other communities, by local and national Federalists. President Washington personally condemned these "self-created societies" for formenting the Whiskey Rebellion. Despite these charges the New York Society continued its activities; Federalists were unable to stifle either this organization or the related political movement. Indeed, the party grew rapidly in strength as artisan electors increasingly gave it their votes. This crucial shift in mechanic support was responsible for the election of the first Democratic-Republican congressman from New York in 1794.[40]

Craftsmen were affected by the most notorious and repressive laws of the 1790s, the Alien and Sedition Acts, only because of their role as Jeffersonian Republicans. In New York the law was implemented against Irish political émigré and newspaper editor John Daly Burk who was forced to close his paper, the *Time Piece,* and flee the country. It also led to the sedition trial and suppression of the New York *Argus,* one of the three most important Republican newspapers. Along with the proceedings against the proprietor of the *Argus,* the state prosecuted and imprisoned a journeyman printer for libel against Alexander Hamilton.[41]

Artisans were subject to less formal repression as well. Federalists were among the wealthiest citizens of New York and employed large numbers of artisans, particularly in mercantile trades. It was not uncommon for Federalists to threaten cartmen and carpenters with loss of their jobs if they voted for the Jeffersonians. The most flagrant such case concerned the cartmen who in one election were forced to line up with red and blue tickets and vote according to the wishes of their "federalist bullies." Federalists expected deference and were unwilling to accept that artisans did not follow their lead and, in fact, possessed a different outlook about the nature of the American state.[42]

In comparison, the LCS suffered much more severe and varied repression. First, the government intimidated many local divisions. Officials pressured tavern and inn keepers to bar their doors to LCS meetings. Secretary Thomas Hardy noted that the "the poor publicans were obliged to submit—there was no appeal—for the Magistrates on Li[c]ensing day have it in their power to stop their licenc[e] without giving a reason why—." Members were forced at times to meet in one another's homes "as none of them [publicans] would admit us into their houses." This harassment remained a problem throughout the era as the divisions scrambled for sites. Several brave license-holders allowed LCS members to meet undetected, but the groups were often on the run.[43]

Besides coercion of tavern proprietors, constables also gave artisan members of the LCS a difficult time. Members of Division 8 in Rotherhite asked the General Committee whether or not they ought to move into the borough because of harassment by constables. Many radical artisans had already lost their businesses and now feared press gangs. In 1795 a meeting of Division 31 was broken up in Blackheath Hundredths by six constables who, while demanding the names of the leaders, acted as if they were about to "pick some out to send aboard a ship." Fearing that a posse composed of all twenty-four of the local constables was prepared for their next meeting, they decided to move to a private house in the country; there, if interrupted, they "determined to defend themselves."[44]

A third measure of intimidation was the use of spies. A number of notorious men volunteered to work for the Home Office. The most infamous, Citizen Groves, sent back reports of society dealings from early 1794 until the trial of Thomas Hardy. He became an intimate of the leadership and even survived a society trial brought on by suspicious members. The home secretary never lacked information on the LCS for as soon as one spy was exposed another became active. Much of what we know of the society today is based on the reports of these spies.[45]

The most powerful repressive weapons in the state's arsenal were judicial and legislative measures. In 1794, without even securing the passage of new laws, the Pitt administration went after the leadership of the LCS by the sudden and harsh arrest and imprisonment of Thomas Hardy, John Thelwall, and others on the charge of high treason. They were held five months and then indicted. After a long and celebrated trial they were acquitted and their lives saved, to the great joy of crowds gathered outside the Old Bailey. Even so Hardy's wife died from the ordeal and he was unable to continue in the society. Without the remarkable defense provided by the noted counsel Thomas Erskine, who successfully argued that the treason laws were limited to a plot directly against the king's life, the state would surely have taken their lives.[46]

The raid on the LCS, along with the seizure of property sharply inhibited further work and greatly diminished membership. When the society revived during the hard economic times of 1795, Home Secretary Lord Dundas turned to legislative means of repression. Following a number of large, open-air meetings that attracted up to 200,000 onlookers, and an alleged attack on the king's carriage by an LCS member, the Pitt administration, which had already suspended *habeas corpus*, introduced and easily secured passage of the notorious "Two Acts." The first declared that to incite "hatred of the king, of his government or of the constitution by either speech or writing" was treason; the second effectively forbade any meetings of more than forty-nine people.[47]

The LCS continued for a number of years after passage of the Two Acts but in a clandestine and increasingly radical and conspiratorial manner. Leaders such as Francis Place became disgruntled and left the organization to radicals often connected to truly revolutionary groups such as the United Irishmen. Finally in 1798, as only a shadow of its original force, the LCS was formally outlawed by an Act of Parliament.[48]

In responding to political intimidation, London artisans in the LCS were clearly in a very different position from those in New York. In America the Federalist administration and Federalist congress, a government much weaker than the Pitt administration, moved against an opposition that was their rival political party. Artisans were but one component of that party. For Pitt, the LCS was *the* opposition. The British government determined that these radical artisans desired the overthrow of the British Constitution and willingly undertook the severest measures to halt them. Both in their attempts at political reform and in their muted public support of France they were anathema.

Not only was the LCS isolated as the opponent of the government, but it had no political party to which it might turn. The whig faction headed by Charles James Fox was sometimes sympathetic, but only to a degree. Fox delayed, for instance, answering the society's request to present a petition in the Commons for universal suffrage, a cause to which he "was not a friend," and then only reluctantly acceded. The LCS decided to decline his services. The motion was eventually presented by another MP, and rejected 282–41. Votes in Parliament in favor of repressive and coercive measures almost always carried by similarly lopsided margins. Moreover, as the war with France proceeded, the reform-minded Whig members largely withdrew from any active participation in the Commons. Consequently, not only were most artisans denied the suffrage, but no political party or faction of any note had their republican goals in mind. Locked out of Parliament and the political process, these men were on their own. They managed to carry on with meetings, lectures, discussion groups, petitions and, in 1795, some immense public meetings. These tactics proved hopelessly inadequate in the face of state opposition.[49]

In the United States, resistance to the Alien and Sedition Acts remained strong throughout the country and was led by figures such as Vice-President Thomas Jefferson and Congressman James Madison. Republican artisans in New York had access to friends in government. They used the republican state they had helped to found, and successfully rejected both the individuals and the policies opposed to their republican ideals. Indeed, the state was their political salvation as they helped drive the Federalists from power through established political processes. How different this was from London, where for republican-minded craftsmen a remote and hostile state attempted to take the lives of their leaders and to close down their society! That they were not executed they owed in part to a tradition guaranteeing trial by jury and the rule of law. But this was a limited victory for a few individuals. The artisans' cause and their society were effectively crushed. The equally hostile Federalists may well have desired a similar fate for Jeffersonian artisans, but they were unable to harness the engines of the new American government into the repressive machine that Pitt assembled. New York's mechanics continued to be strong supporters of the Jeffersonian government in the next decade; London's republican artisans became more and more alienated from their state.

Notes

1. For population statistics and the economic situation of New York and other American port cities see David T. Gilchrist, ed., *The Growth of the Seaport Cities, 1790–1825* (Charlottesville, Va., 1967); for London see George Rudé, *Hanoverian London, 1714–1808* (Berkeley, Calif., 1971), ch. 1; Ian Christie, *Wilkes, Wyvill and Reform* (London, 1962), 17–18.

2. Edmund P. Willis, "Social Origins and Political Leadership in New York City from the Revolution to 1815" (Ph.D. diss. University of California, Berkeley, 1967); Howard B. Rock, *Artisans of the New Republic: The Tradesmen of New York City in the Age of Jefferson* (New York, 1979), chs. 6, 9–10; Sean Wilentz, *Chants Democratic: New York City and the Rise of the American Working Class, 1788–1850* (New York, 1984), 3–60.

3. Rudé, *Hanoverian London* chs., 3, 5; Iorweth Prothero, *Artisans and Politics in Early Nineteenth Century London: John Gast and his Times* (London, 1979), chs. 2–3; M. Dorothy George, *London Life in the Eighteenth Century* (New York, 1925), ch. 4; L. D. Schwarz, "Income Distribution and Social Structure in London in the Late Eighteenth Century," *Economic History Review*, 2d ser., 32 (1979): 250–59. For numerous examples of artisans who fell into debt and dissolution see Mary Thale, ed., *The Autobiography of Francis Place* (Cambridge, 1972).

4. Rock, *Artisans of the New Republic*, intro. and passim; Graham Russell Hodges, *New York City Cartmen, 1667–1850* (New York, 1986).

5. The question of the impact and significance of the LCS is a controversial subject. For opposing views see Ian Christie, *Stress and Stability in Late Eighteenth-Century Britain: Reflections on the British Avoidance of Revolution* (Oxford, 1984) and E. P. Thompson, *The Making of the English Working Class* (New York, 1963), chs. 1, 5.

6. Gary Nash, *The Urban Crucible: Social Change, Political Consciousness, and the Origins of the American Revolution* (Cambridge, 1979), 363; for an overall view of colonial New York politics see Patricia U. Bonomi, *A Factious People: Politics and Society in Colonial New York* (New York, 1971).

7. Roger Champagne, *Alexander McDougall and the American Revolution in New York* (Schenectady, 1975); Leopold S. Launitz-Schurer, Jr., *Loyal Whigs*

and Revolutionaries: The Making of the Revolution in New York, 1765–1776 (New York, 1989), ch. 4; Nash, *Urban Crucible*, 302–5, 362–74; Philip Foner, *Labor and the American Revolution*, (Westport, Conn., 1976), 52–60, 88–95, 117–21; Paul A. Gilje, *The Road to Mobocracy: Popular Disorder in New York City, 1763–1834* (Chapel Hill, N.C., 1987), ch. 2.

8. Nash, *Urban Crucible*, 374; Staughton Lynd, "The Mechanics in New York Politics, 1774–1788," *Labor History* 5 (1964): 225–32; Bernard Mason, *The Road to Independence: The Revolutionary Movement in New York, 1773–1777* (Lexington, 1966), 31, 37–38, 72–73, 149–50; Bernard Friedman, "The Shaping of Radical Consciousness in Provincial New York," *Journal of American History* 56 (1970): 794; the intellectual heritage of Paine is delineated in A. Owen Aldridge, *Thomas Paine's American Ideology* (Newark, 1984) while his relation to artisans is discussed in Eric Foner, *Tom Paine and Revolutionary America* (New York, 1976).

9. Lucy Sutherland, "The City of London and the Opposition to Government," in John Stevenson, ed., *London in the Age of Reform* (Oxford, 1977), 32; John Brewer, "English Radicalism in the Age of George III," in J. G. A. Pocock, ed., *Three British Revolutions* (Princeton, 1980), 323–60; Brewer, *Party Ideology and Popular Politics in the Age of George III* (Cambridge, 1976), 178, 189–90; Christie, *Wilkes, Wyvill and Reform*, 36–37; George Rudé, *Wilkes and Liberty* (New York, 1962); Thompson, *Making of the English Working Class*, 76–78; Rudé, "The Gordon Riots: A Study of Riots and their Victims," in *Paris and London in the Eighteenth Century: Studies in Popular Protest* (New York, 1970), 268–92.

10. Among the important works for this discussion are J. G. A. Pocock, *The Machiavellian Moment: Florentine Political Thought and the Atlantic Republican Tradition* (Princeton, 1976) and "Virtue and Commerce in the Eighteenth Century" *Journal of Interdisciplinary History* 3 (1972): 119–34; Lance Banning, *The Jeffersonian Persuasion: Evolution of a Party Ideology* (Ithaca, N.Y., 1978); idem., "Jefferson Ideology Revisited: Liberal and Classical Ideas in the New American Republic," *William and Mary Quarterly*, 3d ser., 43 (1986): 3–19; Joyce Appleby, *Capitalism and a New Social Order: The Republican Vision of the 1790s* (New York, 1984); idem, "Republicanism in Old and New Concepts," *William and Mary Quarterly*, 3d ser., 43 (1986): 20–34; idem, "The Social Origins of American Revolutionary Ideology," *Journal of American History* 64 (1978): 935–78; Isaac Kramnick, "Republican Revision Revisited," *American Historical Review* 87 (1982): 629–64.

11. Thomas Paine, *Common Sense*, Isaac Kramnick, ed. (New York, 1979); *New York Gazette*, 10, 17 June 1776; Alfred F. Young, "The Mechanics and the Jeffersonians: New York, 1789–1801," *Labor History* 5 (1964): 247–76; Rock, *Artisans of the New Republic*, chs. 6–7, 279–88.

12. Sean Wilentz, *Chants Democratic: New York City and the Rise of the American Working Class* (New York, 1985), ch. 2.

13. Appleby, *Capitalism and a New Social Order*, ch. 3.

14. The most important books dealing with the London Corresponding Society are Albert Goodwin, *The Friends of Liberty: The English Democratic Movement in the Age of the French Revolution* (Cambridge, Mass., 1979); Thompson, *Making of the English Working Class*, chs. 1, 5; and the intro. in Mary K. Thale, ed., *Selections from the Papers of the London Corresponding Society*

(Cambridge, 1983). For an account of the founding of the Society see Thomas Hardy, *Memoir of Thomas Hardy* (London, 1832).

15. Goodwin, *Friends of Liberty*, chs. 2, 6; Thompson, *Making of the English Working Class*, 86–103, 108–13; Thomas Paine, *The Rights of Man* (New York, 1972; orig. pub. London, 1792).

16. Neil McKendrick, John Brewer and J. H. Plumb, *The Birth of a Consumer Society: The Commercialization of Eighteenth-Century England* (Bloomington, Ind., 1982).

17. Schwarz, "Income Distribution and Social Structure," *Economic History Review*, 2nd ser., 32 (1979): 257–58.

18. Lynd, "Mechanics in New York Politics," *Labor History* 5 (1964): 232–38; Alfred F. Young, *The Democratic-Republicans of New York: The Origins, 1763–1797* (Chapel Hill, N.C., 1967), 100–102.

19. For a description of the parade see *New York Packet*, 4 Aug. 1788, and Paul Gilje's essay in this collection, "The Common People and the Constitution: Popular Culture in New York City in the Late Eighteenth Century."

20. On the influence of commonwealth ideology in Britain see Caroline Robbins, *The Eighteenth Century Commonwealthman* (Cambridge, 1959).

21. James Burgh, *Political Disquisitions*, 3 vols. (London, 1774–75), 1:272–74, 298; 2:274–76; J. Cartwright, *The Legislative Rights of the Commonalty Vindicated or Take Your Choice* (London, 1776) x–xxiv, 7, 11, 47–48, 51, 55–56. Arthur Sheps, "The American Revolution and the Transformation of English Republicanism," *Historical Reflections* 2 (1975): 3–28.

22. London Corresponding Society, *Address to the People of Great Britain and Ireland* (London, 1794) 2–3; idem, *Address to the Nation* (London, 1795), 6.

23. Joseph Gerrald, *A Convention the Only Means of Saving Us from Ruin* (London, 1794), 75, 90–92 and passim.

24. LCS, *Address to the People of Great Britain and Ireland*, 7; Goodwin, *Friends of Liberty*, 316–17.

25. Goodwin, *Friends of Liberty*, 175–77, 199, argues that the artisans of the LCS did not accept Paine's republicanism. However, their demands for reform of the House of Commons were uncompromisingly republican, based on demands for universal manhood suffrage, equal representation and annual elections. H. T. Dickinson, *British Radicalism and the French Revolution* (Oxford, 1985) ch. 1.

26. Thale, ed., *Selections from the Papers of the LCS*, 249–50; and Sheps, "The American Revolution and the Transformation of English Republicanism," *Historical Reflections* 2 (1975): 18–28.

27. Alfred Young, "The Mechanics, the Jeffersonians, and New York Politics, 1774–1801," *Labor History*, 5 (1964): 247–76; Arthur Bernstein, "The Rise of the Democratic-Republican Party in New York City, 1789–1800" (Ph.D. diss., Columbia University, 1964).

28. Alan Blau, "New York City and The French Revolution, 1789–1797: A Study of French Revolutionary Influence" (Ph.D. diss., City University of New York, 1973), 114, 130, 184, 262, and passim.

29. Bernstein, "The Rise of the Democratic-Republicans" (Ph.D. diss., Columbia University, 1964), 66; Philip Foner, ed., *The Democratic-Republican Societies, 1790–1800* (Westport, 1976), 151–231; see also Eugene Link, *The Democratic Societies, 1790–1800* (New York, 1942); Young, *Democratic-Re-*

publicans of New York, 393–98, 404–19, 425–28; Wilentz, *Chants Democratic*, 68–71.

30. Linda K. Kerber, *Federalists in Dissent: Imagery and Ideology in Jeffersonian America* (Ithaca, 1970), 173–216; *New York Evening Post*, 16 Nov. 1802; Rock, *Artisans of the New Republic*, 45–51.

31. The Keteltas Affair concerned two ferrymen whom Mayor Varick ordered whipped for insolence without due process. One thereafter died. Attorney William Keteltas protested and petitioned the assembly. When he continued to attack the legislature he was jailed for contempt and became a popular hero. Mayor Varick was also notorious for using his power as licensor of the cartmen to control the votes of this large body of workmen. Young, *Democratic-Republicans of New York*, ch. 22; idem, "Mechanics and Jeffersonians," *Labor History* 5 (1964): 255–60; Hodges, *New York Cartmen*, ch. 8. A number of craftsmen did remain within the Federalist fold. These would likely have included immigrant craftsmen with patriotic feelings towards Britain; prominent and wealthy master craftsmen; craftsmen economically dependent on Federalist employers; and mechanics who willingly deferred to the Federalists as more knowledgeable and better educated. Gilje, *Road to Mobocracy*, 100–112.

32. For a description of British society at this time see Clive Emsley, *British Society and the French Wars, 1793–1815* (Totawa, N.J., 1979) and Dickinson, *British Radicalism and the French Revolution*.

33. Quoted in Graham Wallas, *The Life of Francis Place: 1771–1854* (London, 1951) 25, n. 1; on the loyalist associations see Robert R. Dozier, *For King, Constitution and Country: The English Loyalists and the French Revolution* (Lexington, Ky., 1983).

34. Thomas Paine, *The Rights of Man* (New York, 1969), 121–287; Goodwin, *Friends of Liberty*, chs. 6–7; Dickinson, *Liberty and Property*, 241–57; Thompson, *Making of the English Working Class*, 99–127.

35. For the LCS's *The Address to the French National Convention*, 27 Sept. 1792 see Thale, ed., *Selections from the Papers of the London Corresponding Society*, 20–22.

36. Gerrald, *Convention the Only Means*, 37–40.; LCS, *Address to the Nation*, 12–13.

37. Thale, ed., *Selections from the Papers of the London Corresponding Committee*, 90, 123.

38. Ibid., 106–13, 171.

39. Ibid., 179; the society did condemn Bonaparte in 1798, ibid., 423.

40. Foner, *Democratic-Republican Societies*, 30–40; Young, "Mechanics and Jeffersonians," *Labor History* 5 (1964): 256–64; idem, *The Democratic-Republicans of New York*.

41. Ibid., 204–20, 398–417.

42. Rock, *Artisans of the New Republic*, 51–57; Hodges, *New York City Cartmen*, chs. 7–8; Young, "The Mechanics and the Jeffersonians," *Labor History* 5 (1964): 264–66.

43. Thale, *Selections from the Papers of the London Corresponding Society*, 15, 30, 272.

44. Ibid., 106, 277–81.

45. Ibid., 113n, 215–20, 223–25; 135n., 28n.

46. Ibid., 231–35, 243; Goodwin, *Friends of Liberty*, ch. 9; Thompson, *Making of the English Working Class*, 132–37.

47. Clive Emsley, "Repression, 'Terror' and the Rule of Law in England during the Decade of the French Revolution," *English Historical Review* (1985): 801–25; Goodwin, *Friends of Liberty,* 372–73, 384–86.

48. J. Ann Hone, *For the Cause of Truth: Radicalism in London, 1796–1821* (Oxford, 1982).

49. Thale, ed., *Selections from the Papers of the London Corresponding Society,* 62–64.

ANTHONY GRONOWICZ

4

Political "Radicalism" in New York City's Revolutionary and Constitutional Eras

The ideology of republicanism was regarded as "radical" by the landed classes in late seventeenth- and eighteenth-century England precisely because it was based on land ownership in a land-scarce environment. In an American Eden where landed expansion was held out to the European immigrant and his children as the means to economic independence and social advancement, republicanism could not be radical. Its promise could be fulfilled without disturbing power relationships between upper and lower classes. There was enough land for all. It was only between states that republicanism's expansive potential would lead to fierce conflict, and that would be a civil war between the northern and southern sections of the United States.

At the time of independence, however, freedom from British taxes was the main issue, and republicanism was the ideology of the farmers and urban mechanics who comprised the political majority in the thirteen colonies. After 1791 their spokesman was Thomas Jefferson, whose ideal social order was put forward by the most popular American Revolutionary pamphleteer, Thomas Paine:

> The first useful classes of citizens are the farmers and cultivators. These may be called citizens of the first necessity because everything comes originally from the earth. After these follow the various orders of manufacturers and mechanics of every kind . . . they contribute to the accommodation rather than to the first necessities of life. Next follow those called merchants and shopkeepers. They are occasionally convenient but not important. They produce nothing themselves as the first two classes do, but employ their time in exchanging one thing for another and living by the profits.[1]

Paine sketched a republican pre-industrial capitalist social constellation that made the independent petty producer the star of the social formation. He thereby reinforced the ideas of seventeenth-century English thinker James Harrington, who contended that "if the whole people be landlords, or hold the lands so divided among them that no one man, or number of men, within the compass of the few or aristocracy, overbalance them, the empire (without the interposition of force) is a commonwealth."

Harrington's English followers, real or radical Whigs or commonwealthmen—the *country* party—opposed mercantile empire and the monarchy's arbitrary taxes, especially the excise, the first British tax on propertyless subjects. They maintained that government could stave off corruption by separating its powers. The king would remain chief executive, but should no longer rule by divine right that exercised control over the legislature and the judiciary. As embodied in the *court* party, the monarchy encouraged bureaucracy and corruption through domination of both branches. So extensive was this *court* corruption that Scottish philosopher David Hume could argue that republicanism was impossible in commercial society.[2] Political virtue would be restored when the *country* party, men of independent means and authority such as landowners, were elected to a Parliament that controlled the power of the purse.[3] To those men land did not foster corruption but commerce did.

The *country* party's American republican counterparts proclaimed America's right to an empire, while denying Parliament's right to the same. Unlike the British Empire, America's empire would enable each adult male citizen to secure the land that guaranteed personal autonomy and public virtue.

As a gentleman farmer, James Madison based his writing of the United States Constitution upon the supposition that a land-rich America could avoid Old World social problems. He thought that he had resolved the philosophical contradiction between republicanism and commercial society.[4] In *Federalist No. 10* he sketched the importance of landed expansion to a republic's avoidance of class conflict, and thereby provided the *weltanschauung* for both Jeffersonian republicanism and Jacksonian democracy:

> Extend the sphere, and you take in a greater variety of parties and interests; you make it less probable that a majority of the whole will have a common motive to invade the rights of other citizens; or if such a common motive exists, it will be more difficult for all who feel it to discover their own strength, and to act in unison with each other.

Two paragraphs later, Madison identified the political enemies of his republic. They were men animated by "a rage for paper money, for an abolition of debts, for an equal division of property, or for any other wicked project." Madison's intellectual dependence upon landed expansion also yielded the promise of fiscal solvency that was necessary to keep his political enemies from carrying forward their designs:

> It is now no longer a point of speculation and hope, that the western territory is a mine of vast wealth to the United States: and although it is not of such a nature as to extricate them from their present distresses, or for some time to come to yield any regular supplies for the public expenses; yet must it hereafter be able, under proper management, both to effect a gradual discharge of the domestic debt, and to furnish, for a certain period, liberal tributes to the federal treasury.

Legal precedent for western expansion had been provided in 1787 when Congress passed the Northwest Ordinance, a blueprint for incorporation of future states into a united state system that gave important material and psychological incentives to the yeoman farmer. Slave-holding republican landowners like Madison and Jefferson banked on the fact that the majority of independent agricultural producers would remain the mainstay of the American republic. So long as this vision prevailed, native Americans, women, and slaves were excluded from the economic mainstream. They did not own property, and were therefore deemed "dependent" and ineligible for full political participation.

Republican Radical Whig ideas thus had a negative impact upon all three groups. Native American status declined to the point where by the Declaration of Independence, "most Anglo-Americans view[ed] Indians as significantly different in color from ourselves," while in the nineteenth century they became "red" to the republican eye.[5] Women were not recognized as political beings in the new republic. "The republican beliefs of the Revolution, broadly disseminated among New York laboring men, amplified and strengthened assumptions of female subservience and male authority that were already widely current in eighteenth-century Anglo-American society." For laboring women, "sexual antagonisms . . . grew worse in the next twenty years."[6]

While women were confined to the household, slaves were at the foundation of the economic independence most of the republican founding fathers personally enjoyed. In general "Americans bought their independence with slave labor."[7] Most American farmers and artisans were to the political right of such federalists as Alexander Hamilton on the "negro question." Unlike Hamilton they opposed freeing slaves or enfranchising the few free African Americans. Intellectual justification could be provided by Montesquieu who excluded those who "are in so mean a situation as to be deemed to have no will of their own."[8]

Philosophical support for proslavery republicanism also came from the doctrine's fundamental theorist, John Locke. For him, slaves were:

> captives taken in a just war . . . of nature subject to the absolute dominion and power of their masters. These men, having, as I say, forfeited their lives and with it their liberties, and lost their estates, and being in the state of slavery not capable of any property, cannot in that state be considered as any part of civil society, the chief end whereof is the preservation of property.[9]

Political independence became viable and necessary for America's prosperity when Parliament tried to prevent westward settlement through establishing the Proclamation Line of 1763 that ran the length of the Appalachian Mountains, and levying taxes such as the Stamp Act that diverted capital from land speculation and other investment.[10] Taxation was most especially reviled for curtailing the republican's right to acquire property, which was at the core of his political being.[11]

From the outset a society of white men uprooted and black men chained provided a competitive advantage over Europe in terms of generating capital for agriculture, commerce, and manufacturing. Denial of African rights helped guarantee the franchise for the white male majority.[12] Voting, the lowest order of involvement in a republic, became the process of choosing, from a narrow, pre-determined family-based field, the man best perceived as advancing the economy.

This body of political practice had been laid down early in the colonial experience as British authorities sought to provide a political environment tailored to their economic objectives. On the provincial level in pre-independence New York this policy resulted in an electoral contest between the two richest landed gentry families, Livingston and Delancey.[13]

Consistent with the Lockean view that excluded the "dependent" poor from political participation, artisans supported elite candidates for civic office in the generation before the War for Independence when New York City's boundaries ceased to expand and the population grew by one-half.[14] The rich grew richer and the poor quadrupled in numbers. By 1773 close to 800 persons in the city required public assistance.[15]

Over little opposition, merchants guided political affairs. Until 1763 they enjoyed a majority voice on the Common Council. Thereafter they were joined by a legal profession capitalizing upon the need for adjudication between competing commercial claims.[16]

Upper-class domination was reflected in the 1768 election when the carpenter Amos Dodge received a mere twelve percent of the workingmen's vote—the worst showing among a slate otherwise comprised of merchants and lawyers. A year later, in the last assembly elections prior to the Declaration of Independence, mechanics supported the popular Whigs—merchants and lawyers led by the upper-crust Delanceys.

Before the Revolutionary War began, most men did not support independence. Among the minority that did, disagreement centered on the amount of force required to lift Parliament's restraints upon colonial profits. The more extreme faction, the "Sons of Liberty," who were mainly mechanics led by newer, less secure merchants, burned effigies of British officials, broke countless windows, and looted official residences to gain repeal of the Stamp Act.[17] Their leaders, merchants John Lamb, Isaac Sears, and John Morin Scott, supported the "popular Whig" faction led by James Delancey.[18] In 1770 Lamb successfully exploited tensions between out-of-work citizens and British soldiers competing for scarce jobs, which precipitated the Battle of Golden Hill in New York City.

During the struggle for independence, merchants and lawyers continued to represent artisan mechanics. The most mechanics accomplished in the way of independent political organization was for the prominent among them to found their own "general committee" in 1774.

As pre-industrial manufacturer-producers, artisan mechanics had traditionally employed most of the indentured servants. The psychological corruption borne of having others do work for which one claimed both material and personal credit contributed to the decidedly "middle-class" style of a "working-class" politics[19] that maintained all classes would benefit from removal of British legal restrictions.

Acceptance of elite leadership resulted from this political identification. In *Federalist* No. 35, Alexander Hamilton explained such deferential behavior:

> Mechanics and manufacturers will always be inclined, with few exceptions, to give their votes to merchants, in preference to persons of their own professions or trades. Those discerning citizens are well aware that the mechanics and manufacturing arts furnish the materials of mercantile enterprise and industry. Many of them, indeed, are immediately connected with the operations of commerce. They know that the merchant is their patron and friend; and they are aware, that however great the confidence they may justly feel in their own good sense, their interests can be most effectively promoted by the merchant than by themselves. They are sensible that their habits in life have not been such as to give them those acquired endowments, without which, in a deliberative assembly, the greatest natural abilities are for the most part useless.

Hamilton's analysis may also explain why sentiment for or against the British did not conform to class lines when the First Continental Congress adopted a trade embargo. Although generally supported by mechanics, significant support for the British cause was manifested by the "humble" carters.[20] Those cartmen who did support the revolution accepted merchant leadership in a fashion consistent with Hamilton's description.[21]

Support for the British was also manifested by the non-white population, since British authorities first broke the color line by granting New York City's African Americans the opportunity to obtain carting licenses. This guaranteed that divisions within the labor force would be greater than divisions between employers and employees.[22] The mechanics' radicalism was limited to fostering notions of indirect democracy that did not seek to ameliorate the conditions of nonwhites or the dependent poor. They were aided in these efforts by the fact that common laborers and the poor were not motivated to participate in politics.[23] New York mechanics did not insist that democratic principles be extended to all people like their French counterparts the sans-culottes.[24]

Unlike the French, who produced the revolutionary "Gracchus" Babeuf, New York City radicals behaved like eighteenth-century English radicals who "were preoccupied . . . not with the need to recast the social order nor . . . economic inequality . . . but with the need to purify a corrupt constitution and fight off . . . prerogative power."[25] These radicals took the lead in organizing resistance to British rule through the establishment of extra-legal committees composed of both mechanics and merchants, but dominated by the latter.

At the first recorded New York General Committee meeting, on 16 May 1774, the Committee of Fifty-One was elected to correspond with the other colonies and to enforce nonimportation.[26] Two and one-half months later this coalition was superceded by a sixty-man "committee of observation." The sixty became one hundred following Lexington and Concord and fifty in February 1776, but all were supplanted when the British achieved control of the city in early September 1776.[27] Posh residences were then converted into prisons and houses of prostitution. A fire on 19 September destroyed nearly a fifth of all dwellings, and the population declined from about 20,000 to 5,000.

Throughout these calamitous times spontaneous resistance in New York City was lacking. Between 1776 and 1783 Common Council duties were routinely conducted by nineteen British appointees. There was no trial by jury, but no taxes either.[28] When the British retreated from the city, republican lawyers, freed from earlier restrictions upon their practices, entered politics en masse.[29] In the first local and ward elections held after the war's conclusion, lawyers captured eight of the fourteen aldermen and assistant aldermen seats.[30] A month later, the nine state senate seats in the city went to nine lawyers.[31]

Lawyers played an increasingly important role in a post-revolutionary city undergoing explosive growth where private and public clashes between old and new economic elites set the legislative agenda. Elections resumed almost immediately, as did elite rivalry and the relegation of artisans to supporters of either side. The elite also continued to dominate the administration of justice in New York City.[32]

The main political issues of the early 1780s were the powers of a proposed national government and how it would apportion the war debt. Antifederalists favored only partial repayment to the merchants who had funded the continental army. The antifederal leader in New York, Governor George Clinton, used his power as chief of the state rather than as representative of a powerful family, to fashion the first stable political organization in New York history.[33] He successfully lobbied the state legislature to issue paper money backed by revenues generated from the most productive year in the state's history, 1784–85.

Clinton believed the state did not need a stronger national union. His program of lower taxes and minimal government reflected the desires of a rural constituency. While most of his antifederalist supporters opted for federal land sales rather than property taxes to retire the war debt, only a few radicals demanded confiscation of loyalist estates and cancellation of debts owed them.[34]

Federalists, on the contrary, favored full debt redemption for the merchants through a strong national government that would act as "our anchor in the world of empires."[35] The city's propertyless mechanics supported these efforts,[36] and Alexander Hamilton was instrumental in organizing their nominating meetings and ward organizations.

In the 1786 election, New York City voters rewarded Hamilton's efforts with an assembly seat while electing not one mechanic. In Albany Hamilton wrote the official party tract, personally supervised poll-watchers, and spearheaded the political attack against Clinton in sixteen newspaper articles. He was a popular figure among mechanics.

Nevertheless, the need to construct a strong central government that would command the respect of the European powers as well as support American manufactures led increasing numbers of mechanics to oppose Hamilton's centralizing efforts. In 1784, despite his defense of a proposal before the state legislature to charter the Bank of New York on the grounds that it would act to "strengthen republican government,"[37] no mechanic would sign the petition in support of the bank. Instead, artisans attempted to organize their own bank. In 1787 they designated themselves the General Society of Mechanics and Tradesmen and subscribed £3,000 to a general loan fund whose stated intent was to "promote fellowship, confidence and good understanding among the various descriptions of mechanics; afford relief to distressed members," and to raise more money. This may be considered the first occasion on which New York City's mechanics organized autonomously against the mercantile and legal elite. Political action was aimed at redressing a growing imbalance in productive power perceived as being fostered by a strong federal government. At first limited to masters, the society ultimately grew to almost 400 members in 1791. But no cartmen were members until 1794 indicating that more prosperous artisans dominated.[38]

Dispute over the mechanics' independent action continued. When their society was proposed for incorporation in 1789, merchants succeeded in getting the Council of Revision to veto the bill. Some merchants were expanding their base of operations into manufacturing. Many mechanics could not keep pace. The relative difference in terms of their capabilities in influencing the market place grew wider. Control of the market place was being lost to private entrepreneurs' ever-growing businesses and markets as the freemanship lost its protective shield.

Nevertheless, class cooperation continued. Indicative of this cross-class spirit, which characterized the early stages of the nation's first formal party system, was the Tammany Society. Tammany was established as a secret fraternal order for the self-proclaimed "benevolent purpose of affording relief to the indigent and distressed." It included both federalists and antifederalists in its leadership ranks.[39] The principal founder was the wealthy merchant and federalist assemblyman John Pintard, a partner of William Duer who later became Hamilton's assistant treasury secretary. Pintard defined the Tammany Society as "a political institution founded on a strong republican basis whose democratic principles will serve in some measure to correct the aristocracy of our city."[40] Led by Governor Clinton, its membership was mostly artisans and tradesmen.[41] At the first publicly recorded banquet in 1787 Congress was proferred the third toast and Washington the sixth.

In the 1788 election on the Constitution, federalists won by a large margin in the city. The winning ticket had been nominated at a joint mechanic-merchant meeting chaired by Hamilton. The Grand Federal Procession of 23 July 1788 even sported the *Alexander Hamilton,* a ship float drawn by mechanics. A year after that, Tammany toasted Washington first while Congress was not even included in any of the twelve remaining quaffs.[42]

However, Hamilton's December 1791 *Report on Manufactures* calling for government support of industry turned the mechanics against him. They joined the outraged supporters of Secretary of State Jefferson who advocated a minimal role for government in managing an economy that would continue to favor agriculture.

Federalist merchant-manufacturers, on the other hand, believed that if national interests were shaped by farmers rather than manufacturers, the United States could never become a world power.[43] Hamilton's particular genius was to transform political radical Thomas Paine's notion that the "national debt is a national bond" into the core of the Federalist program to make thirteen states work together as one nation through the establishment of a national bank. He argued that such a move was "inherent in the very *definition* of *Government* and *essential* to . . . the United States.[44]

At the time Hamilton's bank bill was being proposed, Jefferson protested that to establish a bank would create a corporation that could receive grants of land in violation of the Constitution.[45] But not only the city's merchants and speculators benefited from Hamilton's proposals; so did wealthy New York City Anti-Federalists who held federal debt paper.[46] When put to a congressional test, the city's three Republicans voted with the majority to charter the bank.

New York artisans and mechanics, when they did oppose the government, directed their wrath against the Federalist drive to strengthen national power rather than against the upper class in general. Failure of the Federalist-controlled Congress to enact tariff legislation that would protect artisan manufacturers, the rise of corruption, banking, and high taxes and the speculations of Hamilton's Assistant Treasury Secretary Duer that led to the nation's first financial panic in March 1792, harmed the Federalist cause in New York City and elsewhere. That Duer entered prison one day after a branch office of the Bank of the United States opened in the city only exacerbated Anti-Federalist sentiment.

The foreign policy crisis of the 1790s in which British and French enmity threatened to draw Americans into their war also contributed to the decline of New York's Federalist party. The French Revolution presented the politically useful contrast of a newly republican nation under the siege of a monarchist Europe led by Great Britain. The Tammany Society supported the Revolution and soon cooperated with the goals of the Anti-Federalist Democratic Society established in June 1794.[47] With Robespierre's ascendancy, democracy was equated with mob rule by Federalists.

Federalist policies in turn, were polemically equated by Anti-Federalist supporters of Thomas Jefferson with British suppression of republicanism internally among British plebeians through show trials and public executions, and externally against France through war. Among mechanics, Hamilton's dictum concerning the correspondence of interest between merchant and mechanic no longer held political capital for the Federalists. Their shift in party allegiance to the Republicans was accelerated by Hamilton's exertions on behalf of banking and manufacturing in addition to his anti-French sympathies.

In New York City, mechanics had overwhelmingly favored the Federalist party until constitutional ratification in 1788. Nine years later, there were many more Jeffersonian Republican mechanics, and they had attained a strategic political edge over the Federalists.[48] This change in mechanic allegiance, wrought through identifiable mass-based political parties and not through force of arms, was the most important and novel outcome of the radical republican tradition that had originated in England.

Moreover, it represented an important continuity in early New

York political history: mechanics attached themselves to elite factions and parties—first the Delanceys and Livingstons, then the Loyalists and Whigs, then the federalists and antifederalists, and finally the Federalists and Republicans.[49] Because they shared the entrepreneurial goals of their leaders, they found no need to resort to independent political action. New York "radical" republicanism remained socially and politically conservative and helped to soften political differences between the different classes represented within each party.

Led by Thomas Jefferson as president, the Republicans ideologically undermined the Federalists by adopting a loose interpretation of the Constitution in order to double the size of the United States through the Louisiana Purchase.[50] This overwhelmingly popular act set the stage for "Mr. Madison's War" of 1812, which established a military precedent for the conquest of the northern third of Mexico engineered by Jacksonian Democrats.

Landed expansion remained the leitmotif of American political discourse during the antebellum period, while the uses to which new land would be put became the economic cause of the Civil War. "Radical" republicanism had run afoul of the new "radical" Republican party of Abraham Lincoln, which following the war was based upon the industrializing principles of Alexander Hamilton.

Notes

1. *Public Advertiser,* (New York), 30 May 1807.
2. J. G. A. Pocock, *The Machiavellian Moment: Florentine Political Thought and the Atlantic Republican Tradition* (Princeton, 1975), 497.
3. The essays contained in *Three British Revolutions 1641, 1688, 1776,* ed. J. G. A. Pocock (Princeton, 1980), comprise a useful introduction to the relationship between British and American Whig radicalism. Also see *The Origins of Anglo-American Radicalism,* ed. Margaret Jacob and James Jacob (London, 1984).
4. Douglas Adair, "That Politics May Be Reduced to a Science: David Hume, James Madison, and the Tenth Federalist," *Huntington Library Quarterly* 20 (1957): 343–60. Hume's "Idea of a Perfect Commonwealth" in his *Essays, Moral and Political,* published in 1741 is essential to understanding the theoretical framework of the United States' national political system.
5. Alden Vaughan, "From White Man to Redskin: Changing Perceptions of the American Indian," *American Historical Review* 87 (1982): 918.
6. Christine Stansell, *City of Women: Sex and Class in New York 1789–1860* (New York, 1986), 21. See also Joan Hoff Wilson, "The Illusion of Change: Women and the American Revolution," in *The American Revolution: Explorations in the History of American Radicalism,* ed. Alfred F. Young (DeKalb, Ill., 1976), 385–445.

7. Edmund Morgan, "Slavery and Freedom: The American Paradox" in *The Challenge of the American Revolution* (New York, 1976), 142. David Brion Davis echoes this view. *The Problem of Slavery in the Age of Revolution 1770–1823* (Ithaca, N.Y., 1975), 262.

8. Baron de Montesquieu, *The Spirit of Laws*, Book 11: "Of the Laws which Establish Political Liberty with Regard to the Constitution", 62, *Of the Constitution of England.*

9. John Locke, *The Second Treatise of Government*, Sections 85 and 37. Adam Smith borrowed directly from Locke (Section 94) when he wrote, "Civil government, so far as it is instituted for the security of property, is in reality instituted from the defense of the rich against the poor, or of those who have some property against those who have none at all." *The Wealth of Nations* (Canaan edition, 1937), 674.

10. *New York Journal*, 1 Jan. 1767; 9 Jan. 1768; 6 Feb. 1768, 2 Aug. 1770, *New York Gazette & Weekly Mercury*, 4 May 1778. Hendrik Hartog finds that the majority of the petitions to the Common Council in the years from 1735 to 1767 concerned land transactions, with increasing numbers advanced just prior to the War for Independence. Clearly British rule was placing too many restrictions upon such lucrative activity. *Public Property and Private Power: The Corporation of the City of New York in American Law 1730–1870* (Chapel Hill, N.C., 1983), 40–41.

11. *New York Journal*, 2 Aug. 1770. Colin Bonwick places taxation at the core of American radical grievances. *English Radicals and the American Revolution* (Chapel Hill, N.C., 1977), 74. See also Roger J. Champagne, "Liberty Boys and Mechanics of New York City, 1764–1774," *Labor History* 8 (1967): 116. In *The Whiskey Rebellion* (New York, 1986), Thomas Slaughter finds the tax issue determining "the nature of conflict and the parameters of political discourse" despite "three decades of Revolutionary upheaval," 227.

12. Edmund S. Morgan, *American Slavery, American Freedom* (New York, 1975), 363–87.

13. Carl Becker described "the former as being supported by the lawyers and the Dissenters, the latter by the church and the mercantile interest." *The History of Political Parties in the Province of New York 1760–1776* (New York, 1968; originally pub. Madison, Wis., 1909), 18–19.

14. Carl Abbott, "The Neighborhoods of New York, 1760–1775," *New York History* 55 (1974): 38.

15. Gary B. Nash, "Urban Wealth and Poverty in Pre-Revolutionary America" in *Colonial America*, ed. Stanley Katz and John Murrin (New York, 1983), 453, 461.

16. Sidney Pomerantz, *New York: An American City 1783–1803* (New York, 1938), 36.

17. James and John Montresor, *The Montresor Journals* New-York Historical Society, *Collections* (New York, 1881), 336–371, 382–84. Little was made of those occurrences in the city's newspapers.

18. Delancey's "English connections were the most extensive of any native-born New Yorker of the eighteenth century. In fact, he possessed stronger ties with the British government than the royal governor whom he opposed." Stanley Katz, "Between Scylla and Charybdis: James Delancey and Anglo-American Politics in Early Eighteenth Century New York," Katz and Murrin, eds., *Colonial America*, 401.

Bonomi also designates Delancey as a leader. Patricia U. Bonomi, *A Factious*

People: Politics and Society in Colonial New York (New York, 1791), 240–41. Thus Arthur Schlesinger, Sr.'s assessment that "the radical cause lacked . . . an opposition divorced from the control of the merchant class" has not been seriously challenged. *The Colonial Merchants and the American Revolution 1763–1776* (New York, 1939), 255. See also Richard B. Morris, *Government and Labor in Early America* (Boston, 1981: originally published 1946), 189, and the *New York Journal*, 16 Dec. 1773. Edward Countryman, on the other hand, ascribed a revolutionary character to the movement. Yet he concludes that the Delancey faction had no trouble transforming itself from "the 'popular Whigs' of 1768 to the core of royalism by 1775." *A People in Revolution: The American Revolution and Political Society in New York, 1760–1790* (Baltimore, 1981), 112. Lamb, for instance, became chairman of the Federal Republican Society in 1788.

19. Sharon Salinger, "Artisans, Journeymen and the Transformation of Labor in Late Eighteenth-Century Philadelphia," *William and Mary Quarterly*, 3d ser., 40 (1983): 65.

20. Graham Russell Hodges, *New York City Cartmen, 1667–1850* (New York, 1986), 62.

21. Schlesinger, Sr., *Colonial Merchants*, 255. Nash finds the same to be true of Philadelphia. "Artisans and Politics in Eighteenth-Century Philadelphia" in Gary B. Nash, *Race, Class, and Politics: Essays on American Colonial and Revolutionary Society* (Urbana, Ill., 1986), 253.

22. Hodges, *Cartmen*, 64.

23. Eric Foner again finds Philadelphia similar. *Tom Paine and Revolutionary America* (New York, 1976), 52, while Bonwick sees the same for England with "artisan, let alone working class, radicalism . . . still in the future." Bonwick, *English Radicals*, 132.

24. Albert Soboul, *The Sans-Culottes* (New York, 1972), 252.

25. Bernard Bailyn, *The Ideological Origins of the American Revolution* (Cambridge, Mass., 1967), 283.

26. Nash, *Race, Class and Politics*, 369–70. Roger Champagne, "New York and the Intolerable Acts, 1774," *New-York Historical Society Quarterly* 44 (1961): 204.

27. Oscar Barck, *New York City 1776–1783* (Port Washington, N.Y., 1966), 46.

28. Ibid., 54.

29. Pomerantz, *New York City, 1783–1803*, 54.

30. *The Independent Gazette or the New York Journal Revisited*, 20 Dec. 1783; *1787 City Directory*. Four of the others were merchants, one a manufacturer, and the last a "gentleman".

31. *The Independent Gazette or the New York Journal Revisited*, 17 Jan. 1784.

32. Edmund P. Willis, "Social Origins of Political Leadership in New York City from the Revolution to 1815" (Ph.D. diss. University of California, 1967), 13. Catherine Menand, "Juries, Judges, and the Politics of Justice in Pre-Revolutionary Boston," in William Pencak and Wythe Holt, Jr., eds., *The Law In America, 1607–1861* (New York, 1989). This is consistent with Nash's finding concerning Boston's "laboring people" being "conspicuously inactive as a separate group and [making] virtually no demands for their role in the political process." *Race, Class and Politics*, 359.

33. Alfred Young, *The Democratic Republicans of New York: The Origins 1763–1797* (Chapel Hill, N.C., 1967), 575.

34. Staughton Lynd, "The Mechanics in New York Politics," in *Class Conflict, Slavery and the U.S. Constitution* (Indianapolis, Ind., 1967), 98.
35. "In Answer to the Citizen of Rhode-Island on the Five Percent Duty," Philip S. Foner, ed., *The Complete Writings of Thomas Paine* 2 (New York, 1945): 341.
36. Morris, *Government and Labor*, 152.
37. *The Independent Gazette*, 12 Feb. 1784. Lynd, "The Mechanics in New York Politics," *Class Conflict, Slavery and the U.S. Constitution*, 104.
38. Hodges, *Cartmen*, 76.
39. Rushmore G. Horton, *A Brief Memorial on the Origin and Earlier History of the Tammany Society* (New York, 1867), 20.
40. John Pintard to Jeremy Belknap, 11 Oct. 1790, in Edwin P. Kilroe, *Saint Tammany and the Origin of the Society of Tammany or Columbian Order in the City of New York* (New York, 1913), 136–37.
41. Peter Paulson, "The Tammany Society and the Jeffersonian Movement in New York City, 1795–1800," *New York History* 34 (1953): 79; Gustavus Myers, *The History of Tammany Hall* (Dover edition), 2.
42. *New York Journal*, 25 Feb. 1790.
43. Forrest McDonald, *Alexander Hamilton: A Biography* (New York, 1982: originally publ. 1979), 121, 233–34, 411.
44. "Final Version of an Opinion on the Constitutionality of An Act to Establish a Bank," February, 1791, *The Papers of Alexander Hamilton*, eds. Harold C. Syrett and Jacob E. Cooke (New York, 1965) 8:98.
45. "Opinion on the Constitutionality of a National Bank, Feb. 15, 1791", *The Essential Jefferson*, ed. Albert Fried (New York, 1963), 297, 298.
46. *New York Gazette*, 10 Feb. 1790. Young, *Democratic-Republicans*, 172.
47. *New York Gazette*, 15 July 1793.
48. Alfred Young, "The Mechanics and the Jeffersonians: New York, 1789–1801," *Labor History* 5 (1964): 247–76. This essay is the most succinct account of New York City working-class involvement in dominant party politics in the 1790s.
49. Gary Nash finds local republican political structures well in place before the War for Independence. "The Transformation of Urban Politics, 1700–1764," in *Race, Class and Politics* (Urbana, Ill., 1986), 161.
50. It is now almost a century since Henry Adams penned the definitive historical assessment of Jefferson, measuring the worth of eighteenth-century words against nineteenth-century actions as president. Merrill D. Peterson, "Henry Adams on Jefferson the President," *Virginia Quarterly Review* 39 (1963): 201. Henry Adams, *History of the United States of America During the First Administration of Thomas Jefferson* (New York, 1931: originally publ. 1889), 1:142–48, 251, 254–58, 277–78, 404; 2:82–94, 113.

CATHY MATSON

5

Liberty, Jealousy, and Union: The New York Economy in the 1780s

Liberty and Jealousy

In his 1758 essay "Of the Jealousy of Trade," David Hume wrote that "nothing is more usual, among states which have made some advances in commerce, than to look on the progress of their neighbours with a suspicious eye, to consider all trading states as their rivals, and to suppose that it is impossible for any of them to flourish, but at their expense." But enlightened minds, he continues, would reject such a "narrow and malignant opinion" and adopt the alternative view "that the encrease of riches and commerce in any one nation, instead of hurting, commonly promotes the riches and commerce of all its neighbours." Open competition among nations would eradicate the causes of war, costly political bureaucracies, and cure the evil of commercial jealousy.[1]

Hume's prescription for "natural harmony" among consumers and producers was an economic liberal ideal developed in decades of writing about rapidly changing commercial conditions and the character of the Anglo-Americans who experienced them. Theorists and policy makers observed the ranks of rising exporters and manufacturers, and related the extension of England's dominion abroad to the success of its productivity at home. Many economic liberals would join in constructing the mercantile state apparatus that channeled and fettered various commercial activities or fomented the disruptive early modern warfare that was essential to securing national power.[2]

Other economic liberals, Hume included, were critical of mercantilism and sought a more individually inspired and ethical foundation for economic activity. In America, few revolutionists and few newly empowered state leaders stopped to consult Hume's essays. But they did not need to, for many of his notions of *homo economicus* were incorporated into the received wisdoms of public discourse. Time and again, Americans iterated aspects of Hume's more systematic and coherent thoughts about economic activities. His belief in the reciprocal satisfaction of economic desires, individual autonomy in the marketplace, unending expansion across land and water, and peace and a rough equality of condition embodied the dreams of many revolutionary Americans.

This is not to claim a hegemonic position for Humean economic ideas, or for the unchallenged economic liberalism of early state legislative policies in America. Indeed, there were older, formidable discursive traditions that qualified or refuted aspects of economic liberalism throughout the 1780s. One of these was the radical tradition, which eschewed all ethical or political restraints on economic activities. Private liberty, they insisted, lay in continually changing opportunities and voluntarily assumed risks. Open ports and open markets were the best incentives to expand the compass of foreign trade. By seeking to serve economic demand, "free traders" would also create desire for exotic new goods, as well as offer the best quality and lowest prices for necessary ones. Self-interest itself would drive the economy, eventuating in the natural equilibrium of markets. The market place, conceived in the broadest possible terms of universal economic demand and desire, was a sufficient vehicle for social harmony; governments, experience showed, were meddlesome.[3]

Radical economic liberalism found a small, but vocal, following leading up to the revolution. By the 1760s, some Americans were inspired by the general hum of discussion about economic freedom to adopt a radically self-referential image of individuals pursuing distinct economic activities in a self-governing polity. During the imperial crisis radical economic liberals helped shape the goals of political independence, although their ideas were never adopted in unqualified form.[4] But the early months of local military mobilization spurred unimagined opportunities to small traders and shopkeepers of the interior to share the benefits of uninhibited competition. The revolution sanctioned huge private debts in paper obligations, and introduced even more new consumer goods to farmers and frontier families than before the war. By 1776 the remnants of self-restraint promoted during the nonimportation movements gave way to the promise of unfettered private enterprise at all levels of American society. Commerce in the interior as well as on the oceans was now the unexampled means to prosperity. Central to these activities was a strong belief that radical economic liberty was supported in even the most authoritative circles.[5] Indeed, the Continental Congress passed a resolution in April 1776 that endorsed the principle of open ports and international trade reciprocity. The following September some of its delegates committed themselves to the rudiments of economic liberty in an independent America. Trade, said delegates like James Wilson and Christopher Gadsden, would "regulate itself." Their revolutionary discussion, like the earlier notion of free trade that spawned it, was self-referential and radically individualistic.[6]

But at least in the case of New York, this radical vision of economic freedom faded quickly. The constantly attending hand of the new state government and its widely popular authority qualified the opportunities for radical economic liberty. A broad spectrum of commercial farmers, New York City exporters, and ambitious military suppliers found the promise of freer exchanges and greater private advantages compelling, but elusive. These constituencies were threatened with bankruptcy when they lost their "usual channels of trade," unlike the more fortunate public creditors and commissary officials. Farmers complained that embargoes deprived them of markets while commissaries ruthlessly seized grain to sell to the troops at exhorbitant prices. They opposed insensitive state officials who fixed prices of foodstuffs and services, and limited profits to twenty-five percent. New York City exporters joined farmers in protesting their alienation from familiar commercial opportunities by wartime embargoes and requisitions, as well as British occupation of the entrepôt. And neither farmers nor grain merchants could perceive any benefits from the use of depreciating state and continental certificates that they were forced to receive from army departments for their services and goods. Together, they insisted upon generous emissions of paper currency, to which the state government assented because of swollen revolutionary expenses.[7]

Elements of more radical notions of economic freedom persisted alongside the growing authority of a popular state government over the economy. For months citizens of the feeble new state, especially farmers, called for more open trade and refused to pay the taxes that would retire paper currency out of circulation. Hostility toward tax collectors continued well into 1779, forcing the state government to give up making the loathsome levies (with the exception of a feeble attempt in spring 1781).[8] Only one tax was allowed to stand without significant protest: a five percent surtax begun in March 1778 on the profits of trade and manufactures that were made in New York since 1776.[9] But New York City merchants tended to explain in Humean terms that their "trading libertye" was stifled by an excess of open competition in an overly long war. The movement for independence, which was in part "bred of a jealousy of the mother country in her commerce," was now maintained by a worse jealousy among the interests of distinct states that neglected to make private economic opportunities conform to the goals of social order. The states would have to excercise firmer sovereignty over "popular license."[10]

If these New Yorkers wanted to secure economic freedom with the gentle guidance of state government, others believed that economic order would be secure only with firm, centralized political control by a "better sort." Leaders of congressional and military activities tended to draw on another discursive tradition—that of classical republicanism—to explain that too much, not too little, private autonomy had been unleashed during the independence movement. Republicanism was a rich cluster of ideas about public political life.[11] Although by the 1770s republicans recognized the driving force of self-interest, their focus was upon the dangers of elevating private ambitions to preeminence. Many revolutionaries who were strongly influenced by the inheritance of republicanism wondered whether an uncontrollable, consuming, passionate majority had so overcorrected the problems of colonial restraints that the whole revolution was endangered. There did not seem to be sufficient self-denial to support the republican conception of civic virtue. Thus, some state legislators, military suppliers, and public creditors were prepared to take a major step away from economic liberty. Having failed to secure adequate tax revenues or requisitions, they organized an appeal to Congress to urge a national-level response to "local jealousy." In subsequent months they gathered with representatives of other states in conventions to stop the states from issuing paper money and introducing alternative means of paying for military supplies. Meeting with representatives of northern states in Hartford, November 1780, New York delegates proposed that since their separate state remedies were inadequate to meet revolutionary tasks, they should merge their personal economic powers and the state's corporate powers into one congressional effort to raise import duties to pay the public debt.[12] New Yorkers James Hobart, Egbert Benson, and Philip Schuyler attended the Hartford convention; they, and others, agreed with Alexander Hamilton that a stop had to be put to the "excessive licentiousness," the "rage to loose the ties which bind us in orderly commerce," the private "interest which goes by a name of liberty."[13] Out of these concerns would develop much of the rationale for a vision shared by the nationalists, those leading Americans who promoted a Constitution, of a vastly altered political economy.[14] During the revolution they asked all patriots to consider whether they had a sufficient measure of republican virtue to counteract their mutual jealousies in the scramble for economic liberty. And they were some of the first to depart from Hume's explanations of the causes of, and the cures for, the malignancy of commercial jealousy.[15]

Liberty and State Interests

Nationalists' intentions to tame the license of grasping lower- and middle-class citizens in New York met with one frustration after another from 1781 to 1787. The central explanation for this lay with a most important realignment of interests in the state, the emergence of a powerful coalition of commercial farmers, merchant exporters, and state creditors. Many of New York's wholesale merchants who were busy reestablishing trade with non-British ports supported the sovereign state. So did many in the West Indies interest, most of the young retailers and grocers who were connected to long-distance commerce and domestic markets, and most of the "agrarian interest" that hoped to reconstruct an export trade based on higher prices.[16] Although their own differences over specific state policies would qualify their alliance, all of these groupings identified the state as a better safeguard of their interests than the nationalists in Congress. This was most apparent in struggles over two related issues: import duties and the state's external commerce.

The strength of state interests had been clear during the debates over the Articles of Confederation. Congress's apparently hopeless divisions with respect to revolutionary war debts, army pay, and state boundaries underscored how the sentiment for liberty was stronger than the yearning for order and centralization.[17] When a specific proposal to give Congress power to levy five percent import duties reached Philadelphia in February 1781, sufficient congressional opposition defeated it. A follow-up proposal from John Witherspoon to give Congress the right to regulate the various states' commerce also failed. Only with a third attempt did Congress approve an *impost*, "a permanent Fund to support the national Credit and cement more effectually the common Interest of the United States."[18]

At first many of New York's "agrarian interest" combined with some merchant representatives to vote in the state legislature to approve the 1781 national impost act, pending the approval of all other states. Governor Clinton spoke on its behalf. Ostensibly, the impost would help defray New York's growing indebtedness to Congress without resorting to real estate taxes that would normally fall most heavily upon agriculturalists. The impost proposal also won support from merchants who had entered commerce recently or who had not been awarded prestigious wartime responsibilities and supply contracts. They agreed that modest import duties could be traded off for state legislative favors that would give them profits and prestige as their state recovered after the war.[19] Of course, revolutionary suppliers and commissaries, the government's main creditors, were some of the loudest advocates of an impost to bolster Congress's ability to repay its wartime obligations.[20]

But the sovereign states failed to agree about the conditions under which the 1781 impost would be collected. Congress reformulated its appeal for funds on 18 April 1783. This second impost measure asked the states for overall import duties of five percent ad valorem, and a few additional specific duties, for twenty-five years, collectible in the states by state officials. New York's legislature made another bow of approval to the national proposal. Alexander Hamilton, Philip Schuyler, and other New Yorkers who looked toward Congress for greater national stability, opposed the 1783 measure as too weak to simultaneously raise necessary revenues and create a central political authority: so long as the states collected revenues they could also withhold the funds from Congress. But state opposition to federal impost collectors in the various American ports, stronger now in 1783 than in 1781, choked off the chance to found a national revenue anyway.[21]

This second contest between national and state interests indicated that the appeal for economic liberty, kept alive during the revolutionary crisis with reference to individual opportunities, was being reformulated as economic liberty at the level of the sovereign states. When New York repealed its support for a federal impost on 15 March 1783 it was because, as one writer put it, "there grows a *jealousy* among [the states] of our commercial position." First, since all states could not agree about the terms of the impost, New Yorkers would not consent to it and thereby weaken their sovereign position. Moreover, they began to believe that with the 1783 impost a distant Congress sought power that was especially detrimental to economic liberty. Perhaps individuals were insecure in the face of this new power, and only the state should control its trade and revenues.[22]

Shortly after repeal of the national impost proposal the legislature enacted its own state impost. Clinton's hand-picked collector, John Lamb, never favored a national impost but he had stern respect for his responsibility toward the state impost. By 1787 the state received one-third of its revenues from the impost; in 1788 the amount paid into the state treasury by Lamb was £70,298 from the tariff alone. A contemporary estimate set the overall average annual income from the state impost at about £80,000. (In 1774, the year of highest income between 1763 and 1776, import taxes accounted for about £5,000 of New York's income).[23] Such substantial revenues as these drew regular and concerned public attention to how the money would be spent. New York was no different from many states that wanted to build their political sovereignty on the bedrock of financial legitimacy. Debts could not be abolished. But in the eyes of most Clintonians, an independent state had to contain its debts within local spheres as a precondition of its true sovereignty. The state had raised private loans from its own citizens, made state requisitions of supplies, issued various forms of army pay certificates, and emitted paper currency. These debts, argued Clintonians, could remain outstanding and not immediately harm the public welfare. Instead the state would give first priority to abolishing its federal obligations. The federal debt, accumulated since January 1777, was in many forms and in various degrees of accounting disarray or nonpayment. But the journals of Congress and the state legislature, state laws, messages of the governor, and extensive commentary in the newspapers, all attest to the imaginative attempts statesmen made to derive a reliable revenue with which to settle these debts. The early quota system of the Contintenal Congress asked New Yorkers to contribute over $5.5 million from January 1777 to early 1780, of which New York probably sent about $277,500 in specie and state certificates. Congress abandoned this plan in December 1779, and through June 1781 turned to quotas of specific supplies that would be paid for in Continental bills and specie certificates redeemable in the future. New York's share of these quotas was at least $15,400,000 in bills and $243,642 in certificates. Historians Thomas Cochran and E. James Ferguson estimate that the state paid about thirty-nine percent of this obligation to Congress.[24]

In a third phase of congressional finance, superintendent Robert

Morris began to use private contractors to organize and move supplies. The certificates that these contractors gave to private citizens in payments for goods and services were to be accepted by the state. To facilitate these exchanges, Congress established the Loan Office system, in which all the supplies furnished by inhabitants of the states would be reduced to a uniform specie valuation in accounting procedures—so as to erase the effects of depreciation—and 6 percent interest allowed to the supplier from the original time of his transaction with government contractors. Private citizens would be allowed to pay state taxes with the certificates or receive a delayed specie payment. However, because specie grew scarce within months of adopting this procedure, Congress began to credit the states with making payments in yet another form of paper, what became known as "indents." When indents were issued for the interest due, they were designated "6 percents."[25] Unlike other forms of revolutionary debt, the 6 percents were easily and early concentrated in the hands of relatively few New Yorkers (especially in contrast to the numbers who actually contributed supplies and services during the late months of the war).[26] Scarcity of specie also forced Congress to allow states to pay part of their requisitions in indents. From 1 January 1785 to 1 April 1788 four congressional requisitions were levied for the support of the Confederation government, of which New York paid an estimated 65 percent ($648,528) from its specie (derived mostly out of the state impost) and indents.[27] From 1784 to 1787 51 percent of all New York receipts, over $480,000, was paid to Congress against its revolutionary war debts; the state impost accounted for most of this amount.[28]

Nationalists reminded New Yorkers that the initiatives for, and sources of, financial responsibility lay with Congress. Given the state's abysmal record on taxation during the Revolution, there was a certain appeal to the claims of these "consolidators" who "thought continentally" that there ought to be a political union to secure and cement these gains. But it did not stretch New Yorkers' sense of reality to make the alternative claim that the state impost served an array of local interests adequately enough. Public commentators usually attributed these trends to the revival of commerce and the revenues from the state impost that rose with commerce.[29] Support for sovereign state power over the impost and the purse strings was suffused with optimism for a strong postrevolutionary republic with the capacity to expand quickly.

After news of the revolution's impending peace agreement, British merchants, retailers, pedlars, and smugglers began to evacuate New

York City; American equivalents filled some of their places eagerly. In their capacities as former city traders resuming old positions in the city, or new entrants in business taking up places vacated by Tories, many merchants were hopeful about reconstructing the city on the basis of state control.[30] The state impost signalled the returning prosperity of the city, and the confidence of its merchants that the state government would not qualify their self-interest in commerce unduly. Export prices for grain and flour rose steadily during the 1780s, reaching and then surpassing prewar levels by 1785. This prosperity was often attributed to the "favorable situation" of being "left free" of export duties and land taxes. One fear that motivated agrarian support for the state impost, then, was the specter of having to impose land taxes if the state's impost revenues were "drained into a consolidated union" by the nationalists. As John Williams put it in the *Country Journal:*

> What hath kept the taxes so low in this state—the reason is obvious, impost duties. . . . Let our imposts and advantages be taken from us, shall we not be obliged to lay as heavy taxes as Connecticut, Boston, etc.[?][31]

Beginning in 1784 the Confederation government allowed New York state to pay interest due on Loan Office debts to state residents—many of them merchant suppliers—and to redeem indents with future state taxes. In return for relieving Congress of the Loan Office burden, the state recieved credit against its federal requisitions quotas, reinforcing both the effectiveness of its state sovereignty and the appeal of rhetoric about restoring personal liberty by making good the public debt.[32] From 1784 to 1786 the state legislature gathered up more of the purse strings that nationalists could not prevent Congress from giving away. In 1786 New York's Clintonians took the state's financial reputation a step further. They issued $500,000 of paper currency, one-quarter of which was set aside as a fund to pay the interest and principal on the state debt and to fund federal Loan Office certificates and revolutionary-era bills of credit emitted by Congress that were owned by New Yorkers. Within a year securities with a face value of $1,400,000 were retired and *state* securities, with new specie valuations, were issued in their place. In effect New York's state government converted and assumed significant amounts of the federal debt that its citizens owned. By 1790 the state of New York owned federal securities worth over $2,800,000 in specie valuations. About twenty-five percent of New York's freemen took advantage of state assumption, perhaps one-third of the total amount being redeemed by yeomen and small retailers, and two-thirds by merchants, war suppliers, and speculators. The interest due from Congress to New York on these securities more than equalled the annual requisitions on the state by Congress during the confederation period.[33]

In this manner, Clinton tied many public creditors to the state's financial interests and made it less likely that they would support a new national government (for now). He enhanced the political authority of the state, and earned the trust of postrevolutionary creditors who were not already committed nationalists, thereby diminishing prospects for changing the state-oriented policies of the Confederation. He also strengthened the alliance of commercial and domestic agrarian interests by effectively combining a respect for the debt with the useful instrument of paper money, and aggressively legislating the debt into state hands in such a way that many urban merchants and creditors were as happy about the results as those state inhabitants who were in principle opposed to the creation of a distant, powerful national government. He and the legislature neither repudiated the debt (or depreciated it into oblivion with paper money)—a typical "agrarian debtor" response—nor paid the debts with specie at their face values—a typical "merchant creditor" response. New York was being transformed from a debtor state into one of the wealthiest creditor states in the union.[34]

Until 1785 many wealthy dry goods importers supported these state developments. Merchants whose goods and credit tied them to prominent London exporters hoped for the most feasible political means to reconstruct postwar trade. Never much for economic liberty and self-government in the colonial period, dry goods wholesalers now agreed that the state impost was a lower tax on imports than Congress would pass and was, in any event, a necessary political compromise with Clintonians to get other measures enacted. Merchants Bayard, Van Schaick, Taylor, Lansing, and others associated the national impost with competition for their local privileges, especially because its sponsors, like Hamilton, also promoted legislation to assimilate returning Loyalists, regularize sales at auction, and recognize the contributions of British factors living in the city.[35] Even more, Congress's "most favored nation" treaties consistently excluded Britain from American trade beginning in 1783. Yet New York City merchants had been striving actively to reopen channels of commerce and credit with former—and, for them, merely formal—enemies who were now excluded from trade by the congressional restraints.[36] In practice, dry goods merchants simply ignored Congress's paper treaties. In fact, New York received more ships from England than from any other foreign nation from 1784 to 1787. England, contemporaries noted, would continue "to supply our wants, and, more, the productions which our own inhabitants see is beyond their industry." In the absence of their own manufactures why stifle so easy and abundant a connection as England was?[37] Besides, as Jacob LeRoy and others noted from 1783 to 1785, there were few large outstanding debts to English creditors, which was one more reason to cherish that trade.[38]

Only the "West Indies interest" raised serious objections to both the state and national imposts. They reminded fellow New Yorkers that their own consumption of sugar surpassed most European nations, and was more than two times French consumption of table sugar. Other New Yorkers felt that the commodity was no longer even a "luxury" or "superfluity" but a "necessity." Much of the port city's sugar would come from maple syrup in the future, but for now the major portion of it continued to come through the West Indies trade. Merchants like Isaac Roosevelt who imported legally from the British West Indies faced export taxes imposed by England and import taxes at American ports. If they reexported portions of the commodity to consumers in neighboring states they would pay again. Moreover, any impost could only promote the "dishonest" trade of smugglers, since it set up "barriers which are so easily broken" and only inhibited the "reciprocal wants" of the two nations. New York's consumers would face yet another, albeit hidden, tax: the higher price for legally imported sugar compared to cheaper smuggled goods.[39] But the West Indies interest faced more serious postwar circumstances than the impost, and these would drive them to support other measures that strengthened state sovereignty. Beginning in 1784 a series of British acts deliberately sought to subordinate American trade to British interests all over again. British orders in council threw open English ports to American commerce in a dramatic reversal of mercantile precepts and an apparent bow to free trade. But the acts were designed only to revive London merchants' trade with the former colonies; they simultaneously closed British West Indies ports to American vessels, and heavily taxed American commodities destined for West Indies ports. By 1786, the British West Indies trade was restricted largely to provisions, tobacco, and naval stores.[40] In individual cases of hardship increasing numbers of dry good merchants joined their voices to the West Indies interest, whose Caribbean markets were adversely affected by the British acts, to ask for legislative help. "Common Sense," for example, called for Congress to retaliate.[41]

On 30 April 1784, in response to the British acts, Congress asked the states for power to regulate commerce for fifteen years in order to more effectively retaliate against British belligerence; Congress's intention was to ban British imports and exports from American waters. Through July 1785 delegates considered whether it was proper under the Articles of Confederation to relocate power over international— or even interstate—commerce in congressional hands. Since Congress could not ban any imports or exports outright, and since there was strong feeling against any concentration of commercial power, the request never reached state governments. In Congress, at least, representatives still felt more disposed toward currying international detente than cultivating American commerical freedom with hostile retaliation.[42] So, failing to act against British restraints with firm resolve, Congress was forced to allow state legislation to redress merchants' grievances. On 22 March 1784 the New York legislature passed a law to collect 2.5 percent duty on all imports that arrived in New York vessels and were intended for New York consumers, and a five percent duty on British goods entering New York City from the West Indies in British vessels. These acts were renewed repeatedly in the coming confederation years.[43] On 18 November 1784 the New York legislature added duties on goods it deemed "luxuries" and that the British often carried into the city: southern European wines, British West Indies rum, English watches, carriages, and buckles; and, although they were hardly luxuries in New York's agricultural economy, many iron manufactures and tools. Merchants Willet, Lamb, Sears, Rutgers, Stagg, Macolm, Harpur, Van Zandt, Hughes, and others of the Assembly drew upon their experience of the revolutionary period to motivate this "double duty" against British West Indies interests. Only now, instead of arguing that unregulated commerce was the perfect foundation of the public good, they were forced to recognize that unregulated commerce was a chimera so long as some foreign nations imposed another (indeed, more powerful) economic model upon them.[44]

State discrimination against foreign commercial rivals established the legitimacy of discrimination against neighboring states as well. For if the sovereign state defined its economic liberty in distinction to an imperial bulwark of stifling authority, it was a short step to recognize that the same state interests were also autonomous from the interests of other states. Since 1778 New York had tried to keep its own agricultural export prices competitive by placing temporary embargoes on wheat, flour, and meal until local prices rose above those of neighboring Connecticut and New Jersey.[45] But in 1784 it applied long-term direct taxes to the traffic of sister states through New York

City, which brought about a protracted struggle with other northern ports. The general state impost that year, which placed a double tax on all foreign commerce, stipulated that unless other American states' vessels could prove they were non-British (or goods destined for other states were not being shipped by British merchants), the responsible merchants would be liable for the double duty. In late 1784 and again in early 1785 the assembly introduced laws to tax reexports of all foreign goods or interstate commerce through New York City to neighboring states, and imposed an additional five percent tax on all commerce arriving from other American states for sale to New Yorkers.[46]

Of all the northern American ports, New Jersey's were the weakest with respect to harbor facilities and the abilities of its merchants to risk ventures. As a result, its merchants sent small agricultural surpluses coming from the countryside into New York for export; on return trips they drew goods from foreign countries and other states through New York. For decades the colony/state had experimented with "free port" policies in hopes of drawing trade toward itself. But in the wake of the revolution, "Candidus" expressed the fear that New Jerseyites "will have to divide ourselves between the two great States that overshadow us," i.e., New York and Pennsylvania. In late 1784 the New Jersey legislature reiterated its position in favor of free ports at Perth Amboy and Burlington, and threw them open to all nations for twenty-five years. The state dropped all taxes on ships and (with the exception of slaves) all duties on goods, and admitted anyone to freemanship after a one-month residency in its cities. Then the state tried a political expedient that further indicated its weakness relative to New York. Because New Jersey was unable to reciprocate against New York with its own discriminatory legislation, it also refused to pay *national* requisitions on 20 October 1785 until all states agreed to the federal impost. Only in late March 1786 did the New Jersey legislature decide to fall in with Congress's requisition requests, and then face local struggles over what kind of taxes would raise the money to pay Congress.[47]

Connecticut confronted discrimination problems similar to New Jersey's, with respect to dependence on New York for building and outfitting vessels in which its merchants held shares and providing valuable port facilities. A very great portion of Connecticut's agricultural trade continued to flow through New York City. However, unlike New Jersey, the state turned in 1784 from a policy of free ports to place duties on all commerce with other states in an attempt to compete with New York and attract its merchants to new places of business. Despite the strength of Connecticut's agrarian interests, the policy seemed effective in building up New Haven and New London.[48] But it did not undercut New York City's relative strength. Through 1788 about one-third of the imports taxed under New York laws were ordered by Connecticut merchants and retailers (over one half of Connecticut's total imports). Contemporaries estimated that Connecticut merchants paid over $100,000 that year in New York customs duties and fees.[49] It was widely believed that Massachusetts suffered from New York's policies as well, and young Vermont had to import almost all of its commodities through the Hudson River.[50]

It can hardly be surprising, then, to discover that at about the time New York once again raised the amounts of duties it charged neighbors to use its superior ports and services, New Jersey and Connecticut merchants began to support the benefits of a "higher authority" in Congress. While New York's opposition to congressional nationalists derived at least in part from the state's ability to maintain a locally controlled revenue, Connecticut and New Jersey denounced the Clintonian impost as "Approbrius, indecent," a source from which "a Lamb, a Willet, a Smith, a Clinton, and a Yates salaries are paid."[51] Although a federal impost was not otherwise popular in Connecticut and New Jersey, their perceived oppression under New York's state impost would motivate some prominent merchants to turn toward the nationalists.[52] It was not only a merchant's access to particular kinds of markets and goods, but also his relative position in a confederation of thirteen sovereign states, which conditioned his support for economic liberty.

The Clintonian coalition that favored state, as opposed to national, sponsorship of its political and economic agenda was thus much more than an "agrarian interest," although its detractors would continue to tag it as such. In addition to the newly empowered up-state commercial farmers and city artisans and retailers, it included great numbers of rising or returning established merchants in dry goods commerce and some of the West Indies traders who were hopeful that the state could alleviate its particular grievances. A large number of small inland traders, retailers, and transporters hitched their own prospects for new opportunities to the new state government as well. Nationalists were aware of how broad the spectrum of Clintonian support was, and repeatedly warned against the political dangers of confounding economic interests of the lowly and eminent. Alexander Hamilton, among other nationalists, rhetorically divided Americans into agrarian and commercial components in order to propose that the new states intended to serve only the former, while those who "thought continentally" would fuse all interests under a congressional banner. Hamilton's intention was in fact to appropriate and transform the range of concerns that Clintonians were successfully addressing. But in New York a combination of state forces was doing its own appropriating and transforming. On the one hand, the state government had tamed the radical economic liberty unleashed by the revolution, while ensuring that taxation, currency, and regulation of the economy would be controlled by the newly empowered interests. On the other hand, Clintonians invited the traditionally defined elite in commerce to divest itself of overt class biases in order to join a coalition that promised to serve "commerce and agriculture as the twins of our sovereign republic." Until late 1785 the crest of state sovereignty was in fact rising on this dual principle.

Jealousy vs. Union

By mid to late 1785 New York's political balance of forces began to shift toward the nationalists. There are two general forms in which this shift is historically apparent. First, an economic slump from 1785 to 1787 was devastating for certain sectors of the merchant community trading abroad and for some of the newly established lesser merchants, retailers, and grocers in the city. As a result, certain groupings in the Clintonian coalition looked with suspicion on those who continued to prosper and recoiled from the vigor of the state government because it was founded on an articulate popular base that defied traditional responses to economic crises. Second, nationalists assumed an increasingly aggressive posture, evidenced by their inherited fears about "commercial jealousy" and their attempts to place the blame for this jealousy squarely with the states. Nationalist rhetoric about anarchy, crisis, and the imminent demise of the republic reflected their growing concerns about the effective power of new men in local government. Thus, during the debates about the proper form that America's political economy should take, the nationalists added their own interpretation of Hume's "jealousy of trade," an interpretation that borrowed familiar words and broadened them conceptually during this "critical period." What appeared to state interests to be successful implementation of their sovereign rights was, in the wider view of nationalists, a variety of discriminatory impulses emanating from each state that nullified the joint development of all states together. Like Hume's competing nations, the American states had erected barriers to protect their separate, mutually jealous, sovereign statuses.

Before nationalists began a coordinated offensive against rising state interests a serious, although temporary, economic decline raised questions about the state's strength in the face of adversity. Despite episodic reports of returning commercial prosperity, there were even more serious weaknesses in the city's economy by the second half of the 1780s. Private indebtedness rose steeply precisely when public indebtedness began to seem less onerous. Many of the state's small debtors were unable to clear their accounts because of a devastatingly poor harvest in 1785 and a shortage of "circulating medium."[53] As a result, many New Yorkers reverted to a tested colonial remedy when they called for a land bank that would lend paper money on the collateral of real estate. Clintonians accommodated their requests. In fact, the same bill passed in 1786 to help the state assume a large portion of the public debt and also to assuage the demands of the state's private debtors. Out of the emission of $500,000 of paper money, three-fourths of it funded a state land bank.[54]

But merchants who were reliant upon the vagaries of international markets and who needed specie for payments were not as easily placated during the slump. Dry goods and West Indies merchants leveled two apparently contradictory complaints. The former noted the periodic presence of too many goods, gluts that were especially evident after early 1785.[55] West Indies merchants noted the shortage of desireable commodities, persistent blockage of opportunity to trade in old and new markets, and increasingly encumbered port facilities.[56] Yet the two types of complaints derived from the same general discourse about who controlled the New York economy, and for whom. In the case of either gluts or shortages, effective British legislation against the economic freedom of American merchants in international trading arenas made it abundantly clear that New York was not in control of its economy. Dry goods merchants were perennially concerned that New York had no regulations to control auctions, a form of bulk sales of goods at low prices, which gave "interlopers" or foreign merchants' agents in the city a quick turnover and easier disposal of commodities of inferior quality, while many dry goods merchants were forced to sell to city retailers at higher prices in order to recover costs plus markups for profit.[57] Most resident dry goods merchants scorned this business and questioned the viability of the state's position against so formidable a group of "strangers" competing in the city.[58] In addition, after 1785 an increasing number of dry goods merchants were also tied by credit or marriage to London firms, or were themselves Loyalists returned to the city. A combination of state legislation and leftover revolutionary prejudices alienated them from Clintonians as the economic crisis deepened.[59] For the West Indies interest, persistent commercial sluggishness and reports of bankruptcies after 1785 made it appear that British discrimination was the epitome of international jealousy. The Lows, Roosevelts, and others who were accustomed to intense competition in the Caribbean were nevertheless appalled with the foreign regulations heaped upon New York's trade. Although importing continued to rise (75,000 tons of shipping entered New York City in 1788, 55,000 of which were on the credit of New Yorkers), these levels were *perceived* to be lower than merchants could achieve if their "trading libertye" had not been stymied by British orders in council.[60] Moreover, although some West Indies traders continued to specialize in one or two commodities, many began to diversify goods and markets as a hedge against recurrences of the problems they were experiencing. Grain and flour exporters sought longer-distance markets and additional coastal trading. Networks of correspondence and goods wove the interests of New York City merchants with those of all other traders. Out of entrenched self-interest, their expectations for economic opportunity expanded well beyond state boundaries.[61]

Increasingly, members of these two commercial interests grew convinced that the state's policies of retaliation were ineffective against British policies and mutually antagonistic among the states. Despite the successes of New York in recovering from the effects of war in other respects, the all-important matter for many city merchants was access to old and new markets, including relatively unencumbered port facilities in all ports of call. This goal was unobtainable, they began to muse, so long as the various states played a game of outraising their duties against each other and against foreign rivals; the game was all the more dangerous as other domestic interests—mechanics, new manufacturers, and many retailers—sought particular kinds of regulations to protect and extend their interests. But during the slump the state chose to ignore these interests, standing by as some distillers and earthenware and wig manufacturers closed business.[62] Matching international jealousy, then, was a "a species of jealousy in our states" that stultified healthy economic development.[63] By 1787 a group of merchants, which had previously supported the use of legislation to eliminate British competition—even when it entailed port duties—began to favor "a uniform system of commerce" directed from Congress.[64] "Small interests" at the state level denied the central place of international commerce and elevated a plethora of "petty traders" to unearned status, yet ninety-five percent of the value of New York's imported manufactures was handled by the Anglo-American merchants from 1784 to 1788.⁶⁵

Nationalists knew that the argument in favor of consolidating the debts of the states into Congress's hands was appealing mainly to the already converted. Securities brokers, speculators, and army officers were already actively dealing in portions of the unredeemed public debt and knew that a federal schema would best protect their property; they also hoped that redeeming the large amount of federal securities that the state had not assumed (estimated at $3,600,000) could broaden the base of congressional credibility.⁶⁶ But far more significant for the Constitutional debates that surfaced in the midst of the economic slump was the nationalist position on commercial "jealousy." Continued bankruptcies, sluggish circulation of goods, shortages of specie, and rising rents disillusioned many city inhabitants; persistent commercial tensions with neighboring states aggravated other New Yorkers' perceptions of endangered economic opportunity. During the crisis of 1785 to 1787, these immediate concerns were compelling reasons for some New Yorkers to reconsider state sovereignty.

Beginning in spring 1785 defectors from the Clintonian coalition announced themselves in city newspapers and merchants' petitions to the legislature.⁶⁷ On 14 March 1785 John Alsop signed a memorial to the legislature from the Chamber of Commerce—a body of mainly merchants and grocers who had grown disaffected with the state's financial and port policies—lamenting the inability of northern states to cooperate in trade.⁶⁸ Through the following months the nationalist position was reiterated dozens of times in the city press. A typical statement came from an "Appeal of a New York Committee in Behalf of the Impost Amendment" on 30 September 1785 that borrowed the rhetoric of "natural harmony" among class and interstate interests:

> When we see the landholder and merchant seduced with a false idea that their real interests are different it is not to be wondered at (though it must be lamented) that one State should suppose it can derive advantage or may escape danger, from circumstances of injury or oppression to another.⁶⁹

Nationalists denied there was any danger to agrarians of passing a land tax to complement the impost; no such "supplementary taxes" would be necessary, for union would never imply such a gross "imbalance of power" or "divided power" between the states and national government. As for "advantages" of one state over others, nationalists stood on high moral ground arguing that no state should "injure or oppress another."[70] Gerard Bancker, Philip Schuyler, William Floyd, Lewis Morris, Nicholas Roosevelt, Ezra L'Hommedieu, and William Stoutenburgh threw their influences into this debate in the legislature, while Isaac Roosevelt, James Duane, Robert Troup, Isaac Sears, Thomas Lawrence, Ledyard, and Malcolm organized public meetings at Cape's Tavern.[71] "Cimon," "Candidus," "Patrioticus," and others carried on the debate in the *New York Packet*. A national revenue system, they usually argued, was the only sure way to keep trade and industry in America, prevent further rise in luxury consumption, redirect commercial "jealousy" toward foreign rivals rather than each other, and undermine the "anarchy" spreading from the backcountry into American ports.[72]

By the time Virginia's legislators proposed on 21 January 1786 a meeting of delegates from all states at a "commercial convention" in Annapolis, the notion of radically altering the Articles of Confederation was no longer new. When New Yorkers, in their vote for the 1783 national impost request at the 13 April 1786 legislative session, attached unacceptable conditions to Congress's original measure (the state retained its right to collect the impost, appoint collectors, and receive the impost in its own paper money) nationalists agreed that they could no longer delay taking firmer action.[73] On 20 April Hamilton, Robert C. Livingston, and Leonard Gansevoort were appointed by the New York Assembly to the Annapolis convention; on 5 May Robert R. Livingston, James Duane, and Egbert Benson were appointed by the Senate. When delegates of five states finally met in September, barely a month after Clintonians rejected Congress's urgent appeal that New Yorkers reconsider their unacceptable conditions on the impost, the Annapolis delegates recommended to Congress that it "consider how far an uniform system in their commercial intercourse and regulations might be necessary to their common interest and permanent harmony."[74] Congress was only too aware of its own dilemma to ignore the Annapolis proposal. The states were collectively so far in arrears in paying requisitions to Congress that the latter could not pay even the interest on its public debt. And nine days after Congress voted to appoint a committee to consider the Annapolis document it raised troops to quell the Shaysite "anarchy" in western Massachusetts. Congress requested that New York convene its legislature again, repeal its conditions on the national impost, and pledge support for the document as Congress had formulated it.[75]

Nevertheless, from January to March 1787 the press harangued against, and the legislature defeated, bills to give Congress a sure revenue, and instead renewed the state impost.[76] In their spring legislative session, 1787, they clapped new and higher fees on all New Jersey and Connecticut vessels reexporting through New York City, fees that affected every small vessel carrying firewood, every shallop with food supplies, and every boatman transporting personal fare around the Sound.[77] When and how would commercial jealousy end?

Hamilton, Jealousy, and Union

The constitutional convention in Philadelphia represented not so much a federalist defeat of sovereign state hegemony as the supplanting from the state to the national level of a subtle mixture of powers. For New Yorkers the greatest number of converts was won over to the federalist position before the convention and before the most eloquent nationalist writings, including the *Federalist* essays, appeared. Nevertheless, the writings of nationalists like Alexander Hamilton helped to coalesce and articulate in bold statements the piecemeal sentiments of New Yorkers who feared that the accomplishments of the revolution were endangered by the popular majority in power. Even more, his writings gave the elite reading public an intellectual conceptual apparatus that went hand in hand with the political project of nationalists. In a series of essays written in 1781 and 1782, and published in the New York press under the name "Continentalist," Hamilton began to explain his view of the postrevolutionary years.[78] The problem with revolutionary rhetoric about "liberty," he said, was its release of excessive energy, a covetous strain, discriminatory legislation of "jealous" states, and counterproductive trading feuds among individual traders. In the morass of poor economic conditions during the 1780s, private actions could not counteract other private actions to produce a benign political economy.

These conditions were compatible with human nature as Hamilton perceived it. "Men will pursue their interests," he wrote. "It is as easy to change human nature as to oppose the strong current of the selfish passions." He had a pessimistic concern that humans were a mass of uncontrollable urges to get and consume. Hamilton countered free trade optimism with a pessimistic view of our inborn avarice. Out of the "natural competition" to have more than others there arose "natural inequalities," contention for economic power, and the necessity for both checks upon excessive individual desire and protection of those who had legitimately gained in legitimate economic contests."[79] The "Continentalist" essays also made clear how easy it was for these passions to run afoul of social needs. "Liberty," said Hamilton, ought not to be shaped by "selfishness in every part" of the polity but, rather, as a "common liberty." Yet "[i]t is the temper of societies as well as of individuals to be impatient of constraint, and to prefer partial to general interest."[80] There was no better or more immediate case of this in history than the American Revolution when its participants had become "ambitious," "vindictive," "rapacious," "passionate." "Extreme jealousy of power" led to most of the Revolution's "fatal mistakes."[81] Adam Smith may have been correct that human beings will look after their own economic interests in all events; but Smith did not understand the dire consequences of leaving such interests unchecked. Economic activists, in particular, were unpredictable, self-seeking. The sum total of economic activities could not add up to a self-correcting system, but simply to more release of private passions.[82]

Hamilton reminded readers of the "Continentalist" about what happened when the crucial tasks of revolutionary war finance had been left to the sovereign states: "in the midst of dangers too serious to be trifled with, some of the states have evaded, or refused, compliance with the demands of Congress in points of the greatest moment to the common safety" due to "rivalships of commerce" among them.[83] The sovereign

> members of a confederacy have, . . . an advantage in things contrary to the good of the whole. . . . The selfishness of every part will dispose each to believe that the public burthens are unequally apportioned . . . and the ambition of men in office in each state, will make them glad to encourage anti-federal feelings. . . . The particular governments will have more empire over the minds of their subjects, than the general one, because their agency will be more direct, more uniform, and more apparent.[84]

These bad habits were carried forward into the 1780s until "Each state will be afraid to impose duties on its commerce, lest the other states, not doing the same, should enjoy greater advantages than itself; by being able to afford native commodities cheaper abroad [because of the many encumbrances laid upon exports] and foreign commodities cheaper at home [which would raise the costs of labor and hinder productivity in America]." Only the importers of luxuries would be able to withstand this web of "state jealousies," and as these items would become cheaper and more widely consumed, while "necessaries" were neglected.[85]

But firm government guidance would steer passions to productive ends: "A wise legislator will gently divert the channel and direct it, if possible, to the public good."[86] Harkening back to sources like William Petty, whose economic treatises in the 1660s paved the way for a reconceptualization of economic man and new class interests guided by a "science" of "political arithemetic," Hamilton made pragmatic, empirical, interventions for the changing economic needs of America's finance capitalist elite in the 1780s.[87] But instead of proposing to free this new *homo economicus* by leaving him to his own reasoning in the marketplace, Hamilton appealed to the state-directed imperial model for remedies. In addition to sources like Petty, Hamilton probably cribbed from arch mercantilists like Malachy Postlethwayt when he argued that "To preserve the balance of trade in favor of a nation ought to be a leading aim of its policy. The avarice of individuals may frequently find its account in pursuing channels of traffic prejudicial to that balance, to which the government may be able to oppose effectual impediments."[88]

It was also in 1782 that Hamilton began to confront squarely the radical economic liberal vision of America's future that was popular during the revolution: "there are some, who maintain, that trade will regulate itself, and is not to be benefited by the encouragements or restraints of government." These people "will imagine, that there is no need of a common directing power." "This," however, "is one of those wild speculative paradoxes, which have grown into credit among us, contrary to the uniform practice and sense of the most enlightened nations."[89] He continues that "commerce, like other things, has its fixed principles, according to which it must be regulated." Nevertheless, the opposition to wise government regulations arose during the revolution when "injudicious attempts . . . to effect a *Regulation of Prices*" provoked the ridicule of free traders. "It became a cant phrase among the opposers of these attempts, that TRADE MUST REGULATE ITSELF." This opposition, says Hamilton, "misapprehended" "a very ingenious and sensible writer," David Hume. In his essay "Of the Jealousy of Trade," he most emphatically did not propose to leave trade alone to "hold a certain invariable course independent on the aid, protection, care or concern of government." Instead, he said that the commercial success of a nation depended "upon the comparative industry [and] moral and physical advantages of nations; and that . . . there may be a wrong balance against one of them," which would "work its own cure." Thus, wise governments would intervene to bring all "popular jealousies" of the polity into uniform standards of commerce, while the trade among rival nations would reach various changing balances through time. Even Hume recognized that commercial freedom was impossible until standards of proper conduct, derived by consulting the myriad interests arising in commerce and then agreeing upon some "uniform measures" to protect the equal competitive rights of all traders, were discovered.[90]

In the twenty-nine years between 1758 when Hume wrote and 1787 when Hamilton published the *Federalist* essays the differences between them widened. By the latter date many Americans were willing to contemplate Hume's point that mettlesome political interests might interfere with the preservation and extension of beneficial economic interests; but they also knew from painful experience that economic freedom had to be qualified, restrained in some way, lest it destroy the young republic. Hamilton's solution was to unify the acquisitive economic interests that Hume (and others) identified within a political structure that self-consciously avoided a recapitulation of mercantilism, the system from which Americans had just won independence.[91]

Hamilton still held his predecessor's premise that commerce was the engine of all great social changes. Commerce not only circulated the world's existing wealth but it also expanded national production in a world that was increasingly aware of the effects of economic competition.[92] Indeed, Hamilton reiterated received wisdoms in 1787, wisdoms that Hume would have applauded, including praise in *Federalist* No. 6 for the "new incentives to the appetite," the public desire to consume ever more commodities, which aggressive and unfettered commerce could make available to productive nations.[93] In *Federalist* No. 12 he explained that "commerce [is] . . . now perceived and acknowledged by all enlightened statesmen to be the most useful as well as the most productive source of national wealth." Commerce promoted circulation of goods and precious metals, and "in proportion as commerce has flourished, land has risen in value," and the interests of agriculture "are intimately blended and interwoven" with commerce. In addition, commerce "is the faithful handmaid of labor and industry . . . the prolific parent of far the greatest part of the objects upon which [labor and industry] are exerted." Such was merely the "plain truth" of "reason and conviction." Hume and Hamilton (among many others) believed that commerce developed a republic's ability to produce and consume, which in turn enriched the culture.[94] Hamilton also shared with Hume the assumption that jealousy was more than a private passion among covetous individuals. Many early economic liberal writers, regardless of political persuasion, defined jealousy as the regard of corporate, class, or national interests for their prosperity as opposed to that of other interests. Merchants were one of the groups most vulnerable to the interplay of jealous forces in the economy. It followed that while they could be counted as a crucial link between productivity and circulation, they remained self-interested individuals who pursued the single-minded objects of economic opportunity.[95]

However, Hume and Hamilton disagreed about something very important. Hume's corrective to the mercantilists was to loosen the fetters of regulations and allow individuals of all nations to compete freely enough so that the natural levels of mutually harmonious exchanges might be obtained in the long term and trading jealousies thus overcome. Hamilton could not agree that republics that acted jealously in their corporate capacities would enjoy the natural benefits of commerce if simply left free of their economic fetters to compete in the marketplace. Yet Hamilton did not return to mercantile regulations as a panacea either. The American Revolution taught vigilant observers that certain combinations of "designing placeholders" had interests that jarred in irreconcilable ways with the public good. Once merchants left their more thoroughly commercial pursuits and became political activists, says *Federalist* No. 1, these Americans were even more opened up to "ambition, avarice, personal animosity . . . preconceived jealousies and fears,"[96] and proved to be "passionate," "vindictive and rapacious."[97] Thus, the private jealousies of individual merchants could become a more serious threat to the public good when they were mixed with political interests. This was especially true during the 1780s in America, when the tremendous promise of revolutionary accomplishments was threatened by "excessive liberty."[98]

The *Federalist* argues that commercial jealousy hindered the creation of an American empire in two ways. *Internationally,* there were "combinations of European jealousy" that made American commerce "passive." The outrage expressed in the American press over the British orders in council (see above) could have escaped the attention of only those who refused to read or contemplate the "monstrous policies" of that mercantile state which had just been defeated by virtuous republican Americans during the revolution. Certainly the outrage did not escape Hamilton's attention, and he counted on the perceived economic deprivation of "the West Indies interest" to find a remedy to British depredations against "our federal capacity."[99] Hamilton articulated their grievances when he wrote that American merchants were "compelled to content [them]selves with the first price of [their] commodities, and to see the profits of [their] trade snatched from [them]." "That unequaled spirit of enterprise, which signalized the genius of the American merchants and navigators, and which is in itself an inexhaustible mine of national wealth, would be stifled and lost" in the absence of wise governance.[100] Indeed, the "jealousy of power" that led to so many "rivalships and competitions of commerce between commercial nations"[101] would conspire to "waste themselves in ruinous contentions with each other"[102] and inhibit the "true interests" of Americans: the "uniform public good" that was bound inextricably to the "fate of an empire."[103]

If Americans were made "passive" in international commerce by their failure to cooperate in defeating foreign jealousies, their *interstate* quarrels threatened to produce similar dangers to the public good. In 1782 Hamilton's "Continentalist" essays expressed regret that the states had openly abandoned a spirit of cooperation and instead had adopted self-interested policies to an excessive degree. The problem with America's postrevolutionary economy, said Hamilton, was that state politicians had appealed erroneously to republican theory about sovereign republics to explain how the new states might justify a "basis of equal privileges, to which we have been accustomed since the earliest settlement of the country." But, he continued, the principle of "equal privileges" had only led to their mutual "discontent." "[I]nterfering and unneighborly regulations of some states" and "independent sovereignties consulting a distinct interest" were under pressure to promote merchants who "endeavor[d] to secure exclusive benefits to their own citizens." "The infractions of these [exclusive privileges] . . . and the efforts to prevent and repel [these infractions] . . . would naturally lead to outrages" among Americans.[104]

Even worse, during the critical years of the 1780s these private quarrels could become the focus of state politics. The *Federalist* speaks of "the perverted ambition" of men in state posts "who will either hope to aggrandize themselves by the confusions of their country, or will flatter themselves with fairer prospects of elevation from the subdivision of the empire into several partial confederacies."[105] Too many self-serving interests in these sovereign state "confederacies" were willing to "sacrifice . . . national tranquility to personal advantage or personal gratifications." Post-revolutionary economic reconstruction was burdened by a "system of commercial policy" in which each state passed regulations "peculiar to itself" and detrimental to both the general interests of Americans and the special interests that such policies were designed to benefit.[106]

So the revolutionary generation's dream of peaceful expansion and the profitable transformation of Americans from a people of scarcity to a people of bounty and exportable surpluses—a dream very close to

Hume's model of the perfect political economy—had become elusive by 1787. During the decade of the 1780s—its problems catalogued in *Federalist* No. 21—Americans continued to suffer from depreciated paper money and the flight of hard currency, price fixing and forestalling among ambitious farmers and usury among selfish merchants, imported luxuries for which Americans could not pay, and at the same time periodic scarcities of necessary goods.

In the *Federalist* Hamilton used his own state to illustrate this presence of "myriad state jealousies." "New York, from the necessities of revenue, must lay duties on her importations." City merchants bore these financial burdens with relative ease, said Hamilton, because they could pass on their costs in higher prices to consumers. But merchants of neighboring states who used New York port facilities were not so fortunate. "A great part of those duties [collected at New York] must be paid by the inhabitants of the two other States [Connecticut and New Jersey] in the capacity of consumers of what we import." Yet New York received credit from the Continental Congress—the loosely structured national government—for paying these duties to Congress against its postrevolutionary debts. Thus, while the states without adequate ports were assuaged in their consuming "appetites," they were taxed doubly—in the higher price of goods and in the loss of national tax credits—while New Yorkers enjoyed an "exclusive benefit," a privilege that some New England states compared to the monopolies of mercantile interests.[107] Here was but one case of jealously guarded separate jurisdictions, separate state contests for commercial advantages that locked them into persistent economic chaos. Hamilton warned that "Peace between the states is impossible" so long as states persisted in forming "obstacles to a uniformity of [commercial] measures."[108]

Hamilton's contributions in the *Federalist* laid out two serious long-term consequences of state sovereignty over commercial affairs. The first of these was legal and social "anarchy." It would be difficult to regulate the borders of "contiguous American republics," for

> the number of rivers with which they are intersected, and of bays that wash their shores; the facility of communication in every direction; the affinity of language and manners; the familiar habits of intercourse;—all these are circumstances that would conspire to render an illicit trade between them a matter of little difficulty, and would insure frequent evasions of the commercial regulations of each other.[109]

Economic interests would seek natural boundaries to their trade and easily elude the artificial constraints of political jurisdictions. But with one uniform set of regulations there would be only "*one side* to guard—*the Atlantic coast.*"[110]

Paradoxically, then, the activism of state interests that sought to set commerce on a prosperous footing, left American commerce as "passive"—as ineffectual—as the discrimination of foreign nations against Americans had. Americans were no more independent during the 1780s than they were under mercantilism in the British Empire. For Hamilton, the din of competing interests in the 1780s resulted in mutual annihilation of meaningful future development for *any* state. Commercial passivity led to a stagnation of America's development. Passivity, which appeared to be the obverse of the anarchy of mobs like Shays's, was equally likely to deny Americans the satisfaction of their "reciprocal wants." Thus, *Federalist* No. 11 discusses as much about the necessity of providing for an "active commerce" as it does the necessity of taming disruptive tendencies with a "uniform set of regulations." In fact, underactivism called for the same solution as anarchic hyperactivism. But Hamilton's solution in *Federalist* No. 11 derived from his preferences to create an overarching system of regulations that did not discriminate among merchant interests. A "Union" of economic interests

> will advance the trade of each [state], by an interchange of their respective productions, not only for the supply of reciprocal wants, but for exportation to foreign markets. The veins of commerce in every part will be replenished, and will acquire additional motion and vigor from a free circulation of the commodities of every part.

The primary commercial advantage of federal union will be to prevent gluts, scarcities, and unrealized demand in states with less mature capabilities to conduct trade. In their united political condition there will be a

> diversity in the production of different states. When the staple of one fails . . . it can call to its aid the staple of another. The *variety,* not less than the *value* of products for exportation, contribute to the activity of foreign commerce. . . . Particular articles may be in great demand at certain periods, and unsaleable at others; but if there be a variety of articles, it can scarcely happen that they should all be at one time in the latter predicament . . . [of] obstruction or stagnation.

By establishing one general conceptual framework in which "the aggregate balance of the commerce of the United States" circulated according to statutes favorable to all, the country "would bid fair to be much more favorable than that of the Thirteen States" as separate economic republics.[111]

Hamilton tied his appeal for a "uniform system of regulations" to the national impost, that import tax "upon articles of consumption." Since, as *Federalist* No. 21 explained, "there can be no common measure of national wealth, and, of course no general or stationary rule by which the ability of a state to pay taxes can be determined," some members of society must inevitably bear an unequal burden. Taxes on estates or on the produce of land would always fall most inequitably upon the very people upon whom America's virtue is reliant, the independent landholders, agricultural tenants, and the urban middle classes. However, import duties need not harm merchants' profits, for they could pass along costs to consumers such that "duties upon articles of consumption will enable each person to regulate the amount of burden in taxes by the extravagance or frugality of usage."[112] States like New York would no longer be able to discriminate against neighboring states, and the twin evils of "anarchy" and "passivity" would result in a "general harmony" among all economic interests.[113] "One great American system, superior to the control of all transatlantic force or influence," a "domestic union" against foreign nations, was crucial to the survival of "an American empire." A transcendant national political interest would erase the petty political quarrels so that "no partial motive, no particular interest, no pride of opinion, no temporary passion or prejudice . . . or particular interest of the community" could justify jeopardizing "the very existence of the nation."[114]

The Language of Jealousy

The language of "jealousy" had eminent place alongside that of virtue, authority, and self-interest in the eighteenth century, especially in the latter half when so many public spokesmen contemplated the intersection of ethics, politics, and economics. But in the context of what Hamilton called the "circumstances" of the 1780s—what American historians have long called the "critical period"—there is evident a shift in the meaning of "jealousy." For Hamilton it was no more realistic to hope that the American states could set aside their commercial jealousies under the Articles of Confederation government that guaranteed that each state would be a sovereign republic, than it was to expect a natural reconciliation of the jarring interests among nations as Hume proposed. In either case, it was easy to predict the deleterious outcomes of jealousy in these narrow economic contexts. For Hamilton saw that, having separated economics and politics in order to more cooly analyze the "laws" or "science" of each, writers like Hume became involved in a hopeless dialogue about the merits of unfettered commerce or regulation without including due regard for the entanglements of political power. Jealousy, said Hamilton, was perhaps rooted in particular economic interests, but it was coalesced and served in the arena of public political action. With too many arenas, as in the case of the confederation, all effective safeguards to jealousy would rage out of control. Thus, the antidote to state jealousies did not involve introducing new issues or overall objectives; revolutionary Americans and the new states had done a fine job defining them. Rather, the antidote involved a transformative praxis that effectively melded all issues and objectives in one "more perfect union."

Other nationalists also spoke the language of "jealousy." In his popular "Address to the People of the State of New York," John Jay appealed to Americans to consider "consolidation" favorably, since without it, "every State would be a little nation, *jealous* of its neighbors." "Then," he added, "farewell to . . . mutual participation in commerce, navigation, and citizenship. Then would arise mutual restrictions and fears, mutual garrisons,—and standing armies."[115] John Adams wrote at length about the consequences of commercial jealousy. Agreeing that the West Indies was crucial to American interests, and that it was the object of British discriminations against Americans, he insisted that without union the states would remain fragmented and watch England thrive in its postwar economy. Americans were not yet prepared to become self-sufficient in manufacturing—the universal goal of nations at the time—and not capable to send their ships to new commercial markets where belligerents had not yet penetrated. But these weaknesses were merely structural and would be overcome with economic maturity. Worse than these was the "jealousy of American ships, seamen, carrying trade, and naval power" that prevailed because the "States have no confidence in one another." England had the confidence to discriminate against American trade in the West Indies because it appeared that the "states are not, and cannot be united." Adams supported commercial retaliation against the British orders in council, but he wished for one uniform measure administered through Congress.[116] Even Thomas Jefferson believed in 1785 that if England persisted in prohibiting America's trade in the British West Indies the government "must refuse our commerce [to England] or load theirs by odious discriminations in our ports," although this would produce a "species of jealousy" among the states of which he did not normally approve.[117] Tench Coxe put it most stridently when he noted that the "Desultory commercial acts of the legislatures, formed on the impression of the moment, proceeding from no uniform or permanent principles, clash[ed] with the laws of other states and oppos[ed] those made in the preceding year by the enacting state." These, he continued, "can no longer be supported, if we are to continue one people. . . . Commerce is more affected by the distractions and evils arising from the uncertainty, opposition and errors of our trade laws, than by the restrictions of any one power in Europe."[118] The way out of this "anarchy," Hamilton would propose, was to fuse Americans' hopes for economic "energy" in an expansive "empire" with the goal of political "union." Union was the sole means, according to Federalists, to overcome "jealousy" in all its forms.

Hamilton was one of an important few writers during the 1780s to impute to the term *jealousy* more consequential and immanent dangers to political union than Hume and others wrote of, and to heighten public awareness about the need for a more radically altered political economy that emphasized channeled development rather than absence of restraint. Yet he and other Federalists exaggerated the extent of America's economic "anarchy" for their own partisan reasons. Moreover, the *Federalist* reached a small elite whom Hamilton could hope to convince, not a general public.[119] Despite defections of many dry goods and West Indies merchants, as well as some disgruntled small traders, Federalists' success at convincing large numbers of New Yorkers to turn a skeptical eye upon Clintonian liberty and adopt nationalist union happened only very slowly. Interests that had been satisfied with the state's role in assuming the revolutionary debt, raising adequate revenues from a state impost, and more or less effectively discriminating against foreign and domestic commercial rivals would continue to profess that a degree of economic liberty had been won between the revolution and constitution. Their satisfaction with a degree of economic liberty made them reluctant to acknowledge the counterproductive effects of jealousy among states and nations. In fact, the rising popular authority of the state was contagious among other, emerging interests as well. Most important among the new interests were manufacturers who gained an increasing awareness of their entitlement to the rights that the state protected and promoted, and of the state's inadequate attention to those rights. But however much this emerging interest was perceptually clarified by the constitutional discussion that nationalists pressed upon the states, it did not become a united voice or recognizable influence in state or national politics. Moreover, very few members of the Federalist persuasion foresaw the significance of the appearance during the constitutional decade of a manufacturing interest. Even Hamilton's eloquent testimonials to the "seamless fabric of empire" were contextually immediate and it would be left to future battles between the state and national governments, as well as the class interests that transcended political boundaries, to test whether the discourse engendered during the 1780s explained and guided the new realities of economic life.[120]

Notes

1. David Hume, "Of the Jealousy of Trade," in Eugene Rotwein, *David Hume: Writings on Economics* (Madison, Wis., 1955), 78.
2. This is discussed in Cathy Matson and Peter Onuf, "Toward a Republican Empire: Interest and Ideology in Revolutionary America," *American Quarterly* 37 (1985): 496–531, at 502–8.
3. For a discussion of early modern ideas about free trade, see Joyce Appleby, *Economic Thought and Ideology in Seventeenth Century England* (Princeton, 1978), and Cathy Matson, "Fair Trade, Free Trade: Economic Ideas and Opportunities in Eighteenth-Century New York City" (Ph.D. diss., Columbia University, 1985), ch. 2 and footnotes. Compare to Douglass Adair, "That Politics May Be Reduced to a Science: David Hume, James Madison and the Tenth Federalist," *Huntington Library Quarterly* 20 (1957): 343–60.
4. Matson, "Fair Trade, Free Trade" (Ph.D. diss., Columbia University, 1985), chs. 2 and 7; Joseph Dorfman, *The Economic Mind in American Civilization, 1606–1865*, 4 vols. (New York, 1946), 1:280–95; Jacob Crowley, *This Sheba, Self: The Conceptualization of Economic Life in Eighteenth-Century America*, (Baltimore, 1974); and Arthur Schlesinger, *The Colonial Merchants and the American Revolution, 1763–1776* (New York, 1918).
5. Drew McCoy, *The Elusive Republic: Political Economy in Jeffersonian America* (Chapel Hill, N.C., 1980), 86–106.
6. Worthington C. Ford, et al., eds., *Journals of the Continental Congress, 1774–1789*, 34 vols. (Washington, D.C., 1904–37), 5:768–78 (17 Sept. 1776), 5:576–88 (18 July 1776), and 13:231–32 (22 Feb. 1778).
7. On prices and wages, see, e.g., *Laws of the State of New York Comprising the Constitution and the Acts of the Legislature Since the Revolution, from the First to the Fifteenth Session Inclusive*, 2 vols. (New York, 1792), 1st sess., ch. 34, 36 (June 1778), and 3d sess., ch. 43, 106 (9 Feb.–13 Mar. 1780); *Journal of the Provincial Congress, Provincial Convention, Committee of Safety and Council of Safety of the State of New-York, 1775–1776–1777*, 2 vols. (Albany, 1842), 1:299; hereafter *Journals of the Provincial Congress*. On embargos, *Laws*, 1st sess., ch. 10, 10 (June 1778); 3d sess., ch. 21, 82 (4 Sept.–25 Oct. 1779); 4 th sess., ch. 2, 149 (1 Sept.– 10 Oct. 1780); 4th sess., ch. 24, 173 (2 Feb.–31 Mar. 1781); George Dangerfield, *Chancellor Robert Livingston of New York, 1746–1813* (New York, 1960), 114–19; Thomas Cochran, *New York in the Confederation: An Economic Study* (Philadelphia, 1932), 27–39, 46–47, 51–52. For a congres-

sional grant to the states of the right to regulate commerce and trading revenues, see *Journals of the Continental Congress,* 9:826–27, 827–28, 833, 835, 911; 11:569. In general see Richard B. Morris, *Government and Labor in Early America* (New York, 1946, repr. 1965), 103–16. For paper money emissions, Sept. 1775 to Aug. 1777, see *Journals of the Provincial Congress,* 1:133–34, 239, 435, 560. From Aug. 1777 to late 1781 the state issued only certificates from the war departments. On New York state's borrowing $485,000 from private sources, Sept. 1778, see Cochran, *New York in the Confederation,* 39; for borrowing from Oct. 1776 to mid-1780, for congressional requisitions, at four percent to six percent interest through the Loan Offices, see ibid., 41–42. This was the state's strongest attempt to avoid taxing the "agrarian interest;" most of the money was collected between Sept. 1777 and Mar. 1778.

8. On hostility to taxation, see *New York Journal and General Advertiser,* 15 Feb. 26 July 2, 9 Aug. 1779. On requests for freer trade see, "A Farmer," *New York Journal and General Advertiser,* 4 Jan. 1779; ibid., 21 Dec. 1778, 11 Jan. 1779; *Journal of the Provincial Congress,* 1:132.

9. *Laws,* 1st sess., ch. 34, 36 (June 1778).

10. *Journal of the Provincial Congress,* 7:267; *Minutes of the Albany Commissioners of Correspondence,* ed. J. Sullivan (Albany, N.Y., 1923), 1:772.

11. See the discussion and notes in Lance Banning, "Jeffersonian Ideology Revisited: Liberal Classical Ideas in the New American Republic," *William and Mary Quarterly,* 3d ser., 43 (1986): 3–19; Joyce Appleby, "Republicanism in Old and New Contexts," ibid., 20–34; and Matson and Onuf, "Toward a Republican Empire," *American Quarterly* 37 (1985): 502–08.

12. Cochran, *New York in the Confederation,* 38; Morris, *Government and Labor,* 92–119.

13. Alexander Hamilton to James Duane, 3 Sept. 1780, in Harold C. Syrett and Jacob E. Cooke, *The Papers of Alexander Hamilton* (New York, 1961) 1:400–18, at 402, 416–17.

14. The best discussion of the emerging nationalists is in Merrill Jensen, *The New Nation, A History of the United States During the Confederation, 1781–1789* (New York, 1950), chs. 2–3. See also the *New York Packet,* 21 Nov. 1782, which discusses the dearth of currency, highness of prices, and scarcities of goods.

15. On fallen virtue and self-doubt during the revolution, see e.g., George Washington to James Warren, 31 Mar. 1779, in John C. Fitzpatrick, ed., *The Writings of George Washington from the Original Manuscript Sources, 1745–1799* (Washington, D.C., 1931–44), 14:312; further reflections are at ibid., 9:134; 10:192–93, 194; 18:427–28; 20:470. See also John Adams to Mercy Otis Warren, 8 Jan. 1776, *Warren-Adams Letters,* Massachusetts Historical Society, *Collections* (Boston, 1917–25), 2:202, and the discussion in Eric Foner, *Tom Paine and Revolutionary America* (New York, 1976), chs. 3–5.

16. See, e.g., "Rough Hewer," [Yates], *New York Gazetteer* (Albany), 6 Oct. 1783; "A Correspondent," *New York Journal,* 25 Jan. 1787. For general optimism about state policies, see Robert G. Albion, "New York Port in the New Republic, 1783–1793," *New York History* 21 (1940): 388–403; and Sidney Pomerantz, *New York: An American City, 1783–1803* (New York, 1938), 147–59.

17. Jensen, *New Nation,* 83–84.

18. On the 1781 impost, see *Journals of the Continental Congress,* 19:102–3, 110, 112–13 (31 Jan., 1 Feb., 3 Feb. 1781).

19. Jonathan Elliott, *The Debates in the Several State Conventions on the*

Adoption of the Federal Constitution, 5 vols. (Washington, D.C., 1836–45), 2:359; *Laws*, 4th sess., ch. 31, 177 (19 Mar. 1781); *Journal of the Senate of the State of New York*, 4th sess., 79 (16 Mar. 1781); C. H. Lincoln, ed., *Messages from the Governors*, 11 vols. (Albany, N.Y., 1909), 2:120.

20. For commissary and speculator support for the impost, Alexander Hamilton, "The Continentalist," no. 5, 18 Apr. 1782, in Syrett and Cooke, eds., *Papers*, 3:75–82, at 79–81; idem, no. 6, 4 July 1782, 3:99–106; and idem, "Remarks on Appropriating the Impost Exclusively to the Army," 19 Feb. 1783, 3:262.

21. For the 1783 national impost, see *Journals of the Continental Congress*, 24:257–262 (18 Apr. 1783), 24:186–92 (18 Mar. 1783), and 24:195–201 (20 Mar. 1783). For New York's opposition, see *Journal of the Senate*, 6th sess., 1 Mar 1783, 124; *New York Packet*, 19 July 24, 7 Aug. 1783; and Cochran, *New York in the Confederation*, 148–49. On New York's repeal of the impost, see *Laws*, 6th sess., chs. 26–27, 281–82; and *Journal of the Assembly*, 8th sess., (14 Mar. 1785), 88. The state impost and its renewal are at *Laws*, 7th sess., ch. 10, 11–17 (22 Mar. 1784); 8th sess., ch. 7, 180 (18 Nov. 1784); 10 sess., ch. 81, 142 (11 Spr. 1787).

22. For e.g., *New York Packet*, 24 Oct. 1782, and 21 Apr. 1785.

23. For 1783 see Allan Nevins, *The American States During and After the Revolution, 1775–1789* (New York, 1924), 283–84, 510–11, 556–57; for 1784–87, *Journal of the Assembly*, 10th sess., 31–32, (1 Feb. 1787); ibid., Report on Revenue, 11th sess., 14–26, 16 Jan. 1788; and E. Wilder Spaulding, *New York in the Critical Period*, 155; for 1788, *New York Packet*, 23 Jan. 1789; and for estimates of annual averages, J. P. Brissot de Warville, *New Travels in the United States of America, Performed in 1788*, 2 vols. (first publ. New York, 1792; repr. New York, 1970), 1:170–71. For the 1774 comparison, see Governor Tryon to Lord Dartmouth, 1774, *Documents Relative to the Colonial History of the State of New York*, 15 vols. (Albany, 1853–87), 8:452–54.

24. See Cochran, *New York in the Confederation*, 148–49, 167–68; E. James Ferguson, *The Power of the Purse, A History of American Public Finance, 1776–1790* (Chapel Hill, N.C., 1961), 209–10, 239–42, 180–81.

25. *Journals of the Continental Congress*, 26:185–97 (15 Apr. 1784).

26. Cochran, *New York in the Confederation*, 146, 159; Jackson Turner Main, *The Antifederalists: Critics of the Constitution, 1781–1788*, (Chapel Hill, N.C., 1961), 75; Hamilton to George Clinton, 14 May 1783, in *Papers*, Syrett and Cooke, eds., 3:354–55.

27. *Journals of the Continental Congress*, 26:185–97 (5 Apr. 1784), 297–309 (27 Apr. 1784), 311–14 (27 Apr. 1784); 29:765–71 (27 Sept. 1785); 31:461–65 (2 Aug. 1786); 33:649–58 (11 Oct. 1787); 34:433–42 (20 Aug 1788).

28. *Journal of the Assembly*, Report on Revenue, 11th sess., 14–26 (16 Jan. 1788); "Common Sense," *Independent Journal and Daily Advertiser* (New York), 10, 14, 21 May 1784.

29. For example, *New York Daily Advertiser*, 28 Jan. 2, 5 Feb. 1788, reflecting backwards, and *Journal of the Senate*, 8th sess., 48, 50 (17 Mar. 1785).

30. The number of merchants who returned to New York by 1786 is roughly calculated from comparisons of the merchant population in 1774, compiled from my research on New York's prerevolutionary merchant community, and David Franks, *New York City Directory, 1786*, (New York, 1786).

31. John Williams, *Country Journal* (Poughkeepsie), 4 Mar. 1788.

32. E. James Ferguson, "State Assumption of the Federal Debt during the Confederation," *Mississippi Valley Historical Review* 38 (1951): 403–24. For New York's state assumption, *Laws,* 9th sess., ch. 40, 283 (18 Apr. 1786); 9th sess., ch. 64, 326 (5 May 1786).
33. The paper money act is at *Laws,* 9th sess., ch. 40, 283 (18 Mar. 1786). See also Ferguson, "State Assumption," 403–24.
34. For support for paper money, see, e.g., *New York Packet,* 14 Apr. 1785; 18 Feb. 6 Mar. 1786; *New York Daily Advertiser,* 3 Mar 1786; Main, *Antifederalists,* 47–50; Jensen, *The New Nation,* 320–22; and *Journal of the Assembly,* 9th sess., 40–41 (15 Feb. 1786).
35. For example, Bayard, Campell, Pearsall Correspondence, 1751–1806; John Van Schaack Letter Book, Taylor-Cooper Papers, and John Lansing's letters in the Gansevoort-Lansing Papers, all at the New York Public Library. In the *Journal of the Senate,* 8th sess., 17 Mar. 1785, 48, 50, merchants Ward, Klock, Webster, Swartwout, Whiting, Ephraim Paine, Gutherie, Morris, McDougall, Russell, and Stoutenburgh support state duties on commerce. See also Hamilton's letters to Governor Clinton, 12 Jan. 24 Feb. 14 May 1 June 1783, in Syrett and Cooke, eds., *Papers,* 3 : 240–41, 268–74, 354–55, 367–72; "A Correspondent," *New York Journal,* 25 Jan. 1787; "Rough Hewer" [Abraham Yates], *New York Gazetteer* (Albany), 6 Oct. 1783; "Cincinatus," *Independent Journal and General Advertiser* (New York) 10, 14, 21 May 1784.
36. Samuel Flagg Bemis, *The Diplomacy of the American Revolution* (Bloomington, Ind., 1957), 61.
37. Cochran, *New York in the Confederation,* 163–65, 165 n. 6.
38. Bemis, *Diplomacy of the American Revolution,* 103.
39. For example, Brissot de Warville, *New Travels in the United States,* 1 : 463, 464; and Bryan Edwards, *The History, Civil and Commercial, of the British West Indies,* 5 vols. (London, 1819, repr. New York, 1966), 2 : ch. 4. On prewar tensions between dry goods and West Indies interest, see Matson, "Fair Trade, Free Trade" (Ph.D. diss., Columbia University, 1985), ch. 3.
40. For the British legislation of 1784 to 1787, an enumeration is given in Henry B. Dawson, "The Motley Letter," *Historical Magazine,* 2 ser., 9 (1871): 157–201, at 164–69.
41. "Common Sense," *Independent Journal and General Advertiser* (New York), 10, 14, 21 May 1784. See also *Journal of the Assembly,* 126, 130 (30, 31 Mar. 1785), which indicates that both the Assembly and the Senate approved of remitting revenues to Congress in principle, so long as the state controlled the conditions of its collection and submittal.
42. *Journals of the Continental Congress,* 22 : 218n, 237–38 (30 Apr. 4 May 1782).
43. *Laws of New York,* 7th sess., ch. 53, 77, (4 May 1784); 8th sess., ch. 53, 213, (4 Apr. 1785); and 8th sess., ch. 56, 214 (4 Apr. 1785).
44. Ibid. See also C. H. Lincoln, ed., *Messages from the Governors,* 2 : 201; and *Journals of the Assembly,* 7th sess., 3 May 1784, 158, 159–60, which shows agreement with Congress's acts to regulate certain aspects of America's trade with England. However, the state's Council of Revision rejected the terms Congress proposed on the grounds that national laws should not "become the Laws of this State."
45. *Laws,* 1st sess., ch. 10, 10 (June 1778); 3d sess., ch. 21, 82, (4 Sept.–25 Oct. 1779); 4th sess., ch. 2, 149 (1 Sep. 1780); 4th sess., ch. 24, 173 (2 Feb.–31

Mar. 1781); 7th sess., ch. 10, 11 (22 Mar. 1784); 8th sess., ch. 7, 180 (18 Nov. 1784); 10th sess., ch. 81, 142 (11 Apr. 1787).

46. *Laws*, 8th sess., ch. 7, 180 (18 Nov. 1784); ch. 37, 88 (14 Mar. 1785).

47. *New York Packet*, 23 Mar. 1786. However, Congress refused the New Jersey conditions and reprimanded the state for tying state and national interests together in an interstate feud; Nevins, *American States*, 560–61.

48. *New Haven Gazette*, 19 Oct. 1786; *Public Papers of George Clinton, First Governor of New York*, ed. Hugh Hastings, 10 vols. (Albany, N.Y., 1911), 6:174.

49. [Anon.], *New Haven Gazette*, 28 June 1787; 17 Jan. 1788; "An American," *New York Packet*, 27 May 1788. Historian Linda Grant De Pauw says that New York's port duties amounted to about $480,000 for the years 1783–86, or over fifty percent of the state's income; *The Eleventh Pillar, New York State and the Federal Constitution*, (Ithaca, N.Y., 1966), 32. It is more likely that the contemporary source exaggerated Connecticut's dependence on New York, although even De Pauw's figure seems high, given the economic recession.

50. [Anon.], *New York Packet*, 23 Mar. 1786; "Address to the New York Convention," *Pennsylvania Gazette* (Philadelphia), 11 June 1788.

51. *Connecticut Courant* (Hartford), 16 Oct. 1786. See also Hugh Ledlie to General Lamb, 15 Jan. 1788, Lamb Papers, New-York Historical Society.

52. Main, *Antifederalists*, 99–100. For Rhode Island, see H. M. Bishop, "Why Rhode Island Opposed the Federal Constitution," *Rhode Island History* 8 (1949): 1–10; (1949): 33–44.

53. On private debts, e.g., "Petition of Henry Remsen and Others, Merchants of this City," *Journal of the Assembly*, 10th sess., 89 (9 Mar. 1787); and *Journals of the Continental Congress*, 32:124–25 (21 Mar. 1786); 32:176–84 (13 Apr. 1786).

54. *Laws*, 9th sess., ch. 40, 283 (18 Apr. 1786).

55. On gluts, see, for example, David Clarkson's correspondence with London merchants, 1785–86, David Clarkson Letters, New-York Historical Society; and Brissot de Warville, *New Travels*, 1:128.

56. From a comparison of known merchant primary sources. Factors such as relative wealth, status, or length of time at merchant activities did not affect this general complaint from 1785 to 1787.

57. On auctions, see Jerome Paige, "The Evolution of Mercantile Capitalism and Planter Capitalism and the Development of Economic Ideas," (Ph.D. diss., American University, 1982), 101–2. The only law establishing the privilege to auction in New York City before 1790 went to James Barclay, 21 Mar. 1786; *Laws*, 9th sess., ch. 17, 249. Of course, there may have been other auctioneers who did business without official licenses. In 1791 the number of auctioneers was limited to twelve; *Laws*, 14th sess., ch. 27, 353 (8 Mar. 1791).

58. Alfred Young, *The Democratic Republicans of New York: The Origins, 1763–1797* (Chapel Hill, N.C., 1967), 157.

59. My calculation from city directories and known ties of merchants.

60. On bankruptcies, *New York Morning Post*, 10 Mar. 1785; *New York Packet*, 21 Apr. 1785; and *Journal of the Assembly*, 8th sess., 32 (11 Feb. 1785): 181 (27 Apr. 1785), and 9th sess., 100–101 (24 Mar. 1786), for Lawrence Marston, Cadwallader Colden, Thomas Armstrong, John Turner, Thomas Miller, Henry Sickles, Stephen Crosfield, John and Michael Anthony, Benjamin Cole, and others. On tonnage, Minutes of the Chamber of Commerce of New York City, 3 Mar. 1785, New York Public Library.

61. Young, *Democratic Republicans*, 157; Matson, "Fair Trade, Free Trade" (Ph.D. diss., Columbia University, 1985), ch. 4, 5.
62. David Franks, *New York City Directory, 1786*, and idem, *New York City Directory, 1787* (New York, 1787).
63. *New York Packet*, 16 Feb. 1787.
64. Minutes of the Chamber of Commerce, New York Public Library, 1787; Spaulding, *New York in the Critical Period*, 7–8.
65. William Zornow, "New York Tariff Policies, 1775–1789," *New York History* 37 (1956): 40–63, at 48–51.
66. Cochran, *New York in the Confederation*, 159.
67. *Journal of the Assembly*, 7th sess., 132–34 (12 Apr. 1786); *Journals of the Continental Congress*, 31:767–70 (11 Oct. 1786), and 31:785–86 (13 Oct. 1786); Nevins, *American States*, 284.
68. *New York Packet*, 14 Mar. 1785. See also *New York Morning Post*, 10 Mar. 1785; and *New York Packet*, 7, 17 Mar. 2 May 20 June 10 Nov. 1785.
69. "Appeal . . . ," *New York Packet*, dated 30 Sept. 1785, printed 10 Nov. 1785. See also "Consideration," *New York Packet*, 18 Apr. 1785 (which rebutts "Rough Hewer," *New York Packet*, 2 May 1785).
70. "Appeal . . . ," *New York Packet*, 10 Nov. 1785.
71. *New York Packet*, 18, 25 Apr. 2 May 1785; Nevins, *American States*, 284.
72. "Cimon," *New York Daily Advertiser*, 31 Jan. 1787; "Candidus," ibid., 6 Feb. 1787; "Patrioticus," ibid., 13 Feb. 1787. See also *New York Gazetteer*, 7 Mar. 1786; Spaulding, *New York in the Critical Period*, 170–80.
73. New York's votes on the 1783 impost in 1786 is at *Journal of the Assembly*, 9th sess., 85–86 (15 Mar. 1786), 134, 137–38 (13 Apr. 1786), 149–50 (20 Apr. 1786); *Journal of the Senate*, 9th sess., 91–92 (27 Apr. 1786), where Schuyler tried to expunge from the congressional impost the right of the federal government to appoint collectors; he was supported by Stoutenburgh, Floyd, Morris, Roosevelt, and L'Hommedieu. See also *Journals of the Continental Congress*, 30:439–44 (27 July 1786); 31:511–14 (11 Aug. 1786); and 31:515 (14 Aug. 1786).
74. For the Annapolis convention, see *Journal of the Assembly*, 9th sess., 149–50 (20 Apr. 1786), 275, (5 May 1786).
75. *Journals of the Continental Congress*, 31:698–700 (28 Sept. 1786), and 31:891n, 895–97 (20 Oct. 1786).
76. *Journal of the Assembly*, 10th sess., 52 (15 Feb. 1787); *Journals of the Continental Congress*, 30:439–43 (27 July 1786), 31:511–14, 515 (11–14 Aug. 1786). See also *Journal of the Assembly*, 9th sess., 149–50 (20 Apr. 1786), which shows a vote on the 27 Sept. 1785 congressional request for revenues; thirty-five opposed the request, and sixteen favored it: Stagg, Boyd, Glen, Goforth, Denning, Bancker, Malcom, Livingston, John Livingston, Vrooman, Schoonhoven, Bronck, DeWitt, Tayler, Gardner, and N. Smith.
77. *Laws*, 10th sess., ch. 81, 42 (11 Apr. 1787).
78. The "Continentalist" essays ran for six issues in the *New York Packet*, 12, 19 July 9, 30 Aug. 1781, 18 Apr. 4 July 1782; see Syrett and Cooke, eds., *Papers*, 2:649–52, 655–57, 660–65, 669–74; 3:75–82, 99–106.
79. Adrienne Koch, *Power, Morals, and the Founding Fathers* (Ithaca, N.Y., 1961), 52–54.
80. "Continentalist," 19 July 1781, 2:655.
81. "Continentalist," 12 July 1781, 2:650; see also 652.

82. Ibid.
83. "Continentalist," 9 Aug. 1781, 2:660; see also Countryman, *A People in Revolution*, 253–65.
84. "Continentalist," 19 July 1781, 2:655–56.
85. "Continentalist" 4 July 1782, 3:99.
86. E. P. Panagopoulos, *Alexander Hamilton's Pay Book* (Detroit, 1961), intro.
87. "Continentalist," 18 Apr. 1782, 3:75–82. See also Hamilton's speech at the Poughkeepsie convention, 25 June 1788, in Syrett and Cooke, eds., *Papers*, 5:81 (Francis Child's version of the speech), 37.
88. "Continentalist," 18 Apr. 1782, 3:76.
89. Ibid., 77.
90. Ibid., 78.
91. *Federalist*, No. 6.
92. Along with Hume, Hamilton devoted his attention to commerce, and the modest "home manufactures" and predominantly agricultural base that would supply commerce. Hamilton often added (*Federalist* No. 1, e.g.) that westward expansion would serve commercial interests and add to America's sources of revenue as parcels of the national domain were sold. All citations of the *Federalist* are taken from Jacob E. Cooke, ed. and intro., *The Federalist*, (Middletown, Conn., 1961). See also John R. Nelson, Jr., "Alexander Hamilton and American Manufacturing: A Reexamination" *Journal of American History* 65 (1979): 971–95; E. James Ferguson, "State Assumption"; and E. James Ferguson, *The Power of the Purse*, 209–10, 239–42, 180–81; Gordon Wood, "Interests and Disinterestedness in the Making of the Constitution," in *Beyond Confederation, Origins of the Constitution and American National Identity*, eds. Richard Beeman, Stephen Botein, and Edward C. Carter, III (Chapel Hill, N.C., 1787), esp. 103–9; and Albert Furtwangler, *The Authority of "Publius," A Reading of the Federalist Papers* (Ithaca, N.Y., 1984), 40–43 and notes.
93. *Federalist*, No. 6.
94. *Federalist*, No. 12. "Industry" is used here in the more traditional sense of diligent application to work, usually with reference to handicrafts and commercial agriculture. Not all federalists held similar beliefs about commerce, and many of them were more optimistic about America's commercial future as it was developing in the 1780s than Hamilton was. Many of them emphasized prosperity, abundance, and a "flourishing empire" stretching westward under the same "union" Hamilton promoted. Indeed, some antifederalists supported a federalist Constitution once they understood these propositions about commercial agriculture.
95. For some useful suggestions about the connections of jealousy with private passions see, Albert O. Hirschmann, *The Passions and the Interests, Political Arguments for Capitalism before its Triumph* (Princeton, 1977), part One.
96. *Federalist* No. 1. See also *Federalist* No. 37.
97. *Federalist* No. 6.
98. *Daily Advertiser*, 31 Aug. 1786. Hamilton's ideas about commerce began to change even in the crucible of constitutional debates and his differences with writers like Hume increased after 1787–88 as he clarified the role of government in the economy and solidified plans for early industrialization. Lincoln, ed., *Messages of the Governors*, 2:253; *New-York Packet*, 9,

30 May 1785, 12 June 14, 21 Aug. 4 Sept. 1786; *New York Journal,* 23 1786; *Federalist,* No. 11.
  99. *Federalist,* No. 11.
  100. *Federalist,* No. 6.
  101. *Federalist,* No. 6.
  102. *Federalist,* Nos. 6, 31, 36. See also *Federalist* No. 1.
  103. *Federalist,* Nos. 7, 22. See also James Madison's *Federalist* No. 44, on "fluctuating policy" and "sudden changes" of state legislative actions.
  104. *Federalist,* No. 1. His views were tied to the events with Daniel Shays in western Massachusetts that year; as he put it later in *Federalist* No. 6, "If Shays had not been a *desperate debtor,* it is much to be doubted whether Massachusetts would have been plunged into a civil war." Of course the presence of debt and its corresponding tendency to produce "anarchy" were connected to Hamilton's elitism; see his classic statements as "Caesar," in the *Daily Advertiser,* 21 June and 17 Oct. 1787, and *Federalist* No. 35, where he noted that the "multitude" lacked sufficient "majesty" to judge either economic risk taking or the public welfare in politics. In 1784 Hamilton's second "Phocion" essay argued that most Americans were unwilling to allow economic affairs to concentrate into the hands of the few who were able to invest in America's future; they persisted in labelling this monopoly, exclusion, and discrimination, rather (Hamilton implied) than contemplate uniform, centralized commercial order. See "Second Letter from Phocion," Apr. 1784, in Syrett and Cooke, eds., *Papers,* 3:555.
  105. *Federalist,* No. 6.
  106. *Federalist,* No. 7. Some federalists feared that New York would face two great "confederacies," one made up of southern states and the other made up of New England states, which would crush New York if it left the union; see *New York Packet,* 13 May 1788. Other commentators felt that the southern counties of New York could split from the northern ones unless state "jealousies" were resolved; see *New York Packet,* 13 May 1788, and *Pennsylvania Gazette* (Philadelphia), 11 June 1788.
  107. *Federalist,* Nos. 6, 7, 11, 22. Also, Max Farrand, ed., *Records of the Federal Convention of 1787–1788,* (New Haven, 1911, repr. 1966), 18 June 1788, 1:297, where delegate Yates quotes Hamilton; and *Federalist* No. 46 where Madison speaks of the "particular and separate views of the counties or districts," and No. 42 where he supports the national impost's "enlarged and permanent interest" because it will help prevent improper levies of one state upon another.
  108. *Federalist* No. 12.
  109. *Federalist* No. 12. See also *Federalist* Nos. 5, 11, 36, 37, 45.
  110. *Federalist* No. 12.
  111. *Federalist,* No. 11. See also Hamilton, "Report on a Letter from the Speaker of the Rhode Island Assembly," 16 Dec. 1782, *Papers,* 3:213–33, esp. 214–15, 220–21.
  112. *Federalist,* No. 21. Hamilton is never clear who the consumers are—producers (farmers and craftsmen), circulators of goods (merchants), or both.
  113. On "anarchy" and "passivity" see *Federalist,* Nos. 9, 11, 21, 22.
  114. *Federalist,* No. 85. See also *Federalist* No. 21; Lance Banning, *The Jeffersonian Persuasion: Evolution of a Party Ideology* (Ithaca, N.Y., 1978); and

Gerald Stourzh, *Alexander Hamilton and the Idea of Republican Government* (Stanford, Calif., 1970).

115. [John Jay], "An Address to the People of the State of New York," New York, 1788, repr. *American Museum*, June 1788, and Worthington C. Ford, ed., *Pamphlets*, 67–86, esp. at 84.

116. John Adams to _____ Livingston, 14, 16 July 1783, in Wharton, *The Revolutionary Diplomatic Correspondence of the United States*, 6:540–42, 552–53; and John Adams to John Jay, 19 July 21 Oct. 1785, in *Works of John Adams*, 8:281–91, 323–25, 332.

117. Thomas Jefferson to James Monroe, 1785, in Worthington C. Ford., ed., *Writings of Thomas Jefferson*, 4:31, 58, 117–21, 129–30.

118. Tench Coxe, *An Enquiry into the Principles on which a Commercial System for the United States of America should be Founded* (Philadelphia, 1787), 28–33.

119. Spaulding, *New York in the Critical Period*, 253.

120. The struggles between merchants and rising manufacturers will arise for Hamilton (in writing) only in his 1791 *Report on Manufactures*. Until then, Hamilton was still considering a circulation, rather than a production, model with respect to the commodities and trading relations he wants to regulate. For hints of the demands that manufacturers will make in far greater numbers after 1789, see *Journal of the Assembly*, 11th sess., 7 (11 Jan. 1788); mention of a petition from "John Broome, Alexander Robertson, and others, Merchants and Manufactures of New York," which calls for more protection for nails, spades, shovels, axes, sythes, hoes, and the like in *Journal of the Assembly*, 11th sess., 94–95 (27 Feb. 1788); Hamilton to George Clinton, 14 May 1783, Syrett and Cooke, eds., *Papers*, 3:354, 355; Cochran, *New York in the Confederation*, 146; and Main, *Antifederalists*, 75.

SAUL CORNELL

6

Politics of the Middling Sort: The Bourgeois Radicalism of Abraham Yates, Melancton Smith, and the New York Antifederalists

Partisan politics and cultural pluralism, two vital characteristics of modern American political culture, were already well-established features of life in the middle Atlantic on the eve of the struggle over the United States Constitution. Given the presence of these seemingly modern qualities, it is easy to see why a number of historians have looked to this region as the birthplace of modern electoral politics. If the middle Atlantic was the embryo of a new political order, if it did point the way toward liberal capitalism, what role did the ideological debates between federalists and antifederalists play in promoting this transition? At least a partial answer to this important historical question can be obtained by examining the character of antifederalist ideology in New York. Antifederalists in New York produced some of the most powerful critiques of the Constitution, and mounted one of the most successful campaigns against ratification in any state.[1]

Historians have been divided over the question of which side in the ratification struggle contributed most to the emergence of a distinctly modern liberal ethos. Most historical commentators have generally assumed that it was the federalists who paved the way for the rise of liberalism. Proponents of this view have relied on Publius as the authoritative guide to the political thought of the framers of the Constitution and have placed special emphasis upon Madison's analysis of factions in *Federalist* No. 10. Casting Madison as the intellectual father of liberalism led to the inescapable conclusion that the federalists championed a form of modern interest-group politics. Antifederalists were usually portrayed as backward-looking proponents of a homogeneous yeoman republic. In this scheme, the losers in the ratification struggle appeared as the mirror image of the winners. If the federalists were far-sighted modern liberals, then the antifederalists were parochial and narrow-minded traditionalists who failed to grasp the revolutionary character of the Constitution.[2]

It has become increasingly clear to scholars working on the Constitutional period that Madison did not intend *Federalist* No. 10 to serve as a justification for interest-group politics. Instead, Madison hoped that the multiplicity of factions in an extended republic would ensure that no single faction would dominate government. Out of this stalemate of competing interests, he believed, disinterested men of vision would emerge who would be able to discern the common good.[3]

If federalists like Madison were not the direct lineal progenitors of modern liberalism, what then of the antifederalists? Recently, historian Gordon Wood has argued that it was antifederalists, not federalists, who articulated an interest-oriented theory of representation that contained the seeds of a liberal conception of politics. While Wood has captured an important proto-liberal element of antifederalist political thought, his emphasis on this aspect of antifederalism does slight the many traditional republican ideas contained within antifederalist ideology. To understand the full breadth and complexity of the antifederalists, it is important to acknowledge both the republican and liberal character of their thought. New York antifederalists rejected the traditional gentry ideal of virtue and substituted in its place a vision of politics that championed the superiority of a middle-class polity.[4]

The role of the "middling sort" in early American politics has been neglected in recent scholarship.[5] While intellectual and political historians have traditionally devoted considerable attention to elites, and social historians have probed the lives of working men and women, hardly anything has been written about the political ideology of the middling sort. Leading antifederalists in New York were drawn from the broad ranks of this class of men. Some, like Abraham Yates, rose from humble origins and relative obscurity to considerable prominence. Others, like Melancton Smith, improved their position within the ranks of the middle class. The political ideology of these middling men holds the key to understanding antifederalism in New York.[6]

Abraham Yates and the Triumph of the Middling Sort

Among New York antifederalists no one better symbolized the dramatic rise of the middling sort than Abraham Yates, who became a potent symbol for federalists and antifederalists alike. To appreciate why Yates came to be the lightning rod for federalist criticisms and a leading spokesman for antifederalist aspirations it is necessary to look closely at his own political career.

In contrast to most of his federalist opponents, Yates stood outside the narrow circle of great landed families who controlled New York politics. Born in 1724 to a respectable family of the middling sort, he initially plied his trade as a cobbler but left the ranks of Albany's artisan community to become a clerk in the law offices of Peter Silvester. By 1754 he had attained a seat on the Common Council of Albany. Still success in New York politics required a powerful patron. While Yates had initially enjoyed the support of the Livingston faction, he lost it in his campaign for an assembly seat in 1761. Dissatisfied with the system of patronage politics, Yates set about building a more popularly-based political organization. The events of 1776 accelerated Yates's rise to prominence. He rose rapidly in the revolutionary government, played an active role in the Albany Committee of Correspondence, and eventually became its chairman. Yates also served as chairman of the committee that drafted the State Constitution of 1777. During the Confederation period he gained considerable experience in state and national politics, becoming one of the most vocal spokesmen for the many "new men" who had entered the highest levels of New York politics thanks to the Revolution. Adopting the pseudonyms "Sidney" and "Rough Hewer," he frequently took up his pen to defend his own interpretation of the Revolution's principles.[7]

The ascendency of this "yeoman-artisan 'middle class'" was not welcomed by everyone. Yates and his allies earned the enmity of a powerful group of politicians who later became federalists. Among his opponents were John Jay, Gouverneur Morris, and Alexander Hamilton.[8] Hamilton bitterly denounced Yates and noted condescendingly that "the people have been a long time in the *habit* of choosing him in different offices . . . he . . . being a preacher to their taste." Hamilton felt that Yates's political views were in part motivated by a distrust born of envy. It was obvious to Hamilton that Yates "hates all high-flyers, which is the appellation he gives to men of genius."[9] By 1785 the power of Yates and his allies had grown to the point where Hamilton felt that it was urgent to elect men to "the Legislature whose principles are not of the *levelling kind*" and thus restore the *"security of property."*[10]

The elitism and condescension of federalists angered anti-federalists. Self-educated men of the middling sort like Yates were determined to demonstrate that wisdom and knowledge were not the exclusive property of a small, privileged elite. Unfortunately for Yates, his attempts to compensate for his lack of education made him an easy target for federalists who mocked the pedantry of his essays. In the "Anarchiad" several leading federalist "men of letters" satirized Yates's pretensions in rhyme:

> The blunt *Rough Hewer,* from his savage den,
> With learned dullness loads his lab'ring pen;
> In muddy streams his rumbling wit combines
> Big words convolving on the turbid line.[11]

In the eyes of federalist gentlemen, Yates's affected displays of learning only confirmed that he was "a man whose ignorance and perverseness are only surpassed by his pertinacity and conceit."[12]

In addition to attacking his lack of breeding, Yates's enemies denounced him as a hypocrite and a self-serving politician. Philip Schuyler described him sarcastically as the "Honorable Abraham Yates Esq. one of the Senate of this State, a member of the Council of Appointment—one of the Committee of the City and County of Albany, Recorder of the City of Albany—and Postmaster General, late Cobler of Laws and Old Shoes."[13] Schuyler believed that only the richest men, drawn from the ranks of a natural aristocracy, could act in the public interest. A self-made man like Yates, who used political office to rise above his natural station in life, was incapable of acting in a disinterested fashion.[14]

At the heart of the struggle between this yeoman-middle class and the supporters of the old elite was the question of who should rule at home. This debate was fought within the terms of the prevailing language of whig republicanism. Each side utilized the symbols and vocabulary of republicanism to justify its own conception of a just political order. Not surprisingly, the vision of society articulated by each side tended to legitimate its own interests.

The Education of a Bourgeois Radical

Men like Abraham Yates reshaped the dominant language of whig republicanism to reflect the aspirations of an emerging middle class. The leading opponents of the Constitution in New York were heirs to a revolution that had elevated members of the middling classes to positions of considerable power. Eager to preserve their recent victory, these bourgeois radicals drew inspiration from their own vision of middle-class hegemony.

Antifederalists like Yates hoped to diminish the authority and prestige of leading federalists like Washington and Franklin. To achieve this end, Yates asked his fellow countrymen a simple question: how could men like Washington and Franklin be held up as "infallible judges of civil government" when their claims about the Constitution were contradicted by "Montesquieu, Locke, Sidney, and many other celebrated authors upon government."[15] The enduring power of deference in post-revolutionary society worried antifederalists. "Even in the late discussion," Yates noted, "we meet with observations . . . that the consent of General Washington and Dr. Franklin, is not only a conclusive argument" but incontrovertible proof of the necessity of adopting the Constitution.[16] Equally disturbing was the contempt directed at any who presumed to challenge the authority of these men. Everything Yates wrote reiterated the message that freedom required one to "ask no favors . . . [and] fear no man's frown." In his view independence required respect but not deference.[17]

Whig republican theorists played a major role in shaping Yates's political philosophy. In England whig opposition was most closely identified with the "country party," a tenuous alliance that included disenfranchised Tories, oppositional whigs, and Commonwealth radicals.[18] While these groups shared a common language of protest, they differed widely in their compositions and in their commitments to reform. Even among the radical wing of the "country party," there were considerable differences separating the three distinctive traditions that contributed to eighteenth-century radicalism: religious dissent, plebeian protest, and bourgeois radicalism. Although there was some common ground that united whig radicals, ultimately each tradition of protest derived its commitment to political radicalism from a different socioeconomic base, and each group interpreted the leading theorists of whig ideology in distinctive ways. Brought together by their opposition to the entrenched power of the "court party," radical whiggery was an unstable alliance of convenience.[19]

Bourgeois radicalism was strongest in the towns and cities, where the lesser merchants, tradesmen, shopkeepers, and prosperous artisans sought to assert their growing economic strength and dismantle the corrupt political system inaugurated with the ascendancy of Walpole. The involvement of the emerging urban bourgeoisie in the traditions of "country protest" ironically gave rise to a new urban variant of "country ideology." Throughout the eighteenth century "middling men" agitated for a more equitable redistribution of power and an end to government corruption. They rallied around John Wilkes and expressed considerable sympathy with the cause of the American colonists over issues like the Stamp Act.

For the struggling members of the emerging middle class, political reform was closely tied to economic reform. Nothing was so crucial to men of the middling sort as an alteration in the system of taxation. Unlike many groups within the "country tradition," bourgeois radicalism was not anticommercial. Such men distinguished between productive labor and speculative commercial ventures. The former enriched the nation and bound members of society together in a network of interdependent relationships while the latter redistributed wealth upwards, robbing the industrious middle sort and enriching a privileged elite.[20]

Bourgeois radicalism stood between patrician society and plebeian culture. Unlike plebeians, bourgeois radicals embraced Lockean ideas and viewed property rights and contractual obligations as sacrosanct. In addition to parliamentary reform they sought to alter the English financial system and create a stable system of credit. Wherever possible they attacked privilege and monopolies. Nor were men of the middling sort entirely comfortable with many aspects of plebeian culture like price controls or rough music. Increasingly over the eighteenth century the rising middle class struggled to distinguish itself from the lower orders.

Bourgeois radicals generally favored reducing the power of government. Country ideology provided a powerful critique of centralized authority that contributed to this minimalist conception of the state. Some bourgeois radicals endorsed Adam Smith's new understanding of political economy, while others clung to an older ideal that glorified the virtuous tradesmen whose honesty and frugality were the cornerstones of productivity and wealth. Men of the middling sort had much to fear in eighteenth-century England. Uncertainty marred their lives; instabilities were a constant danger due to the rapid fluctuations in the credit economy. These instabilities, many argued, were precipitated by the unscrupulous activities of "placemen" and "stock jobbers." To combat the influence of these "harpies," men of the middling sort sought to minimize government involvement in the economy.[21]

Government, bourgeois radicals argued, posed the greatest threat to equality. As E. P. Thompson has noted, "this was a predatory phase of agrarian and commercial capitalism, and the State was itself among the prime objects of prey."[22] Inequality, bourgeois radicals theorized, did not grow out of the relations of production. Governmental corruption, not economic exploitation, led to the impoverishment of the honest and industrious. Men of the middling sort had relatively little to fear from the wealthy so long as they did not use government as an instrument of class domination. The unscrupulous activities of placemen and courtiers threatened the security of the middling sort in a variety of ways. Taxation drained wealth away from virtuous yeoman, mechanics, and merchants. The unstable credit economy created by speculation fostered a business climate that was filled with uncertainty.

America provided an ideal climate to nurture the growth and development of bourgeois radicalism. The American Revolution opened up new possibilities for bourgeois radicals like Abraham Yates. Although men like Yates eagerly joined in the Revolutionary cause, it is important to acknowledge that the political vision of the middling sort stopped well short of the most radical goals of the Revolution. The men who became leading New York antifederalists were not advocates of majoritarian democracy or universal suffrage. Commenting on the debates over the New York State Constitution of 1777, "Sydney" apparently took a moderate position on the issue of expanding the suffrage. His position was a halfway point between those who argued for stricter requirements and those who advocated granting the vote to all resident citizens aged twenty-one or older.[23]

This view of suffrage was characteristic of bourgeois radicalism because it was less concerned with expanding the number of voters and more concerned about guarding against electoral corruption. Yates believed that the great landed estate holders might exert undue influence on the lesser yeomen who lacked the economic means to insure their own independence.[24] This problem continued to worry

Yates and his supporters all through the Confederation period. During the debates over the ratification of the Federal Constitution Yates's antifederalist allies expressed considerable concern that "the well meaning yeomanry" would not be able to "follow the dictates of their consciences" and would be forced to do the bidding of their "masters," who were part of the "Ban[e]ful Manor Interest."[25] Having only recently challenged the power of New York's great landed gentry, Yates and his supporters thought that the old elite would seek to use its economic power to regain political control of the state. If the old elite triumphed, Yates feared that the interests of the middling sort would be undermined.

Bourgeois Radicalism and Antifederalist Political Economy

Middling antifederalists in New York articulated a procommercial economic vision that set them apart from both their federalist opponents and many other antifederalists.[26] Abraham Yates wrote extensively about political economy during the Confederation period, often opposing attempts to increase economic regulation. This position put him at odds with some radical whigs and many conservative whigs. Nationalists like Robert Morris and Alexander Hamilton eagerly sought to establish a funded national debt to prosecute the war effort and strengthen the nation's economy. Among the "lower orders" there was considerable support for the protection afforded by government price controls. Yates came to oppose both of these attempts to involve government in the economy. Bourgeois radicals like Yates believed that the interests of the middling sort would be best served by minimizing government involvement in the economy.[27]

Rather than developing a coherent statement of his principles of political economy, Yates espoused a negative vision of government, one marked by economic restraint. He had seen the havoc wrought by wartime intervention in the economy. In his view government interference in the economy did "more honour to our zeal than our discretion." He reminded his readers that "the price of salt was regulated in Albany in the spring of the year 1776 and the worst consequences attended that pernicicious measure." Regulation, he added, caused "great quantities of salt that then was in, to be carried out in the neighboring states, where no such restrictions existed."[28]

The economic vision of bourgeois radicals like Yates set them apart from plebeians. Yates's economic ideology differed from the producer ideology of small farmers and poorer artisans. He opposed inflationary paper money policies that often benefited debt-ridden small producers. His economic philosophy did not favor debtors or seek to restrain the prerogatives of creditors, but instead remained faithful to the sanctity of contractual obligations.[29]

Few issues were more important to Yates than the depreciation of currency and the war debt. In late 1779 Yates wrote to New York's congressional delegation regarding the problems of wartime finance. He added his voice to many others who believed that the nation's woes could be cured by a collective exercise of republican virtue.[30] He chose a compelling metaphor to express these sentiments when he advised Americans to act like "the crew of a sinking vessel." The ship of state, he advised, would be saved by "a joint exertion" with all "hands upon deck" searching "out every hole and corner for leaks" so as to "keep the vessel adrift." In his mind the cause of the depreciation was closely linked to the extravagance of Congress. To cure this ill he offered advice that evinced his own essentially bourgeois perceptions of economics. "Oeconomy will be the best antidote against that mischiefe." Failing in such measures the public must "conclude that the money must sink to nothing as naturally as they judge of a spend thrift in private life."[31]

Yates returned to this general theme during the ratification debate, once again stressing the importance of virtuous economic behavior. As "Sidney," he argued that the economies of nations depended on the same principles of virtue as did the economic success of individuals. "Respecting *glory* & *public credit,* I will readily admit that *reputation;* that is, to be considered a man of *truth, honesty* and *oeconomy,* is necessary to an *individual,* and to *virtue, righteousness* and *truth;* to the *prosperity, exaltation* and *glory* of a republic." Economic problems could easily be cured by the exercise of republican virtue.[32]

Political economy was closely connected to personal economy in Yates's mind. The popular advice literature that filled the pages of newspapers was an important influence on the thinking of the middling sort. Yates would have agreed with the suggestions offered in the *Country Journal, and the Poughkeepsie Advertiser.* "There is . . . a certain happy medium between penuriousness and indiscreet expense, which can be obtained only by a habit of attention as well as of self government." Virtue required that "expenses . . . be regulated by the income we enjoy" and that all financial matters "lie under one's own management, and not subject to the deceit and abuse of servants."[33]

Another significant economic problem confronting the new nation was the war debt. Yates never doubted the need to pay the debt.

Rather, he questioned the wisdom of the proposals put forward by nationalists like Morris and Hamilton. The attempt by Morris to persuade Congress to adopt a plan to raise a revenue independently of the states struck Yates as an ominous sign that the nationalists sought to transfer power away from the states to a distant central government. A government far removed from the people, with vast powers to tax and levy imposts, would invariably become corrupt and would be utilized by a small minority to advance their own interests at the expense of the people. Yates doubted that investing Congress with additional control over economic matters would help the American economy. He continued to believe that more virtuous behavior held the key to economic prosperity. Even if the nationalists were correct in their economic views, Yates thought that any possible short-term economic improvements obtained by greater government control over trade and taxation would be offset by the dangers resulting from giving too much power to a distant government. Antifederalists like Yates continued to affirm the radical whig ideology of the Revolution and its suspicion of strong centralized government. By doing so, however, they lost an important source of support among urban merchants and artisans that had been crucial to their initial political success in 1776.[34]

The continuity between the ideology of the Revolution and antifederalism was readily apparent in Yates's attitudes toward the nationalists' economic program. He clearly thought that the nationalists sought to create a funded national debt modeled on the English system. Once again, it seemed, corruption threatened to undermine liberty.

As early as 1782 Yates warned several of his political allies in New York that Robert Morris "had too much power already and that Congress had better curtail him."[35] Morris's economic program conjured up the worst images associated with English "court" politics. By creating a funded debt, America would encourage the sort of corruption and intrigue that infected every aspect of English government. Financial instabilities would follow as "money men" engaged in uncontrolled speculation in securities. Such a climate would encourage venality and lead to the establishment of a "court-style" system of patronage politics.

Yates's apprehensions were not wild imaginings but rather reflected his careful reading of republican history. Corruption, he noted, had permeated recent English history with its "South sea and Mississippi Bubbles." The plottings of Morris and Hamilton were only the most glaring examples of how the unscrupulous few sought their own aggrandizement. Yates advised Americans "to look back into the history of former times; where it will be found, that ever since the days of Pharaoh, it has been a principle with tyrants and usurpers, when they conceive themselves in danger of losing, or mean to usurp a power; to distress, distract, and impoverish the people" through onerous taxes.[36]

For bourgeois radicals like Yates, corruption, patronage, and privilege stood in the way of equality. This belief led them to stress the need for governmental restraint in matters of economic policy. Yates's position was consonant with the "country" critique of the "court." Fears about the undue influence of dishonest officials merged easily with the bourgeois desire to eliminate arbitrary privilege. Yates therefore set himself against "not only officers, courtiers, idle gentry and soldiery, but also those that would be such" corrupt officials who would "plunder and rifle the citizens and country people, and so by the corruption of the government enrich themselves, or attain to grandeur."[37]

The history of New York in the pre-revolutionary period provided abundant evidence to vindicate Yates's theory. Writing as "Sydney," he analyzed the nature of class domination during the colonial period. His essays captured the central concerns of bourgeois radicalism: "under the colonial government there existed violent parties. . . . The *ins* being nearest to the disposition of the offices of honor and profit . . . had the means of making use of undue influence to retain their situations" through "obtaining patents for vacant lands."[38] By simply curtailing the power of government, Yates believed that vast inequalities of wealth would largely disappear. With privilege dismantled, virtuous tradesmen, artisans, and merchants would prosper or fail solely through their own exertions.

Yates's political economy fused conventional republican principles and middle-class radicalism. In his view the American Revolution had wiped away much of the corrupt class structure of English society. Yates accepted the prevailing myths of American exceptionalism; echoing Benjamin Franklin, he acknowledged that post-revolutionary America was largely characterized by a "happy mediocrity" populated by industrious yeomen, artisans, and merchants. Federalist schemes for a stronger central government and a funded national debt threatened this middle-class vision.[39]

The negative vision of the state that was an essential feature of bourgeois radicalism should not be confused with modern libertarian doctrine or modern liberal individualism. The ideology of bourgeois radicalism more closely resembled a set of doctrines that historian

Yehoshua Arieli has described under the rubric of collective individualism. This ideology represented a radical variant of Lockean doctrine. Property rights were sacrosanct as long as ownership was gained through industry or labor. Adherents of collective individualism deemed property illegitimate only when it was obtained through unfair access to government privileges, monopolies, or favors. Furthermore, unlike modern notions of liberal individualism, the economic vision associated with collective individualism was essentially cooperative, not competitive. Yates's image of the ship of state embodied a vision of political economy in which a mutuality of wants and needs united individuals as they pursued their own economic interests.[40] It was collective individualism that nourished antifederalists' faith in a form of libertarian politics. Antifederalism thus combined elements from both liberalism and republicanism. Indeed, the idea of collective individualism provides a partial explanation of how the antifederalists could unite traditional republican political economy with a strong emphasis on individual liberty. For antifederalists there was no conflict between the pursuit of the common good and the pursuit of individual liberty.

Notions of collective individualism are evident in the thought of another influential antifederalist political leader, Melancton Smith. Like Yates, Smith was among the most articulate spokesmen within the ranks of the New York antifederalists. Writing under the pseudonym of "A Plebeian," Smith addressed himself to the "common people, the yeomanry of the country." He informed his readers that "when a tyranny is established, there are always masters as well as slaves; the great and the well-born are generally the former, and middling class the latter." In this particular pamphlet Smith sought to contrast the oppression that would follow in the aftermath of the adoption of the Constitution with the harmony, liberty, and economic freedom that he associated with life during the Confederation period. He asked his readers several rhetorical questions about the quality of economic life in the post-revolutionary era: "does not every one follow his calling without impediments and receive the reward of his well-earned industry? The farmer cultivates his land. . . . The mechanic is exercised in his art. . . . The merchant drives his commerce, and none can deprive him of the gain he honestly acquires; all classes and callings of men amongst us are protected in their various pursuits."[41] His discussion emphasized both the moral context of acquisition and the overall sense that within the broad range of middle-class economic pursuits all interests were mutually beneficial. The Constitution threatened the utopian vision that was an important feature of the bourgeois radicalism inspiring New York antifederalists. The apprehensions of Yates, Smith, and others were a logical response to their perception that the new frame of government would undermine the position of the middling sort.

The Superiority of the Middling Sort: The Antifederalist Theory of Representation

New York antifederalists departed significantly from traditional whig ideology in their understanding of the idea of political virtue. Virtue in traditional whig republican thought was closely identified with disinterestedness; only members of the gentry and other gentlemen of refined views were deemed capable of rising above their narrow interests and discerning the common good.[42] Rather than identifying virtue with leisured affluence, New York antifederalists proudly asserted that the protection of the rights and liberties of the people "depended on the middle sort of people," whom he defined as "the yeomanry . . . the husbandmen and the mechanics."[43]

Contrary to the traditional republican ideal of disinterestedness, bourgeois radicalism championed the idea of mediocrity. New York antifederalists shared the view expressed by an anonymous author in the *Country Journal* who noted that "the Middle State of life is preferable to superfluity or indigence" and superior to "wealth or opulence." Acknowledging that this view appeared "paradoxical to the unthinking," the author asserted that a careful investigation of the effects of leisured affluence would demonstrate its incompatibility with republicanism. "The principle danger of an exalted station lies in an habitual levity of mind, which excludes the cultivation of moral improvements." Those who inhabited such a position were likely to be distracted by "a long glossy train of magnificent show" that "diverts the mind from substantial and worthy concerns. . . . they become an easy prey to the temptations, peculiar to their wealthy situation." The middle state "wherein men enjoy a sufficiency, or competency, to secure them from temptations to dishonesty and pitiful advantages on the one hand, and from cringing dependence and flattery on the other" was in the end the most enviable.[44]

If Abraham Yates was inclined by interest to historical analysis, seeking in the past the clues to understanding the sources of his nation's problems, Melancton Smith is best understood as a political sociologist, seeking to discover the social forces shaping politics in his society.[45] While recognizing that "the same passions and prejudices govern all men," Smith believed that ultimately it was rank or class that exerted the greatest influence on character.

> Those in middling circumstances have less temptation; they are inclined by habit, and the company with whom they associate, to set bounds to their passions and appetites. . . . hence the substantial yeomanry of the country are more temperate, of better morals, and less ambition, than the great.[46]

Moreover, "when the interest of this part of the community is pursued, the public good is pursued, because the body of every nation consists of this class, and because the interest of both the rich and the poor are involved in that of the middling class."[47]

Like John Adams, Smith accepted that America contained an identifiable class of natural aristocrats. Smith, however, was far less impressed by their salutary impact on society.[48] He saw little to distinguish the wealthy and powerful in America from Europe's hereditary nobility and cautioned his countrymen "to guard against the government being placed in the hands of this class."[49] Rather than attempt the impossible and banish them from government, Smith hoped to use expanded representation to neutralize aristocratic power and ensure the dominance of the middle class.

Antifederalists viewed the manner of representation proposed under the Federal Constitution as an attempt to institutionalize an aristocratic counterrevolution. If ratified, the Constitution would threaten the new and unprecedented power of the middling classes. At least two-thirds of the debate in the New York state ratifying convention concerned representation. In addition, a number of the most important antifederalist pamphleteers and essayists published in New York, including Brutus, Cato, and *The Federal Farmer,* discussed the failure of the Constitution to guarantee adequate representation. The greatest weakness in the design of the legislative branch, New York antifederalists argued, was the likely exclusion of the middling classes from the new government.[50]

Melancton Smith spoke forcefully on behalf of the interests of the middling sort in the state ratifying convention. Representatives, Smith argued, ought not to be disinterested men of leisure but should be intimately familiar with and accountable to those they represent. Indeed, he moved well beyond the notion that representatives ought to act as agents for those they represented to suggest that this was only possible if representatives actually resembled those they served.

> The idea that naturally suggests itself to our minds, when we speak of

representatives, is, that they resemble those they represent. They should be a true picture of the people, possess a knowledge of their circumstances and their wants, sympathize in all their distresses, and be disposed to seek their true interests.[51]

In contrast to the traditional notion that "the knowledge necessary for the representative of a free people" was "acquired by men of refined education, who have leisure to attain to high degrees of improvement," Smith thought that a representative's knowledge "should also comprehend that kind of acquaintance with the common concerns and occupations of the people, which men of the middling class of life are, in general, more competent to than those of a superior class."[52]

Among New York antifederalists, Smith displayed an acute understanding of the forces governing political life in the new nation. His acumen led him to probe the social basis of electoral politics and expose the unspoken assumptions guiding federalist ideas about representation. The key to Smith's vernacular sociology was his analysis of the concept of natural aristocracy. He borrowed John Adams's definition of the term when he addressed the New York State Convention.[53] A natural aristocracy, he observed, was characterized by its advantages of "birth, education, talents, and wealth." Members of this class, Smith reminded the convention, "command a superior degree of respect." He further observed that when the number of elected offices were small, political position would invariably be "highly elevated," thus discouraging "substantial men, who have been used to walk in the plain and frugal paths of life." In practice "the great will generally . . . succeed in elections" because they "easily form associations" and "unite their interests" and invariably "government will fall into the hands of the few." The superior social standing of federalists, their wealth and education, would work in conjunction with the continuing persistence of deference to ensure their dominance in politics. To counteract such advantages, Smith proposed an enlarged legislature. "By increasing the number of representatives, we open a door for the admission of the substantial yeomanry of our country." With an enlarged legislature and smaller electoral districts, representatives would have stronger ties to their constituents. Prestige, fame, wealth, or education, he reasoned, would be less likely to confer undue advantages on members of a natural aristocracy in small electoral districts. Representatives would thus closely resemble those whom they represented.[54]

Smith rejected his opponents' scheme of representation. Federalists sought to restructure government to favor the election of members of a natural aristocracy, thereby diluting the power of local government and strengthening a more distant national government. One important component of this strategy was to increase the size of electoral districts to allow men of established reputation and broad vision to triumph over men more localist in their views. Although no process could assure that all representatives would be disinterested men, federalists hoped their scheme would filter and artificially encourage the selection of refined gentlemen of enlarged views.[55]

Alexander Hamilton attacked Smith's views of natural aristocracy in the New York state ratifying convention. Hamilton confessed to his fellow delegates: "For my part, I hardly know the meaning of this word, [aristocracy] as it is applied" and countered with the observation that "every distinguished man is an aristocrat." It was only natural, he argued, that the "people . . . elect their most meritous men," and asked his opponent, "is this to be considered as an objection," adding that "it is a harsh doctrine that men grow wicked in proportion as they improve and enlighten their minds."[56]

Robert Livingston went further than Hamilton, asking who besides members of the natural aristocracy would be suitable representatives. His sarcastic answer pointed out the problem with Smith's formulation of the concept of natural aristocracy.

> Whom, in the name of common sense, will we have to represent us? Not the rich. . . . Not the learned, the wise, the virtuous, for they are all aristocrats. . . . He [Smith] would have his government composed of . . . the rogue and the robber . . . the poor, the blind, and the lame.[57]

Smith's definition of natural aristocracy failed to distinguish between two meanings of this term. Antifederalists like Smith were most concerned about the dangers of an aristocracy of wealth, power, and privilege. The problem of an aristocracy of talent was hardly an issue. Smith sought to demonstrate, rather unsuccessfully, that federalists were supporters of an aristocracy of privilege, not an aristocracy of virtue. His rhetorical assault was undermined by the structure of republican discourse itself. Within republicanism there was no simple way to distinguish between the concept of aristocracy and natural aristocracy. Unable to pin down this vital distinction so that federalists could not turn this idea to their own advantage, Smith was powerless to formulate a convincing rebuttal. The federalists cleverly utilized the inherent ambiguity within the concept of aristocracy to portray Smith as an enemy of virtue rather than privilege.

The exchange between Smith and his federalist adversaries highlights an important quality of American political culture. One of the most important myths in American history has been the idea of classlessness. Louis Hartz captured an important dimension of this myth when he observed that "America has presented the world with the peculiar phenomenon, not of a frustrated middle class, but of a 'frustrated aristocracy' . . . trying to break out of the egalitarian confines of a middle class life."[58] Ironically, it was the ruling class in America who suffered from false consciousness, not the masses. For Hartz, federalists like John Adams and Alexander Hamilton were frustrated aristocrats who failed to grasp that the true genius of American politics resided in its liberal middle-class ethos. Although extremely suggestive, Hartz's characterization of federalist thought failed to capture an important difference between Adams and Hamilton. Adams accepted a traditional republican conception of politics that acknowledged the necessity of a natural aristocracy. Hamilton also accepted a positive role for natural aristocracy even though he shied away from defending this belief in public debate. Federalists like Hamilton understood that to acknowledge the existence of a *class* of natural aristocrats would arouse the fears and indignation of antifederalists. Although Hamilton was far less intellectually honest in this respect, ultimately, he proved to be far more politically astute than John Adams, who openly defended the necessity of a *class* of natural aristocrats. By affirming the success of the Revolution in freeing America from the last vestiges of the old world class structure, Hamilton co-opted the radicalism of the Revolution to deflect the radicalism of his opponents. Hamilton understood the power of utilizing the concept of classlessness to disarm his enemies' attempts to employ a crude class-based critique. Federalists like Hamilton were not the unwitting victims of a dominant ideology, as Hartz suggests, but instead were its shrewd manipulators.[59]

The debate over natural aristocracy is a classic illustration of how the rhetoric of political radicalism could be used to achieve conservative ends in American public discourse. By allowing his opponents to set the terms of the debate, Melancton Smith left himself open to Hamilton's rhetorical counterattack. The mythic character of the American Revolution and the language of revolutionary republicanism ultimately favored Hamilton, not Smith. It would, however, be a mistake to blame Smith for his failure. Antifederalists like Smith operated within the constraints imposed upon them by the range of available political ideas. Bourgeois radicals like Smith were quite successful in redefining republican virtue and investing it with a new meaning that reflected the experiences and interests of the middling sort. Yet, neither traditional republicanism nor bourgeois radicalism provided a political vocabulary adequate for the type of class analysis that antifederalists sought to use against their federalist opponents. The fact that Smith accepted the notion that the Revolution had effectively freed America from the shackles of a European class system only compounded his difficulties in trying to make an argument about the continuing reality of class distinctions. Moreover, the notion of natural aristocracy, particularly the way it was defined within republican discourse, contained an inherent contradiction that was easily exploited by federalists. Since natural aristocracy could be defined both in terms of social class and in terms of virtue, an agile debater like Hamilton could easily exploit this ambiguity and turn it to his advantage by making Smith seem to be opposed to the idea of virtue itself. The concept of natural aristocracy was too slippery, too easily co-opted, and ultimately, was turned against Smith and his supporters.[60]

From Republicanism Toward Liberalism

Antifederalists in New York like Abraham Yates and Melancton Smith spoke for an emerging middle-class polity. Middling radicals like Melancton Smith and Abraham Yates were able to reappropriate concepts from traditional republican thought and invest them with new meanings that reflected their experiences and aspirations. The attempt by New York antifederalists to reshape republican thought is just one example of the elasticity of political discourse in the post-Revolutionary period.

New York antifederalists left a mixed legacy: they were neither wholly traditional republicans nor thoroughly modern liberals. In politics they looked forward, while in matters of political economy they glanced backward. Their greatest contribution to the growth of liberalism lay in their reformulation of an older notion of republican virtue and in their defense of a liberal theory of representation.ABraham Yates's and Melancton Smith's thought represent a transitional period in American history when an older ideal of disinterestedness was giving way to a newer notion of accountability. At this point in American history the language of republicanism coexisted with an emerging theory of interest-oriented politics. During the 1780s a traditional republican discourse was being molded to suit the needs of a developing capitalist social order. New York antifederalists inched backwards toward modernity, little realizing that their reformulation of republican principles paved the way for a distinctly modern middle-class ideology.

Notes

ACKNOWLEDGMENTS

This essay is based on a revised version of a chapter of my Ph.D. dissertation, "The Political Thought and Culture of the Anti-Federalists," University of Pennsylvania, 1989. I would like to thank the members of my dissertation committee for their help and encouragement: Richard Beeman, Richard Dunn, Bruce Kuklick, and Michael Zuckerman. While researching and writing this essay I was fortunate to have had a chance to discuss my ideas with David Narrett, Robert Gross, and Gordon Wood, who each helped me sharpen the focus of my argument. Several participants at the New-York Historical Society conference on "New York in the Age of the Constitution" provided useful suggestions, especially Stefan Bielinski, Patricia Bonomi, and Peter Hoffer.

1. On the middle Atlantic as the birthplace of modern American liberalism, see Patricia U. Bonomi, "The Middle Colonies: Embryo of the New Political Order," in Alden T. Vaughan and George Athan Billias, eds., *Perspectives on Early American History: Essays in Honor of Richard B. Morris* (New York, 1973), 63–92 and, more recently, Michael Zuckerman, ed., *Friends and Neighbors: Group Life in America's First Plural Society* (Philadelphia, 1982). For a brief overview of how the antifederalists fit into the current historiographic debate over the transition from republicanism to liberalism, see Saul A. Cornell, "The Changing Historical Fortunes of the Anti-Federalists," *Northwestern University Law Review* 84 (1989): 39–73. Two recent overviews of the struggle over ratification in the states are: Patrick T. Conley and John P. Kaminski, eds., *The Constitution and the States: The Role of the Original Thirteen in the Framing and Adoption of the Federal Constitution* (Madison, Wis., 1988); and Michael Allen Gillespie and Michael Lienesch, eds., *Ratifying the Constitution* (Lawrence, Kan., 1989).

2. Many modern scholars have followed the lead of Martin Diamond, who suggested that the *Federalist* is the best guide to the political ideas of the Constitution. "What the Framers Meant by Federalism," in Robert A. Goldwin, ed., *A Nation of States: Essays on the American Federal System* (Chicago, 1961), 21–41. Modern misreadings of Madison's intention are discussed by Paul F. Bourke, "The Pluralist Reading of James Madison's Tenth *Federalist*," *Perspectives in American History* 9 (1975): 271–95. The negative assessment of the antifederalists was most powerfully argued by Cecelia Kenyon in her influential article, "Men of Little Faith: The Anti-Federalists on the Nature of Representative Government," *William and Mary Quarterly*, 3d ser., 12 (1955): 3–43. For the most recent effort to portray the antifederalists as backward-looking republicans, see James H. Hutson, "Country, Court, and Constitution: Antifederalism and the Historians," *William and Mary Quarterly*, 3d ser., 38 (1981): 337–68.

3. Robert J. Morgan, "Madison's Theory of Representation in the Tenth *Federalist*," *Journal of Politics* 36 (1974): 852–85.

4. On the liberal character of antifederalism, see Gordon S. Wood, "Interests and Disinterestedness in the Making of the Constitution," in Richard Beeman, Stephen Botein, and Edward C. Carter II eds., *Beyond Confederation: Origins of the Constitution and American National Identity* (Chapel Hill, N.C.,

1987), 69–109. For two views of antifederalism that stress the preference of both liberal and republican ideas, see Saul Cornell, "Reflections on 'The Late Remarkable Revolution in Government': Aedanus Burke and Samuel Bryan's Unpublished History of the Ratification of the Federal Constitution," *Pennsylvania Magazine of History and Biography* 112 (1988): 103–30, esp., 103–18; Isaac Kramnick, "The 'Great National Discussion': The Discourse of Politics in 1787," *William and Mary Quarterly*, 3d ser., 45 (1988): 3–32. On the gentry ideal, see Robert H. Wiebe, *The Opening of American Society: From the Adoption of the Constitution to the Eve of Disunion* (New York, 1984), 1–90.

5. On the social history of the middle class, see Stuart M. Blumin, *The Emergence of the Middle Class: Social Experience in the American City, 1760–1900* (Cambridge, 1989).

6. Historical discussions of antifederalism in New York that set ratification within the larger context of New York politics include: Alfred F. Young, *The Democratic Republicans of New York: The Origins 1763–1797* (Chapel Hill, N.C., 1967); Edward Countryman, *A People in Revolution: The American Revolution and Political Society in New York, 1760–1790* (Baltimore, 1981). Important studies of ratification in New York include: Staughton Lynd, *Anti-Federalism in Dutchess County, New York* (Chicago, 1962); Linda Grant De Pauw, *The Eleventh Pillar: New York State and the Federal Constitution* (Ithaca, N.Y., 1966); Robin Brooks, "Alexander Hamilton, Melancton Smith, and the Ratification of the Constitution in New York," *William and Mary Quarterly*, 3d ser., 24 (1967): 339–538; Steven R. Boyd, *The Politics of Opposition: Antifederalists and the Acceptance of the Constitution* (Millwood, N.Y., 1979), chs. 3–4; Stephen L. Schechter, ed., *The Reluctant Pillar: New York and the Adoption of the Federal Constitution* (Troy, N.Y., 1985). On individual antifederalists, see Staughton Lynd, "Abraham Yates's History of the Movement for the United States Constitution" *William and Mary Quarterly*, 3d ser., 20 (1963): 223–45; Robin Brooks, "Melancton Smith: New York Anti-Federalist, 1744–1798" (Ph.D. diss., University of Rochester, 1964); Theophilus Parsons, Jr., "The Old Conviction versus the New Realities: New York Antifederalist Leaders and the Radical Whig Tradition" (Ph.D. diss., Columbia University, 1974); Stefan Bielinski, *Abraham Yates, Jr., and the New Political Order in Revolutionary New York* (Albany, N.Y., 1975); Bernard Friedman, "Hugh Hughes, a Study in Revolutionary Idealism," *New York History* 64 (1983): 229–59. Antifederalist ideology in New York is discussed by Richard W. Crosby, "The New York State Ratifying Convention: On Federalism," *Polity* 9 (1976–77): 97–116; David E. Narrett, "A Zeal For Liberty: The Anti-Federalist Case Against the Constitution in New York," in Narrett and Joyce S. Goldberg, eds., *Essays on Liberty and Federalism: The Shaping of the U.S. Constitution* (College Station, Tex., 1988). Rather than focus on a more popular political figure like George Clinton, I have chosen to concentrate on Yates and Smith because they took a far more active role in shaping antifederalist political rhetoric.

7. Among the more important offices Yates held were: state senator, loan officer for the Continental Congress, delegate to Congress from the State of New York. For further biographical details, consult Bielinski, *Abraham Yates*.

8. Jackson Turner Main, "Government by the People: The American Revolution and the Democratization of the Legislatures," *William and Mary Quarterly*, 3d ser., 23 (1966): 391–407. The broader impact of the Revolution on the democratization of American culture is discussed by Gordon S. Wood,

"The Democratization of Mind in the American Revolution," in Robert H. Horwitz, ed., *The Moral Foundations of the American Republic*, 2d ed. (Charlottesville, Va., 1979), 102–28. Historians like Staughton Lynd, Alfred Young, and Jackson Turner Main all identify Yates with the middling sort. See n. 6 above.

9. Alexander Hamilton to Robert Morris, 13 Aug. 1782, *The Papers of Alexander Hamilton*, ed. Harold C. Syrett (New York, 1962), 3:139.

10. Alexander Hamilton to Robert Livingston, 25 Apr. 1785, ibid., 3:609.

11. "The Anarchiad," *New-Haven Gazette, and the Connecticut Magazine*, 5 Apr. 1787.

12. Alexander Hamilton to Robert Morris, 13 Aug. 1782, *Hamilton Papers*, 3:139.

13. Quoted in Lynd, "Abraham Yates's History," *William and Mary Quarterly*, 3d ser., 20 (1963): 225.

14. For a similar attack on another leading antifederalist figure, see Schuyler's remarks about Governor George Clinton, in Schuyler to John Jay, 14 July 1777, *The Correspondence and Public Papers of John Jay*, ed. Henry P. Johnston, 3 vols. (New York, 1890–93), 1:147.

15. [Abraham Yates], "Essays by Sidney," in Herbert J. Storing, ed., *The Complete Antifederalist: New York and Conclusion*, 6 vols. (Chicago, 1981), 6:91.

16. [Abraham Yates], "Essays by Sidney," in Storing, *The Complete Antifederalist*, 6:91.

17. Abraham Yates, *Political Papers, Addressed to the Advocates for a Congressional Revenue in the State of New-York* (New York, 1786), 4.

18. Backward-looking Tory variants of "country ideology" are explored in Isaac Kramnick, *Bolingbroke and His Circle: The Politics of Nostalgia in the Age of Walpole* (Cambridge, Mass., 1968). For another view of Tory involvement in this tradition, see Linda Colley, "Eighteenth-Century English Radicalism before Wilkes," *Transactions of the Royal Historical Society*, 5th ser., 31 (1981): 1–19. Plebeian political ideology is a central concern in the work of E. P. Thompson, see especially: "The Moral Economy of the English Crowd in the Eighteenth Century," *Past and Present* 50 (Feb. 1971): 76–136; "Patrician Society, Plebeian Culture," *Journal of Social History* 7 (1973–74): 382–405; "Eighteenth-Century English Society: Class Struggle Without Class?" *Social History* 3 (1978): 133–65. For more on traditions of popular radicalism, see Craig Calhoun, *The Question of Class Struggle: Social Foundations of Popular Radicalism during the Industrial Revolution* (Chicago, 1982); for a different view, see Harold Perkin, *The Origins of Modern English Society, 1780–1880* (London, 1969).

19. Some of the most important and useful works on republicanism, country ideology, and whig culture are: Bernard Bailyn, *The Ideological Origins of the American Revolution* (Cambridge, Mass., 1967); J. G. A. Pocock, *The Machiavellian Moment: Florentine Political Thought and the Atlantic Republican Tradition* (Princeton, 1975); as well as Pocock, ed., *Three British Revolutions: 1641, 1688, 1776* (Princeton, 1980) and *Virtue, Commerce, and History: Essays on Political Thought and History, Chiefly in the Eighteenth Century* (Cambridge, 1985); Gordon S. Wood, *The Creation of the American Republic, 1776–87* (Chapel Hill, N.C., 1969). Historiographical assessments of these themes can be found in Robert Shalhope, "Toward a Republican Synthesis: The Emergence of an Understanding of Republicanism in American Historiography," *William and*

Mary Quarterly, 3d ser., 29 (1972): 49–80, and Shalhope, "Republicanism and Early American Historiography," ibid., 39 (1982): 334–56; Joyce Appleby, ed., "Republicanism in the History and Historiography of the United States," *American Quarterly* 37 (1985): 463–631.

20. The ideology of bourgeois radicalism is treated in the following works: John Brewer, "English Radicalism in the Age of George III," in J. G. A. Pocock, ed., *The British Revolutions*, 323–67 and Isaac Kramnick, "Religion and Radicalism: English Political Theory in the Age of Revolution," *Political Theory* 5 (1977): 505–34; Geoffrey Gallop, "Politics, Property and Progress: British Radical Thought, 1760–1815" (D. Phil. diss., Oxford University, 1983). Other works on Anglo-American radicalism worth consulting include: Isaac Kramnick, "Republican Revisionism Revisited," *American Historical Review* 87 (1982): 629–64; and Margaret Jacob and James Jacob, eds., *The Origins of Anglo-American Radicalism* (London, 1984).

21. See previous note.

22. Thompson, "Eighteenth-Century English Society," *Social History* 3 (1978): 139.

23. [Abraham Yates], "Address by Sydney," in Storing, *The Complete Antifederalist*, 6:115.

24. A fragment containing Yates's draft proposal for revisions to the Constitution is in the Yates Papers, New York Public Library (hereafter cited as NYPL). It is worth comparing his draft with the document that was eventually adopted, *The Constitution of the State of New York* (Fishkill, N.Y., 1777). The best discussion of the drafting of the state constitution is Bernard Mason, *The Road to Independence: The Revolutionary Movement in New York, 1773–1777* (Lexington, Ky., 1966), 212–53. Mason places Yates in the moderate camp, 247. See also Young, *Democratic-Republicans*, 86.

25. Abraham Lansing to Abraham Yates, 20 July 1788, Yates Papers, NYPL.

26. Jackson Turner Main, *The Antifederalists: Critics of the Constitution, 1781–1788* (Chapel Hill, N.C., 1961), portrays the opponents of the Constitution as subsistence farmers beyond the reach of the market. This view clearly fails to capture the economic vision of many New York antifederalists. Peter Onuf and Cathy Matson, *A Union of Interests: Political and Economic Thought in Revolutionary America* (Lawrence, Kan., 1990), stresses the pro-commercial aspects of antifederalism. For an overview of antifederalist political economy, see Saul A. Cornell, "The Political Thought and Culture of the Anti-Federalists" (Ph.D. diss., University of Pennsylvania, 1989).

27. On the relationship between Hamiltonian economics and "court" traditions, see John M. Murrin, "The Great Inversion, or Court Versus Country: A Comparison of the Revolution Settlements in England (1688–1721) and America (1776–1816)," in Pocock, ed., *Three British Revolutions*, 368–453. On artisans, see Eric Foner, *Tom Paine and Revolutionary America* (New York, 1976).

28. Yates, manuscript copy, "Speeches to the Delegates in Congress, 1786," Yates Papers, NYPL.

29. Abraham Yates, "To the Delegates who Advocated the Propriety of Vesting a Revenue and an Exclusive Jursidiction in the Congress of the United States of America," draft copy located in the Yates Papers, NYPL. For a discussion of Yates's opposition to many aspects of plebeian economic ideology, see the Rough Hewer Mss., 24 Feb. 1786, Yates Papers, NYPL. On

producer ideology in this period, see Ronald Schultz, "The Small Producer Tradition and the Moral Origins of Artisan Radicalism in Philadelphia, 1720–1810," *Past and Present* 127 (May 1990): 84–116.

30. See the discussion of "rage militaire" in Charles Royster, *A Revolutionary People At War: The Continental Army and American Character, 1775–1783* (Chapel Hill, N.C., 1979), ch. 2.

31. Abraham Yates Letterbook, "To the Delegates for the State of NY at Congress Dec. 31, 1779," Yates Papers, NYPL.

32. "Essays by Sidney," in Storing, *The Complete Antifederalist*, 6:100. For other expressions of similar ideas by antifederalist writers in New York, see [Melancton Smith] *A Plebeian; Brutus, Jr.;* and *The Federal Farmer.* For a general discussion of the importance of virtue to economic thought in this period, see J. E. Crowley, *This Sheba, Self: The Conceptualization of Economic Life in Eighteenth-Century America* (Baltimore, 1974).

33. *Country Journal, and the Poughkeepsie Advertiser*, 1 Nov. 1786. Yates's "Sidney" essays appeared in the *Country Journal* as did *The Letters of A Federal Farmer*, another important antifederalist essay that articulated a simliar ideological position.

34. On the importance of the fear of corruption to the ideology of the American Revolution, see Bailyn, *Ideological Origins*. Artisan support for the Constitution deprived antifederalists of an important base of urban support. On the evolution of political ideology among New York artisans, see Howard B. Rock, *Artisans of the New Republic: The Tradesmen of New York City in the Age of Jefferson* (New York, 1979); and Sean Wilentz, *Chants Democratic: New York City and the Rise of the American Working Class, 1788–1850* (New York, 1984).

35. Draft of a letter from Abraham Yates to the Honorable James Duane and Ezra L' Hommedieu, 19 Oct. 1782, Yates Papers, NYPL.

36. [Abraham Yates], "Essays by Sidney," in Storing, *The Complete Antifederalist*, 6:102–3. The importance of taxation ideology to radical whig political thought is discussed by Thomas P. Slaughter, "The Tax Man Cometh: Ideological Opposition to Internal Taxes, 1760–1790," *William and Mary Quarterly*, 3d ser., 41 (1984): 566–91.

37. Abraham Yates, "Speeches to the Delegates in Congress 1786," Yates Papers, NYPL.

38. [Abraham Yates], "Address by Sydney," in Storing, *The Complete Antifederalist*, 6:114–15. Yates developed these themes at greater length in several historical essays. Although he never finished these histories, the rough drafts of several of these essays may be found in the Yates Papers, NYPL. See in particular, "Notes on Early History of Albany" and "Notes on Early History of New York."

39. Yates quoted Franklin's writing about America's "happy mediocrity" in [Yates], "Essays by Sidney," in Storing, *The Complete Antifederalist*, 6:96–97. One of the clearest invocations of this concept occurred in Benjamin Franklin's widely reprinted essay, "Information to those who would Remove to America." A portion of this essay is reprinted in Phillip B. Kurland and Ralph Lerner, eds., *The Founders Constitution*, 5 vols. (Chicago, 1987), 1:531. For another discussion of this idea, see the *Country Journal*, 27 Dec. 1786.

40. Yehoshua Arieli, *Individualism and Nationalism in American Ideology* (Cambridge, 1964), 173, 175.

41. [Melancton Smith], "Address by a Plebeian," in Storing, *The Complete Antifederalist*, 6:142,131.
42. Wood, "Interests and Disinterestedness," in Beeman et al., *Beyond Confederation*.
43. Abraham Yates, "Speeches to the Delegates in Congress 1786," Yates Papers, NYPL.
44. *Country Journal*, 17 Jan. 1787.
45. The idea that debate over ratification involved a disagreement over "an essential point of political sociology" is developed by Wood, *Creation of the American Republic*, 485.
46. Jonathan Elliot, ed., *The Debates in the Several State Conventions on the Adoption of the Federal Constitution . . .*, 2d ed., 5 vols. (Philadelphia, 1836–45), 2:247. It is worth comparing Elliot with Smith's own notes of the debate in the Melancton Smith Papers, New State Library, Albany, New York.
47. Elliot, *Debates*, 2:247–48.
48. Adams's discussion of natural aristocracy appears in *A Defence of the Constitutions of Government of the United States . . .* (London, 1787–88). Adams felt that any danger arising from this class might be controlled by sequestering them in an upper house much like the British House of Lords.
49. Elliot, *Debates*, 2:248.
50. In "The Authorship of the *Letters from the Federal Farmer*," *William and Mary Quarterly*, 3d ser., 31 (1974): 299–308, Gordon S. Wood suggests that this essay was probably written by a New Yorker. The most recent attempt to identify the Federal Farmer argues that he may have been Melancton Smith; see Robert H. Webking, "Melancton Smith and the *Letters from the Federal Farmer, William and Mary Quarterly*, 3d ser., 44 (1987): 510–28. The ideological affinity between the *Farmer* and Smith's own thinking on the issue of representation, especially with regard to the critique of federalist theories of representation, certainly reinforces Wood's original thesis even if it falls slightly short of providing positive proof of Webking's assertion.
51. Elliot, *Debates*, 2:245.
52. Ibid.
53. For a discussion of the concept of vernacular sociology and the role that it played in the critique of natural aristocracy articulated by more radical antifederalists, see Saul Cornell, "Aristocracy Assailed: The Ideology of Backcountry Anti-Federalism," *Journal of American History* 76 (1990): 1148–72.
54. Elliot, *Debates*, 2:246–47, 244. Edward Countryman's own conclusions about the impact of the expansion of the number of government offices on the social composition of the New York State Legislature lends support to Smith's claim that an enlarged representative body would offer more opportunity to men of the middling sort, *A People In Revolution*, 198.
55. For a discussion of federalist theories of representation, see Jean Yarbrough, "Representation and Republicanism: Two Views," *Publius* 9 (1979): 77–98; and Wood, *Creation of the American Republic*, chs. 12–13. The views of leading New York federalists may be sampled in Elliot, *Debates*, esp. 2:254–57.
56. Elliot, *Debates*, 2:256–57.
57. Elliot, *Debates*, 2:277.
58. *The Liberal Traditon in America: An Interpretation of American Political Thought since the Revolution* (New York, 1955), 8.

59. For an analogous argument about the way federalists used the rhetoric of democracy against the democratic demands of their opponents, see Wood, *Creation of the American Republic*, 562; a useful discussion of the relationship between Adams's political thought and that of other Federalists may be found on 567–92.

60. On the general tendency of mainstream politics to co-opt radical alternatives, see Richard Hoftstadter's classic study, *The American Political Tradition and the Men Who Made It* (New York, 1948). The ability of a dominant political discourse to shape and limit radical alternatives is discussed by T. J. Jackson Lears, "The Concept of Cultural Hegemony: Problems and Possibilities," *American Historical Review* 90 (1985): 567–93.

MARTA WAGNER

7

Education and Politics in Revolutionary Albany

In September 1783 Simeon Baldwin, an Albany schoolteacher, delivered a farewell address to his students. In it he expressed his belief that education provided them "even in childhood a superiority over those . . . who are still bedarkened with native ignorance," but that the benefits of learning lay open to all who would take advantage of the opportunities it offered. In the final lesson he taught at the academy, Baldwin declared that "the Muses are not respecters of persons—all are welcome to the choice prizes of her bounty & it is assiduity alone that they reward with the Blessing of Merit." He knew his view did not coincide with opinions that generally prevailed in Albany. Baldwin was leaving to accept an appointment as a tutor at Yale, where he had graduated two years earlier, and in his private writings he conveyed his delight over returning to Connecticut, his native state. Since his arrival in the city in August 1782, he had become convinced that New Yorkers did not appreciate his intellectual accomplishments. In Albany Baldwin had confronted two competing factions, neither of which shared his attitude toward knowledge. On the one side stood the entrenched local elite, who saw education as a means of reinforcing status based on birth. Their opponents, who had gained access to power through political organization, also put loyalty to the group as a whole over notions of individual merit like Baldwin's.[1]

Baldwin thus had encountered more than different philosophies of education; he had entered a political situation for which his previous experiences had not prepared him. As a teacher at the Albany academy, Baldwin occupied a central position in a struggle between the two factions, who were contending for positions in local, state, and national government. By 1788, these groups would form the basis for Albany's federalists and antifederalists in debates over the ratification of the United States Constitution. Even then, a two-party system in the modern sense had not achieved legitimacy anywhere in America. Nonetheless, in Albany the structure and scope of political participation changed substantially in the course of the American Revolution. Although party development remained limited in 1788, at the beginning of the War for Independence a far different political vision had held sway in Albany. The colonial paradigm assumed that each individual in a community contributed to a single public good that promoted the interests of all. Baldwin and the school at which he taught played a small part in the transformation of Albany politics away from the traditional corporatist model toward a more modern pattern of institutionalized conflict between two coalitions of interest groups.[2]

* * *

The challenge to the entrenched Albany elite began in 1761, the year of Baldwin's birth, when Abraham Yates, Jr., ran for the colonial assembly. With the backing of the region's powerful Livingston family, he had held a seat on the City Council since 1753, but now he met with opposition from his former friends. After this incident Yates worked to build his own set of supporters, joining with others who believed they had more to gain from organizing against Albany's established elite than in trying to earn its favor. The Yates faction particularly sought to win the loyalty of newcomers recently settled in the area. This category included former New Englanders who lived in the city or in the surrounding countryside of Albany County, where small farmers were developing antagonisms toward large landlords like the Livingstons. In 1771 Robert Yates joined his relative on the City Council and the following year one of Abraham's nephews, Peter W. Yates, began to represent the first ward.[3]

These victories for the challengers made the next City Council election, in 1773, an especially heated contest. A Yates relative by marriage, William Winne, tried to unseat incumbent John Ten Broeck, a member of the established elite. At the same time, one of Ten Broeck's allies, Thomas Hun, sought to oust Abraham Yates. The contest resulted in a disputed election. Efforts to recruit new supporters by both sides required the establishment of a written set of rules to determine voters' eligibility. Although these new regulations were supposedly "founded on the Customs," they disfranchised some voters who had participated in earlier elections and one who had even held office. While Albany officials did not ignore the Yates faction's charges of bribery, they did not disqualify anyone on that account. Instead they focused on residency requirements, demonstrating a need to define the position of newcomers and transients. Testing each of the contested votes against these standards, the City Council declared Yates and Winne the losers. This level of conflict between the established elite and the challengers led by Abraham Yates still did not reach anything like party organization, but intensifying competition between the two factions introduced more formal procedures into Albany politics by the early 1770s.[4]

Colonial resistance against British policies added another dimension to the area's internal political struggles. Members of both factions united in order to contend with the considerable number of Loyalists in their midst, but their differences continued to emerge. After the outbreak of fighting in Massachusetts in 1775, Albany's Committee of Correspondence took on many functions of local government as the City Council, reluctant to oppose British rule, began to meet less frequently. New difficulties arose, however, when the Continental Congress began to appoint representatives of the established elite to offices that enabled them to exercise national authority back on the local scene.[5]

In July 1775, the resentment of privilege by members of the Yates faction surfaced in an anonymous broadside satirizing a parade welcoming home Philip Schuyler, a member of Albany's established elite. The Continental Congress had recently appointed him a general, with command of the army's Northern Department. The broadside described the order of procession:

    I   The Congressional General
    II   The Deputy Chairman and who is only Chairman Pro Tempore
    III Mr. Ten Broeck—thro' a mistake
    IV   The Chairman
    V   The Committee
    VI   The Troop of Horse, most beautiful and Grand Some Horses long tail[e]d, some bob Tailed and some without any Tails, and attended with the Melodious Sound of an incomparable fine Trumpet
    VII The Association Company

Although the comments on the horses and the trumpet cast aspersions on the whole effort by making it sound amateurish, a more important source of controversy concerned the publicity given to divisions within the Committee of Correspondence. The document implied that an impropriety had occurred in allowing its deputy chairman, Samuel Stringer (a close associate of Schuyler) and Ten Broeck (a member of the established elite) to precede the chairman, Abraham Yates. The broadside criticized this order of march for allowing social standing to take precedence over the political honor the committee had accorded to the challenger Yates.[6]

This attack, however, would not necessarily prove popular among Albany's Patriots, who were invoking the traditional corporatist model of politics in order to stifle internal dissent in the face of British and Loyalist opposition. Less than a week after the parade, the committee discovered that the author of the broadside was one of its members and its chairman's nephew, Peter W. Yates. He admitted that he had written the commentary on the procession, but he denied having "any Intention to injure the Cause of Liberty" and expressed his regret for the "imprudent" action that had "drawn on [him] the Resentment of the public." Without any opposing votes, the other members agreed to accept his "Concession and acknowledgement."[7]

The controversy did not end with this confession, even though it followed precedents for absolution of guilt within a traditional corporatist community. When Yates apologized for producing the broadside, he addressed not only the committee but also the "Citizens of Albany." The previous day the committee had exonerated Yates from a charge of Loyalism. When news of the second instance of leniency circulated, "a Number of the Inhabitants of [the] City assembled together" to challenge the committee's decision. The crowd demanded that Yates "be expelled . . . and that the Proceedings [regarding him] be published in Hand Bills." The next morning the committee "received" his resignation, but a second crowd soon gathered at City Hall, insisting on a larger role in the proceedings. This throng was willing to forego an examination of the committee's records, an uncustomary intrusion into official conduct, for Yates's "public Concession in Person to the People [t]here Assembled." They threatened to invade the committee's jurisdiction unless the members compelled Yates to perform publicly the traditional ritual of atonement for violating the norms of the community and gave them a part in bringing the deviant individual back within common bounds. The committee and Yates complied with the request.[8]

The extent to which the corporatist ideal invoked by Albany's Patriots existed in reality came further into doubt when the first ward held a new election to replace Yates. The voters chose him again. The electoral process contradicted the assertion that the crowd spoke for the whole against one isolated individual and revealed the fact of political conflict. The standoff finally ended when Yates declined to serve.[9]

Throughout these events, Peter W. Yates retained his seat on the City Council, which did nothing in this period to offend either the British government or Albany's Loyalists. With one exception, it took no formal notice of any actions taken by the Committee of Correspondence. In March 1776, the committee asked Albany officials to join in strengthening the night watch. They responded by ordering council members to poll their constituents on the issue but the minutes ended two days later without a report. That summer the committee declared the mayor, Abraham C. Cuyler, "notoriously disaffected" and banished him.[10]

With the Declaration of Independence and the removal of high-ranking Loyalists like Cuyler, new structures of government shifted the political balance further in favor of the Yates faction. In 1777 New York adopted a new Constitution and elected George Clinton governor, which enlarged the power of the Yates faction at both the state and local levels. The new state government reactivated Albany's City Council in February 1778. Abraham Yates, a member of the New York Council of Appointment, filled the key post of city recorder under Mayor John Barclay. The council began meeting again in April 1778, with members chosen by the voters of their wards to serve until the usual election day in September. In the hands of assured Patriots, it assumed responsibility not only for its old duties but also for a number of "clean-up" operations necessitated by the war and some functions of the Committee of Correspondence. The minutes of that body ended with one session to settle accounts in June, but it had ceased to meet regularly in April. Measures against Loyalists came under the jurisdiction of a state-wide Commission for Detecting and Defeating Conspiracies. Members were appointed for each county in April 1778. Those in Albany took over the remainder of the tasks formerly performed by the Committee of Correspondence.[11]

That same month, April 1778, both of Albany's political factions began organizing at the county level in preparation for the annual state elections. According to Loyalist William Smith, confined on parole at Livingston Manor, a group of twenty-five supporters of the established elite met at Albany to name a slate for lieutenant governor, one state senator (another "they left Tryon County to nominate"), and ten members of the assembly, including eight incumbents. Six men present at the meeting appeared as candidates. Smith indicated that this strategy arose in response to the activities of the Yates faction: "The Caballing at Albany is to disappoint Abraham Yates the outed [*sic*] Senator who tis said has had several Meetings for setting up Candidates."[12]

At this stage of party development, tickets usually included some incumbents belonging to the opposing faction who would certainly win re-election. Such seeming nonpartisanship attempted to fool voters who disapproved of overt campaigning as a break from traditional corporatism. Smith demonstrated the secrecy involved by mentioning the elite's lack of knowledge about Yates's candidates. Once a faction decided on a ticket, it had to solicit support at the local level. Walter Livingston told Smith that his faction "had sent two Persons to everyone of the 18 Districts to secure the Votes for the List agreed upon at Albany."[13]

The Livingston strategy apparently worked in the county, because the assembly slate named by Smith won, but their candidates for lieutenant governor and state senator, Abraham Ten Broeck and Philip Schuyler, did not carry. However, a new opportunity for Albany's established elite arose early in 1779 when John Barclay died. In February the New York Council of Appointment, on which Dirk W. Ten Broeck had replaced Abraham Yates, named Abraham Ten Broeck mayor of Albany.[14]

The political scene in Albany that Simeon Baldwin would enter in 1782 had been set by the spring of 1779, even before the founding of the academy at which he would teach. Both the established elite and the challengers were in the process of building organizations with which to win elections by getting faithful voters to the polls. Although most New York politicians kept up the appearance of faithfulness to the corporatist ideal and did not openly espouse the legitimacy of partisan tactics, Albany politics revealed a sharp division. The Yates faction, now allied with Governor George Clinton, comprised one side, while the other consisted of large landlords like the Livingstons, Schuylers, and Ten Broecks, along with such urban supporters as Samuel Stringer and Thomas Hun.

* * *

A year after Albany's local government began operating again, even as officials dealt with Loyalists and the danger of another British invasion, the city turned its attention to education. On 9 April 1779 Mayor Abraham Ten Broeck took to the council a proposal "by sundry of the Inhabitants of the City and County of Albany for the establishment of a Seminary in [their] City, for the promotion of

Useful Knowledge and the Education of Youth." The members "unanimously Resolved that" they would "most chearfully take the said Seminary under their protection, direction and care, and that they [would] at all times do every thing which may tend to its support and aggrandizement."[15]

The unanimity shown by the council members' vote reflected the general conviction among Americans of the time that education furnished an excellent protection for republicanism. Even with the war still raging, Albany's officials needed to turn their attention to establishing institutions to preserve the common good of the whole community. The corporatist ideal now required public virtue to underpin the relationship between the rulers and the ruled. Under a representative government, properly educated citizens would recognize their duty to serve the interests of all in exchange for their electoral power.[16]

In addition Abraham Ten Broeck, the mayor, had a personal motive for wanting the venture to succeed. The previous year he had become sole guardian of his nephew Stephen, the fifteen-year-old heir to the Manor of Rensselaerwyck, whose mother was a Livingston. Founding an academy in Albany would solve the problem of providing a suitable education not only for Stephen but also for his younger brother, who was also the mayor's ward, and for Ten Broeck's own son, almost the same age.[17]

These two factors, the one altruistic and the other practical, did not eliminate the possibility that partisan considerations may also have contributed to the school plan. For both of Albany's factions the proposed academy provided an opportunity to build their political organizations by gaining control over what they perceived as a crucial institution. Leaders from both sides were no doubt aware of the controversies and the influence that was contested for in political struggles waged over educational establishments elsewhere. Conflicts over the founding of King's College in New York City in the 1750s revealed ethnic and religious antagonisms and included a Livingston challenge to Delancey power. More recently the College of Philadelphia, in the city where Philip Schuyler and other New Yorkers attended the Continental Congress, faced a charter battle between its existing officers and the radical Constitutionalists in the Pennsylvania legislature. In these other cases, state and local politics had permeated educational matters.[18]

The appearance of unity about the school that cloaked political divisions among Albany officials continued to prevail two months later when they faced an external threat—the prospect of a competitor in the vicinity. Two proponents of "a Plan for erecting a College in the Town of Schenectady" attended a council meeting, seeking "the concurrence" of the Albany government. Advocates of the Schenectady proposal needed to demonstrate widespread approval of it before submitting it to the state legislature that summer. Before the War for Independence, only nine colleges had operated in the American colonies. Each new one had struggled to attract students from its nearest rival. Although affiliation with a particular religious denomination played a significant part in a family's choice of a school, geographic location had a greater impact. War had disrupted the existing institutions, including King's College in British-occupied New York City. These misfortunes, combined with the general increased republican interest in education, created opportunities for new ventures. Nevertheless, for a particular locality to gain authority from the state for such an establishment, it had to show agreement on the site in the region from which the greatest proportion of students would come. At the Albany council meeting considering the Schenectady project, the members voted to table consideration of the request. Their reaction suggested that they put their desire to control their own institution ahead of their general support for education.[19]

City officials favoring an academy in Albany had to consider the competition a nearby college might pose. To enter an eighteenth-century American college, applicants took an examination, for which they might have studied at an academy, but admission required no prior degree. A well-prepared candidate often earned advanced standing, thereby receiving a diploma at substantially reduced tuition costs. As a result, the time and money a student spent at either institution varied greatly and depended largely on personal preferences. Several colonial colleges associated themselves with classical academies to ensure qualified candidates without a loss of revenue. An academy and a college as near to each other as Albany and Schenectady, but not jointly run, would find themselves competing rather than cooperating. Whatever success the Schenectady institution might have would detract from that of a school within the exclusive realm of influence of the Albany council.[20]

A second factor in tabling the Schenectady proposal arose from the kind of education associated with a college. The Albany council had supported an institution dedicated to "the promotion of *Useful Knowledge* [emphasis added]," a function more often credited to colonial academies than to colleges. Although academies prepared some of their students for higher learning, not everyone made the move. On this issue, both Albany factions—the local elite and the challengers—could agree for different reasons. Certainly many families of the middling sort regarded practical training as the best means for their children to advance. While financial considerations explain many cases, more affluent families often deemed further schooling a waste of time and money or even a threat. Members of an elite based on birth and wealth could contend that their heirs did not need to excel in the classics in order to preserve their standing in a city like Albany. Moreover, the hurdles of expense and family background did not automatically bar all those of lesser status whose ambition and aptitude might allow them to outshine academically their social betters. Paradoxically, subjecting elite youth to rigorous tests of scholarship could as easily undermine their position as reinforce it.[21]

In August 1779, the sponsors of the Schenectady institution submitted a petition to the New York legislature asking for authority "to erect an Academy or College," without designating a preference. This strategy removed some objections to the plan, or at least delayed further controversy. Nonetheless, it could not overwhelm the opposition of Albany residents who wanted their own school. When the proposal went to the state assembly, it had attached to it 842 supporting signatures from Albany and Tryon Counties and 131 from Charlotte County. The numbers of people backing the school compensated for the indecision of Albany's City Council.[22]

Although "the unsettled state of affairs" in June 1779 served as the official justification for tabling Schenectady's proposal, Albany officials nonetheless began recruiting instructors for their own school. In this effort, the established elite, headed by Mayor Abraham Ten Broeck's family, took the lead. By July 1779 the City Council had assumed the role of the academy's governors. In that capacity, it had contacted three educators, probably to solicit recommendations. Two of the council's three correspondents had clear connections to Albany's elite. John Addison headed an academy in Kingston, New York, that Stephen Van Rensselaer had attended. Peter Wilson, living in northeastern New Jersey, had forged strong links with the Dutch Reformed church and its college, Queen's, now Rutgers. Stephen Van Rensselaer's step-father, Eilardus Westerlo, minister of Albany's Dutch Reformed church, had served as a trustee of that college, as had Philip and Robert Livingston. The third individual, William Thompson, who wrote from Pottsgrove, now Pottstown, Pennsylvania, may have made contact there with New York's delegates to the Continental Congress.[23]

During the summer of 1779, Albany's elite extended its connections in another direction. Since the local academy did not yet exist, Mayor

Ten Broeck decided to put the young patroon under the care of John Witherspoon, president of Princeton's College and member of the Continental Congress. When Witherspoon returned from official business in Vermont, he escorted Stephen Van Rensselaer to the grammar school attached to his college. Although the boy's father had also studied there, he had left before Witherspoon became president and had gone on to graduate from Yale in 1763.[24]

The tie to Princeton under Witherspoon may soon have seemed a mistake to the Albany elite. While Stephen Van Rensselaer was preparing for college, he had a suit made in Philadelphia, for which he paid more than £367. Witherspoon generally did not approve of such conspicuous displays or of the aristocratic behavior customary for the future lord of the manor. He clearly preferred expressions of republican simplicity in his students' words and deeds.[25]

Apparently unaware of or unconcerned with this potential clash of values, members of Albany's elite eager to find an instructor for the city academy actively recruited a Princeton graduate of the class of 1779, George Merchant. Having finished college just as Van Rensselaer was entering, Merchant apparently taught in the preparatory school during the intervening year. Witherspoon may have recommended him as early as 1779, giving him time to mature before going to a distant city to take charge of an academy. The council offered Merchant the school on 15 July 1780. When he failed to reply by 15 August, the minutes reflected a sudden note of urgency. The city officials not only sent him a duplicate of their earlier correspondence; they also asked Philip Schuyler, who was then near Princeton and who would soon become the young patroon's father-in-law, to intercede in person. Although Merchant took until 15 September "to deliberate," he then accepted the proposal and promised to arrive as soon as he finished "settling [his] business."[26]

* * *

On the very day that the Albany officials received Merchant's reply, 29 September 1780, internal political divisions within the City Council erupted again, in the form of a disputed election. Peter W. Yates, who had not served in the city government since its hiatus between 1776 and 1778, defeated one of the incumbent aldermen from the first ward, John Price, an ally of the established elite. Price claimed that his ouster had occurred because "a number of the voters who polled" for Yates and for the victorious incumbent, John Roorbach, "were not entitled to, or had a right to vote." This challenge alluded to the rules for eligibility formulated during the controversy in 1773. On that occasion, Roorbach had sided with the Yates faction. Unlike the earlier contest, however, the matter never came to a vote or even a "scrutiny" by the council, because Price abandoned his protest.[27]

Price may have calculated that he did not have enough support on the council to win his challenge. The outcome of a parallel case considered six months later by the same set of officials suggests what verdict Price would have obtained. Early in April 1781 John Ten Broeck, the mayor's cousin and the alderman who had defeated Abraham Yates in 1773, received a commission as Albany County sheriff from the state Council of Appointment. He then resigned as alderman, in compliance with a constitutional provision against dual officeholding. The council accepted his resignation and ordered a special election to fill the place. When Ten Broeck sought to take his oath as sheriff, however, the members voted seven to four *against* allowing him to qualify. The names recorded fit a consistent pattern of alliance for the established elite on one side and for the Yates faction on the other. The maneuver did not alter the council significantly because the third ward returned Thomas Hun, a Yates opponent, to John Ten Broeck's seat. Nevertheless, the incident demonstrated the contest for power raging during the period when the academy was getting started under George Merchant.[28]

After Peter W. Yates returned to the council, his supporters gained key committee assignments regarding the Albany academy and struggled to wrest control of it from their political rivals, the established elite. On 9 November 1780 the city records announced that "the public School" would open the following Monday. Two days later the council appointed three of its members "to examine the School Room with Mr. Merchant the Rector . . . and confer with him respecting the Appointment of an English Master." The committee consisted of three political activists: Peter W. Yates, John Ten Broeck, and John Roorbach. On 12 November, Mayor Abraham Ten Broeck reported on a meeting of the academy's subscribers, who recommended a candidate for the position. A new committee, established almost two weeks later to confer with the prospective teacher, did not include Yates, but all three members—Roorbach, John N. Bleecker, and Robert McClallan—would vote against Ten Broeck as sheriff. The minutes suggest that they did not hire this assistant. On 29 November the council considered an application for "Usher or second Master" from Sewell Chapin, a recent graduate of Dartmouth College. A committee of Yates, Roorbach, and Stringer examined him. With their approval and that of Merchant, Chapin agreed to accept the council's offer.[29]

Having participated directly in the establishment of the academy, including interviewing and hiring staff, Albany officials continued to take an active role in its affairs. In December 1780 they appointed Cornelius Cuyler "Treasurer to [the Council] for the special purposes of auditing and settling all the accounts and demands which may be brought against [it] for and on account of the Seminary." The following February they authorized their own clerk to send out bills "to the subscribers of the Academy requesting them immediately to pay to the Treasurer appointed for that purpose one Quarter's Tuition Money." At the same meeting, the council accepted an invitation from Merchant "to attend the public examination of the School." This occasion permitted Albany officials not just to determine personnel and curriculum but also to judge formally the performance of the students. The exercises would show whether the education provided by the academy enabled the children of Albany's elite to maintain their status or whether it opened opportunities for less privileged youth to achieve at least a high academic standing. After the examination, the city records revealed a renewed search for a third teacher. In March 1781, the council directed Peter W. Yates and Leonard Gansevoort, Jr., a member of the established elite, to draft a letter "with all convenient speed." In May the Albany officials set a three-week vacation at the school.[30]

With Price's futile challenge to the election in 1780 and the defeat dealt John Ten Broeck in the spring of 1781, the September city elections brought new controversies. While Peter W. Yates prevailed again in the first ward, John Price appeared to have made a comeback in winning John Roorbach's seat until Cornelius Cuyler, the academy treasurer, contested the vote. The council's scrutiny resulted in a tie, requiring a new election, which Cuyler won. He may have increased his chances of victory, among both city officials and first ward voters, by serving in the school post. This episode provided additional evidence that Albany's politicians struggled for influence over the institution not just for the sake of education but also to advance their factions. It also indicated that controlling the academy could strengthen a group's electoral prospects, at least at the city level.[31]

Despite the role of Abraham Ten Broeck, Stephen Van Rensselaer, and their relatives in hiring George Merchant, they wound up with a rector whose background fit the pattern of the newcomers who were uniting with the Yates faction against Albany's traditional political elite. Merchant's parents had immigrated in the 1740s from Germany to New Jersey, where they translated their name from Kauffman. The participation of the Yates faction in selecting his assistant also produced a potential ally. Born in western Massachusetts, Chapin came from an old New England family. Both represented the pool of non-Dutch immigrants to Albany whose increasing numbers gave the Yateses the opportunity to build a political organization with which to outvote the dominant families.[32]

At Princeton, Merchant had come under the influence of Witherspoon, who valued republican simplicity and discouraged aristocratic ostentation. At least some of the Albany academy's students, especially those seeking to maintain their inherited status, could not have found very reassuring the standards with which Witherspoon had inculcated Merchant. A sign of this discontent appeared in the council minutes in November 1781 when city officials, once again exerting their authority over the school, "requested [Merchant] from time to time to report to [the] Board . . . Students . . . guilty of wantonly breaking any pains [sic] of Glass or other things belonging to the Academy." Histories of educational institutions and studies of the behavior of privileged youth during this period have shown that broken windows often indicated more than indiscriminate rowdyism. This scholarship has concluded that the occasions, perpetrators, and targets of such incidents demonstrate a pattern of protest against academic rankings that did not conform to traditional social hierarchies. This conflict, which probably explains the destruction committed at Merchant's school, certainly contributed to the discomfort Simeon Baldwin would feel in Albany a year later.[33]

On the same day that the Albany council intervened in the academy's disciplinary problem, the city's established elite maneuvered to overcome the growing influence of the Yates faction in school affairs. Mayor Ten Broeck, on behalf of the academy subscribers, proposed to locate a new building on property belonging to Albany's Dutch church. At the same time, city officials contacted "his Excellency Governor Livingston of New Jersey requesting him to recommend a proper person as a third Teacher in the Academy." William Livingston, an ally of the Albany elite, had taken a leading part in the political controversy surrounding the founding of King's College in the 1750s. Advice from him could have resulted in a candidate whose background would have countered the gains made by the Yateses in the arena of education.[34]

Efforts to hire an instructor sympathetic to the Albany elite failed in late 1781 and early 1782. The City Council tendered an offer to John Bogart, a Queen's College graduate with Dutch connections, but negotiations bogged down. By May Bogart and John Taylor, a Queen's College tutor to whom the council had also offered a position, had both declined jobs at the Albany academy. In the meantime, Merchant had indicated his desire to leave the academy.[35]

Members of Albany's established elite did not want to abandon without a fight the opportunity presented by the two educators connected with Queen's College. Their representative, Leonard Gansevoort, Jr., an assistant on the City Council, went to New Jersey to see the candidates in person, perhaps to negotiate with them over money or other terms of employment. His mission failed, however. The following August Gansevoort billed the city "for his expenses in going down to New Jersey for the purpose of procuring Teachers for the Academy," when he learned that the Yates faction had outmaneuvered the elite in obtaining instructors for the school who would presumably strengthen the challengers' political organization among Albany's transplanted New Englanders.[36]

When Gansevoort returned from his unsuccessful trip, Peter W. Yates reclaimed the initiative. With the authorization of the Albany council and a letter from the mayor, he "went to New Haven and there . . . engaged two Teachers for the Academy," Simeon Baldwin and John Lovett, a 1782 Yale graduate. They agreed to begin in August, at a "Salary [of] £150 Y[ork] M[oney] Silver per annum," which minus "Board & washing 100 Doll. per ann. le[ft] £110." Soon after Yates's return, the council "unanimously [approved his] conduct and the contract he . . . entered into with the said Teachers . . . and . . . thanked [him] for his services."[37]

* * *

The backgrounds of both Baldwin and Lovett, from modest families in eastern Connecticut, put them in the same group of newcomers to Albany as Merchant and Chapin. If the new academy instructors found the place strange, they were by no means alone in their situation. People of diverse origins, but especially New Englanders, were arriving and sometimes moving on to take up lands and other opportunities around and beyond the city. Other single young men, besides the teachers, mingled with the offspring of colonial families. Newcomers and transients included junior officers in the army and young lawyers, studying or practicing in the state court, located in Albany.[38]

When Baldwin and Lovett first arrived in Albany, both political groups welcomed them socially. They ate, drank, and rode with members of the established elite, including various Van Rensselaers and Ten Broecks. The Yates faction not only entertained Baldwin and Lovett, but they also lived in the home of Peter W. Yates. Soon

Baldwin, who had begun to study law in Connecticut, took up his reading again under Yates's direction.³⁹

Before long, however, trouble arose. By the end of September Lovett moved out, although his relationship remained unchanged with Baldwin, who also quit lodging at the Yates house in the middle of November. Early in December Baldwin visited Peter W. Yates, who received him with what he called in his journal "hypocritical professions of friendship." The attorney urged Baldwin not to neglect his law books, implying that with his patronage Baldwin might win admission to the bar in less than the three years prescribed by the court. In his journal, he expressed his contempt for Yates's "ready promises." Unwilling to trust political power like Yates's to advance his career, Baldwin expected to earn esteem in Albany by displaying the academic and personal accomplishments for which Yale had rewarded him. He refused to ally with Yates, in order to promote through his position at the academy the system of merit he had excelled at in college.⁴⁰

Unfortunately for Baldwin, the Yates faction's political rivals did not accept him on his own terms either. Albany's established elite embraced some outsiders who conformed to their values, but Baldwin had difficulty understanding them. Just before the academy students put on a public performance, the instructors received a small rebuke from Mayor Abraham Ten Broeck for "not giving the [city] Corporation a *formal written* information & Invitation to [the] Exhibitions." Since members of the council had recently witnessed an examination at the school, Baldwin and Lovett did not expect them to attend the entertainment in their official capacities. The young New Englanders misjudged how much involvement Albany officials wanted in their academy's affairs.⁴¹

Just as Baldwin would not turn his intellectual attainments to the political purposes of the Yates faction, so he remained uncomfortable with the attitudes toward education held by Albany's traditional elite. Baldwin did not realize that his superior learning did not automatically give him a privileged position in a system of inherited status. He took offense when his acquaintances conversed in Dutch in his presence. In his journal Baldwin recounted an incident that exemplified the conflict he found between his knowledge and theirs:

> Was a few nights [ago] in a Circle of mix'd Company . . . during the whole of which scarce a subject could be introduced without some of their disagreeable *Douts sprauter*—they knew I understood none of it, therefore broke the chain of conversation & of course it would be difficult for me to sustain my part of it—I had frequently given *gentle*

hints—I was determined now to give a *loud one*. I introduced a short discourse with a friend in Lattin [*sic*], ended with *visne ambulare* [do you care to walk?]; ans[wer:] *etiam Domine* [yes, sir], with that we left them.

Never voicing any admiration for the Albanians' bilingualism, Baldwin did not try to learn the language in order to fit into the local social scene. Instead he considered foreign customs erroneous. In a similar vein, Baldwin interpreted unfamiliar courtship practices as rejections and thereby eliminated the most common method of assimilation into the city's family networks. He attributed any coolness toward him as rudeness instead of an example of social structures that rewarded personal qualities other than the ones he cultivated.[42]

Baldwin directed perhaps his greatest hostility toward the city's elite youth, whom he termed the Albany Gallants. He particularly condemned their excessive consumption of alcohol in ritualized patterns that placed the cohesiveness of the group over the autonomy of individuals. In the spring of 1782, when unofficial rumors of peace reached the city, they celebrated the news in a manner that illustrated this conflict. After a supper the party sat down to drink, electing a president to supervise the proceedings. The person chosen "required absolute powers." On this occasion, Baldwin attempted to alter their conduct democratically, but to no avail: "the Vote went against me, & the event soon proved my fears to be true, if any refused to drink what he was ordered, a funnel was introduced & some of the Company ordered to oblige him to it, nor might any leave the room without Leave." Accustomed to getting ahead by exercising self-control, not only while under the influence of alcohol, he resisted the idea of winning friends, even important ones, by taking his turn alongside the others at appearing powerless.[43]

Baldwin returned to New Haven, not only loath to deal with the Yates faction's political battle, but also uncomfortable with the challengers' foes, the established elite. Unwilling to attempt to change the situation through his role as a teacher he simply lamented the lack of recognition New Yorkers accorded to the kind of learning he possessed. Lovett, however, remained in Albany, where he practiced law and obtained land and political offices through the connections he developed. Although he did not marry into an Albany family, he proved that a New Englander could turn a Yale degree into an asset in New York at the end of the eighteenth century. To succeed, however, newcomers had to struggle to shape the conditions they encountered.[44]

* * *

Most significant of all, however, remained the continued development of political organizations in Albany. Through the 1780s the two factions intensified their contests for national, state, and local elections on the basis of popular participation—getting a disciplined electorate to the polls. In 1788, as the county's federalists and antifederalists, the established elite and the Yates challengers fought heatedly over the choice of delegates to New York's ratification convention. Both groups formed campaign committees that circulated partisan pamphlets, published lists of candidates, held meetings, and designated poll watchers. Rainy weather and the resulting bad road conditions during the election meant that only highly motivated voters cast their ballots. Nonetheless, about one-half of the adult white males turned out. The antifederalists won by an almost two-to-one margin among the 7,449 votes counted in Albany County. According to one supporter, they won every district, except the city itself.[45]

The federalists of the City of Albany, winners in their immediate locality, could not convey their sentiments across the surrounding antifederalist county to the state level. By the end of June, however, knowing that the required nine states had adopted the Constitution, they could again see success for their cause within reach. News of Virginia's ratification arrived on 3 July and increased the pressure on the antifederalist majority at the Poughkeepsie convention to join the new union. It gave Albany's federalists an occasion to gloat over the eclipse of their opponents at the national level. The timing happened to coincide with the anniversary of American independence, which the citizens of Albany united to commemorate on the Fourth of July. But before the day ended, the festivities turned into a partisan conflict that erupted into violence.[46]

A month later, however, after New York's convention had ratified the United States Constitution, its Albany supporters celebrated the event without interference from the antifederalists. They held a parade that resembled almost exactly the format adopted elsewhere, most notably in New York City and Philadelphia. The salient features of each included a boat (in Albany a fur trader's bateau instead of a symbolic "ship of state") and groupings of artisans, with insignia of their trades and floats containing workshops. The Albany procession included eminent citizens, musicians, farmers, government officials, merchants, lawyers, physicians, teachers, students, church officials, and militia officers, as well as the artisans. Although the violence on Independence Day indicated that two-party competition had still not won full legitimacy by 1788, the arrangement of the ratification parade represented the new nation as a coalition of interest groups, described theoretically by James Madison in *Federalist* No. 10. In response to their defeat, Albany's antifederalists organized to win the congressional seat created by the United States Constitution.[47]

Notes

1. Simeon Baldwin, "Farewell to the Albany Academy," 24 Sept. 1783, Baldwin Family Papers, Sterling Memorial Library, New Haven, Conn.; Simeon E. Baldwin, *Life and Letters of Simeon Baldwin* (New Haven, n.d.), ch. 4; Franklin B. Dexter, *Biographical Sketches of the Graduates of Yale College*, 6 vols. (New York, 1903–12), 4:178.

2. Richard Hofstadter, *The Idea of a Party System: The Rise of Legitimate Opposition in the United States, 1780–1840* (Berkeley, Calif., 1969), 1–80; Alfred F. Young, *Democratic-Republicans of New York* (Chapel Hill, N.C., 1967), chs. 2–4; Edward Countryman, *A People in Revolution: The American Revolution and Political Society in New York, 1760–1790* (Baltimore, 1981), 292–95; Stefan Bielinski, *Abraham Yates, Jr., and the New Political Order in Revolutionary New York* (Albany, N.Y., 1975), 48–50.

3. Albany Common Council, "City Records," in *Collections on the History of Albany*, ed. Joel Munsell, 4 vols. (Albany, N.Y., 1865–71), 1:231, 239; Bielinski, *Abraham Yates*, 4–13; Countryman, *People in Revolution*, 78, 222–25; Alice P. Kenney, *The Gansevoorts of Albany: Dutch Patricians in the Upper Hudson Valley* (Syracuse, N.Y., 1969), 84–88. The City Council referred to throughout this paper consisted of the mayor, the recorder, six aldermen and six assistants, with two aldermen and assistants from each of three wards. The colonial and later the state government appointed the mayor and recorder. The minutes rarely recorded roll call votes and on those occasions the mayor voted only in the case of a tie.

4. Albany Council, "City Records," 1:250–57; Bielinski, *Abraham Yates*, 12; Countryman, *People in Revolution*, 78, 223, Kenney, *Gansevoorts*, 86.

5. Albany Council, "City Records," 1:271–72; James Sullivan, ed., *Minutes of the Albany Committee of Correspondence, 1775–1778*, 2 vols. (Albany, N.Y., 1923–25), iv–vi, 23–25; Countryman, *People in Revolution*, 104, 108–16, 121–22, 151–52; Paul V. Lutz, "The Damnation of the Disaffected," *Manuscripts* 31 (1979): 25–45, 108–26; Kenney, *Gansevoorts*, 94–97.

6. Peter Force, *American Archives*, 9 vols. (New York, 1972 [1837–53]), 4th ser., 2:1615; Benson J. Lossing, *Life and Times of Philip Schuyler*, 2 vols. (New York, 1860), 1:346–49; Don R. Gerlach, *Proud Patriot: Philip Schuyler and the War of Independence, 1775–1783* (Syracuse, N.Y., 1987), 19–20; Sullivan, *Albany Committee*, 127–28, 134, 137, 139.

7. Sullivan, *Albany Committee*, 139, 141, 156–57.

8. Ibid., 152, 156–57, 159–60.

9. Ibid., 164, 169–70.

10. Albany Council, "City Records," 1:273–76; Sullivan, *Albany Committee*, 355; Lutz, "Disaffected," 35–45.

11. Albany Council, "City Records," 1:276 fol.; Sullivan, *Albany Committee*, 962–63; Victor H. Paltsits, ed., *Minutes of the Commissioners For Detecting and Defeating Conspiracies in the State of New York: Albany County Sessions, 1778–*

1781, 3 vols. (Boston, 1972 [1909–10]), 79; Robert M. Calhoon, *The Loyalists in Revolutionary America, 1760–1781* (New York, 1973), 409; Young, *Democratic-Republicans*, 17–29, 39–46; Countryman, *People in Revolution*, 313–14; Bielinski, *Abraham Yates*, 26–37.

12. William H. W. Sabine, ed., *Historical Memoirs of William Smith*, 2 vols. (New York, 1956–58), 2:354. "The Persons who met last Week at Albany to fix upon Candidates for the Elections were . . . Gen. Schuyler, Gen. Ten Broeck, Jacob Cuyler, Cornelius Cuyler, John Ten Broeck, Abraham Cuyler, Jerem. Van Renselaer, John N. Bleecker, John M. Beekman, Thos. Hunn, Andries Douw, James Duane, Col. Lansing, Cornelius Swits, John H. Beekman, Henry Wendle, Ph. V. Renselaer, Walter Livingston, Leonard Gansevoort, James V. Renselaer, John Taylor, John H. Ten Eyck, Volkert P. Douw, M. G. Van Bergen, Stephen J. Schuyler. . . . These named . . . for Assemblymen—John Taylor,* James Gordon,* Wm. B. Whiting,* Walter Livingston,* Killian V. Renselaer,* Peter Vroman,* Stephen J. Schuyler,* Robt. V. Renselaer,* Jacobus Teller, Leonard Gansevoort [punctuation added, incumbents starred]."

13. Ibid.

14. New York Council of Appointment, "Minutes," in *New York Historical Society Collections* 58 (1925): 59; Countryman, *People in Revolution*, 314–15.

15. Albany Council, "City Records," 1:297.

16. Carl F. Kaestle, *Pillars of the Republic: Common School and American Society, 1780–1860* (New York, 1983), 4–8; Robert Middlekauff, *Ancients and Axioms: Secondary Education in Eighteenth-Century New England* (New Haven, 1963), 116–17; Gordon S. Wood, *The Creation of the American Republic, 1776–1787* (New York, 1969), 426–27.

17. William Bertrand Fink, "Stephen Van Rensselaer: The Last Patroon" (Ph.D. diss., Columbia University, 1950), 6–7; Jonathan Pearson, "Contributions for the Genealogies of the First Settlers of Albany," in *Collections of the History of Albany*, ed., Munsell, 4:171.

18. Donald F. M. Gerardi, "The King's College Controversy," *Perspectives in American History* 11 (1977–78): 147–96; Edmund P. Cheyney, *History of the University of Pennsylvania, 1740–1940* (Philadelphia, 1940), 119–25.

19. Albany Council, "City Records," 1:297; Donald G. Tewksbury, *The Founding of American Colleges and Universities Before the Civil War* (New York, 1932), 58–59; George P. Schmidt, *The Liberal Arts College* (New Brunswick, N.J., 1957), ch. 1; Beverly McAnear, "The Selection of an Alma Mater by Pre-Revolutionary Students," *Pennsylvania Magazine of History and Biography* 73 (1949): 429–40.

20. Middlekauff, *Ancients and Axioms*, 149; James McLachlan, *American Boarding Schools: A Historical Study* (New York, 1970), 31–35.

21. Middlekauff, *Ancients and Axioms*, 119–27; McLachlan, *American Boarding Schools*, 31–34; Phyllis Vine, "The Social Function of Eighteenth-Century Higher Education," *History of Education Quarterly* 16 (1976): 409–24.

22. *Votes and Proceedings of the Assembly of the State of New York, Third Session* (Fishkill, N.Y., 1779), 26 August 1779; Andrew V. V. Raymond, *Union College*, 3 vols. (New York, 1907), 1:3–5.

23. Albany Council, "City Records," 1:298; Richard A. Harrison, *Princetonians, 1776–1783* (Princeton, 1981), 379; Daniel D. Barnard, "Life and Services of Stephen Van Rensselaer," in *Annals of Albany*, rev., ed. Joel Munsell

(Albany, N.Y., 1869), 211–12, 215; Fink, "Stephen Van Rensselaer," 6–7; Allen Johnson and Dumas Malone, ed., *Dictionary of American Biography*, 20 vols. (New York, 1928–36), 20:341 (hereafter *DAB*); *Magazine of the Reformed Dutch Church* 2 (1827): 99–100; John Howard Raven, ed., *Catalogue of the Officers and Alumni of Rutgers College* (Trenton, N.J., 1916), 7–9; George H. Ryden, "The Relation of the Newark Academy of Delaware to the Presbyterian Church and to Higher Education in the American Colonies," *Delaware Notes* 9 (1935): 41.

24. Albany Council, "City Records," 1:298, 304; Harrison, *Princetonians, 1776–1783*, 379–80; Barnard, "Stephen Van Rensselaer," 212–14; Fink, "Stephen Van Rensselaer," 7–13.

25. Harrison, *Princetonians, 1776–1783*, 380–81; Fink, "Stephen Van Rensselaer," 13–15.

26. Albany Council, "City Records," 1:308–9, 311; Harrison, *Princetonians, 1776–1783*, 273; Jack N. Rakove, *The Beginnings of National Politics: An Interpretive History of the Continental Congress* (Baltimore, 1979), 278; Gerlach, *Proud Patriot*, 395.

27. Albany Council, "City Records," 1:310.

28. Ibid., 1:322–23. For Ten Broeck: Recorder Leonard Gansevoort, Samuel Stringer, Leonard Gansevoort, Jr., Isaac D. Fonda. Against Ten Broeck: Peter W. Yates, John N. Bleecker, John Roorbach, Robert McClallan, Peter W. Douw, Cornelius Swits, Matthew Visscher. Two council members who voted with the Yates faction, Bleecker and Swits, and relatives of a third, Douw, had attended the Livingston meeting in 1778. Apparently they switched allegiances when the Yates faction demonstrated the advantages of its alliance with Governor George Clinton at the state level, possibly as early as 1779.

29. Ibid., 1:313–15; George T. Chapman, *Sketches of the Alumni of Dartmouth College* (Cambridge, Mass., 1867), 26.

30. Albany Council, "City Records," 1:316, 320–22, 324.

31. Ibid., 1:331–34. Cuyler, like some other council members now allied with the Yates faction, had attended the Livingston meeting in 1778. He married a Yates about that time. Pearson, "Genealogies," 4:112.

32. Harrison, *Princetonians, 1776–1783*, 272–73; Gilbert Warren Chapin, *The Chapin Book*, 2 vols. (Hartford, Conn., Chapin Family Association, 1924), 1:33; Bielinski, *Abraham Yates*, 8–13; Kenney, *Gansevoorts*, 88.

33. Albany Council, "City Records," 1:335; Joseph F. Kett, *Rites of Passage: Adolescence in America, 1790 to the Present* (New York, 1977), 54–61.

34. Albany Council, "City Records," 1:335–36; *DAB*, 11:325–36.

35. John Bogart, *Letters* (New Brunswick, N.J., 1914), 31–32, 34–36, 39, 44; Raven, *Rutgers*, 7, 67; Albany Council, "City Records," 1:339; Harrison, *Princetonians, 1776–1783*, 274.

36. Albany Council, "City Records," 1:339–41, 343.

37. Albany Council, "City Records," 1:341–43; Abraham Ten Broeck to Ezra Stiles, 25 June 1782, Ezra Stiles Papers, Beinecke Library, Yale University, New Haven, Conn.; Franklin B. Dexter, *The Literary Diary of Ezra Stiles*, 3 vols. (New York, 1901), 3:29, and *Biographical Sketches*, 4:178–80, 227–29.

38. Dexter, *Biographical Sketches*, 4:178–80, 227–29; Kenney, *Gansevoorts*, 118–32.

39. Baldwin, *Life and Letters*, 85, 90–93.

40. Ibid., 96, 107–8, 114–15.
41. Ibid., 107–9.
42. Ibid., 103–5, 131, 140–41.
43. Ibid., 127, 135–36.
44. Dexter, *Biographical Sketches*, 4:227–29.
45. John P. Kaminski, "New York: The Reluctant Pillar," in *The Reluctant Pillar: New York and the Adoption of the Federal Constitution*, ed. Stephen L. Schechter (Troy, N.Y., 1985), 92–94.
46. Linda Grant De Pauw, *The Eleventh Pillar: New York State and the Federal Constitution* (Ithaca, N.Y., 1966), 206–16, 266–68; Young, *Democratic Republicans*, 110, 119; Richard Leffler, "The Constitution of the United States: The End of the Revolution," in *Reluctant Pillar*, ed. Schechter, 46–47; *New-York Journal*, 14 July 1788.
47. Whitfield J. Bell, Jr., "The Federal Processions of 1788," *New-York Historical Society Quarterly* 46 (1962): 5–40; De Pauw, *Eleventh Pillar*, 268–69; Joel Munsell, *Annals of Albany*, 10 vols. (Albany, N.Y., 1850–59), 1:330–34; Merrill Jensen, Robert A. Becker, and Gordon DenBoer et al., ed., *The Documentary History of the First Federal Elections, 1788–1790*, 4 vols. (Madison: University of Wisconsin Press, 1976–89), 3:202–3, 500–512; Countryman, *People in Revolution*, 294.

Contributors

SAUL CORNELL, Assistant Professor of History, Ohio State University.

PAUL A. GILJE, Associate Professor of History, University of Oklahoma.

ANTHONY GRONOWICZ, Assistant Professor of History, Pennsylvania State University at Hazleton.

GRAHAM RUSSELL HODGES, Associate Professor of History, Colgate University.

CATHY MATSON, Associate Professor of History, University of Delaware.

WILLIAM PENCAK, Professor of History, Pennsylvania State University at Ogontz.

HOWARD B. ROCK, Professor of History, Florida International University.

MARTA WAGNER, Harvard Law School, Cambridge, Massachusetts.

Index

Adams, John, 167
Addison, John, 184
"Address to the People of the State of New York" (John Jay), 140
African Free School, 39
Afro-Americans. *See* Blacks
Albany, 17–18, 176–93; Committee of Correspondence, 153, 179–81; Common Council, 176–78, 183, 185; education, 176–93; elite, 177, 188–91; Gallants, 191; Loyalists, 178
Alien and Sedition Acts, 74, 90, 93
Allinson, Samuel, 18
Alsop, John, 129
Anglican Church, 23–26, 34, 39
Annapolis Convention (1786), 130
Antifederalists, 104–8, 151–68, 192. *See also* Clinton, George; Jeffersonian Democrats; Tammany Society; Yates, Abraham
Appleby, Joyce, 79
Arieli, Yehoshua, 161–62
Ariès, Philippe, 65–66
Articles of Confederation, 121, 130, 151
Artisans, 16, 48, 53–63, 74–93, 102–3. *See also* French Revolution; London Corresponding Society
Attucks, Crispus, 40

Babeuf, Gracchus, 103
Bakers (in Grand Federal Procession), 61
Baldwin, Simeon, 181, 188–91

Bank of New York, 105–7
Barbados, 130
Barclay, John, 180
Bawdy House Riot, 15, 49–50, 66–69
Bedlow, Henry, 67–69
Benson, Egbert, 116, 130
Bergen County (New Jersey), 22
Bicentennial (of American Revolution), 50
Black Brigade, 15, 24–39
Black Guards, 24, 31
Black Pioneers, 24, 31–33
Blacks, 15, 20–40
Bleecker, John, 186
Bleuke, Stephen, 30, 33, 39
Bogart, John, 188
Bonaparte, Napoleon, 88
Book of Negroes, 15, 29
Bourgeois radicalism, 18, 151–57, 168
Bristol, 88
British Constitution, 80–84
British–United States relations, 80–82
Brutus, 164
Burgh, James, 80
Burk, John Daly, 90–91
Burke, Edmund, 86
Butchers (in Grand Federal Procession), 61

Cabinet makers (in Grand Federal Procession), 61
Carey, "Mother," 67–69

199

INDEX

Cartmen, 52, 61, 103
Cartwright, John, 80
Catskills, 14
Chair makers (in Grand Federal Procession), 61
Chapin, Sewall, 186–88
Charlotte County (New York), 184
Cincinnati, Order of the, 52, 57
Civil War, American, 108
Class: problems of, 98–101
Clinton, George, 17, 19, 89, 104, 117–30, 180–81
Clinton, Sir Henry, 23, 32–34
Cochran, Thomas, 118
College of Philadelphia, 182
Colleges, American, 176–93
Columbia College. *See* King's College
Commerce (New York), 112–40
Committee on Behalf of the Impost Amendment, 129
Committee of Correspondence (Albany), 178
Committee of Fifty-One, 98–101, 104
Common Council (New York City), 102–4
Congress, Continental, 114–23, 130, 158–60
Connecticut, 124–25
Constitution, British. *See* British Constitution
Constitution, United States, 14–19, 58–63, 48–69, 81–85, 101–2, 151–52, 155, 164, 181, 192–93
Constitutional Convention (New York), 160, 165, 192
Cordwainers (in Grand Federal Procession), 62
Cornwallis, Lord, 39
Council of Revision (New York), 105–6
Country (party, ideology), 98–99, 153–57
Coxe, Tench, 141
Craftsmen. *See* Artisans
Crowds (New York), 48–70
Cuyler, Abraham, 180
Cuyler, Cornelis, 187

Darnton, Robert, 51

Dartmouth College, 186
Davis, Susan, 49
Death: attitudes toward, 63–65
Debt (New York), 117–18
Declaration of Independence, 74, 180
Defoe, Daniel, 68
Delancey (family), 93, 102, 108
Democratic–Republicans, 107–8. *See also* Antifederalists; Jeffersonian Democrats; Tammany Society
Doctors' Riot, 49, 63–65
Dodge, Amos, 102
Duane, James, 130
Duer, William, 106–7
Dundas, Lord, 91
Dunmore, Lord, 21, 23, 27
Dutch Reformed Church, 184

Economy (New York), 105–8, 115–41
Education, 176–93
English. *See* British Constitution; British–United States relations
English Manumission Society, 39
Erskine, Thomas, 91
Essex County (New Jersey), 22
Ethiopian Regiment, 31

Federalist Papers, 17, 50, 100, 134–40, 151–52
Federalists, 18, 29–30, 40, 43–48, 106–8, 131, 134–40, 166–67
Federal Procession (1788), 15, 48–63, 69–70, 106
Ferguson, E. James, 118
Fox, Charles James, 92
Franklin, Benjamin, 155
Franklin, William, 35
French Revolution, 74, 82–93, 103–8

Gadsden, Christopher, 114
Gansevoort, Leonard, 187–89
Genet, Edmond, 85
George III (King of England), 26
Gerrald, Joseph, 83–85, 88
Ginsburg, Carlo, 51
Gluckman, Max, 52
Golden Hill, Battle of, 102

INDEX

Goldsmiths' Company (New York), 78
Gordon Riots, 78
Grand Federal Procession. *See* Federal Procession
Grave robbers, 50–51, 64
Green Mountain Boys, 14
Groves, Citizen, 91

Habeas Corpus, 83, 91
Haiti, 22
Hallet's Cove (Long Island), 25
Hamilton (float in Federal Procession), 58–61, 106
Hamilton, Alexander, 17, 61–62, 101–8, 116–17, 130–41, 152, 154, 158–67
Hardy, Thomas, 80, 89–91
Harrington, James, 99
Hartz, Louis, 167
Hobsbawm, Eric, 51, 53
Hogarth, William, 68
Holland Land Company, 14
Hollis, Thomas, 80
Hospital (New York), 64
House of Commons (British), 84, 92
Howe, Sir William, 23, 30
Huddy, Josiah, 38–39
Hume, David, 17, 99, 112–15, 126, 136–37, 140–41
Hun, Thomas, 181, 186

Impost, 116–18
Indians. *See* Native Americans
Irving, Washington, 14
Isaac, Rhys, 51–52

Jacksonian democracy, 100, 108
Jay, John, 140, 154
Jay Treaty, 86
Jealousy of Trade, 112–15, 131–41
Jefferson, Thomas, 79, 92, 106–8
Jeffersonian Democrats, 79–80, 93, 106–8. *See also* Antifederalists; Democratic Republicans; Tammany Society
Jones, Thomas, 33

Keteltas Affair, 86
King, Boston, 23

King's College, 182–83, 187

Ladurie, Emmanuel Le Roy, 51, 62
Lamb, John, 102, 118, 123–24
Lawyers, 104
Lee, Charles, 23
L'Enfant, Pierre, 56
Lincoln, Abraham, 108
Linebaugh, Peter, 65
Livingston, family, 57, 102, 108; Peter, 85, 177; Robert, 57, 130; William, 184, 188
Loan Officer (Continental), 118–19
Locke, John, 78–79, 100–2, 155, 161
London, 48, 74–93. *See also* Artisans; London Corresponding Society
London Corresponding Society, 74–93
Louis XVI (King of France), 86
Louisiana Purchase, 108
Lovett, John, 189–91
Low, Isaac, 128
Loyalists: in Albany, 178–80; Black, 20–40

McClallam, Robert, 186
Madison, James, 17, 93, 99–100, 151–52, 192
Magna Carta, 82
Manumission Societies (English and American), 39
Margarot, Maurice, 83
Massachusetts (trade with New York), 123–24
Mechanics and Tradesmen, General Society of, 105
Medical Society (New York), 64–65
Merchant, George, 185–87
Merchants (in New York politics), 121–24
Middle class (in politics), 151–68
Middlesex (England), 75, 78
Monmouth County (New Jersey), 34–37
Montesquieu, Baron, 155
Morris, Gouverneur, 154
Morris, Robert, 118, 158–61
Muhlenberg, Henry, 23, 24

Nationalists, 118–20. *See also* Federalists
Native Americans, 35
Navigation Acts, 134–38
New Jersey: blacks in, 20–40; trade with New York, 123–24
New York *Argus*, 90
New York City and State. *See* specific topics
Northwest Ordinance, 100
Nova Scotia, 20–21, 24

Paine, Thomas, 77–80, 85, 87, 98, 106
Parliament, British, 92, 98, 106
Peace of Paris (1783), 81
Pennsylvania (trade with New York), 123–24
Peters, Thomas, 32
Pewterers (and Flag in 1788 Federal Procession), 48, 56
Philadelphia (artisans), 48–49
Pintard, John, 106
Pitt, William, 91
Place, Francis, 87, 91
Pope Day, 52
Popery. *See* Roman Catholicism
Popular culture, 48–70
Postlethwayt, Malachi, 133
Pottsgrove (Pottstown), Pennsylvania, 184
Poughkeepsie Convention. *See* Constitutional Convention (New York)
Price, Richard, 80
Princeton College, 184–88
Proclamation of 1763, 101
Prostitution, 66–69, 104

Quakers, 14, 25
Queen's Rangers, 24, 31, 37

Radicalism, 98–108; middle class, 151–68
Refugeetown, 35–37
Reid, John, 29
Reign of Terror, 85
Rensselaer. *See* Van Rensselaer
Republicanism, 74–75, 79–81, 107–8, 151
Rituals and traditions, 52–54

Robespierre, Maximilien, 85, 107
Roman Catholicism, 84–85
Romanticism, 65–66
Roorbach, John, 185–87
Roosevelt, Isaac and Nicholas, 122, 128, 130

Sandy Hook, New Jersey, 35–36
Sawyer, Lanah, 67–69
Schenectady, 182–84
Schuyler family, 181
Schuyler, Philip, 65, 102, 116, 130, 154, 181, 185
Scott, John Morin, 102
Sears, Isaac, 102
Sidney, Philip, 153, 155, 160
Sierra Leone, 39
Silvester, Peter, 153
Simcoe, John Graves, 24, 35, 37
Slavery. *See* Blacks
Smith, Lawyer. *See* Bedlow, Henry
Smith, Melancton, 18, 153, 163–68
Smith, William, 180–81
Smock, Barnes, Hendrick, and John, 36–37
Society for the Propagation of the Gospel, 10
Somerset County (New Jersey), 32
Sons of Liberty, 102
Stansell, Christine, 67
Staten Island, 22, 36–38
Stringer, Samuel, 177, 186

Tammany Society, 85, 106–7
Taxation: under Articles of Confederation, 116–23 (*see also* Impost); Robert Yates on, 157, 160–61
Taylor, John, 188–89
Ten Broeck, Abraham, Dirk, and John, 177, 181–90
Thelwall, John, 91
Thompson, E. P., 51, 151
Thompson, William, 184
Trade: with West Indies, 122–24. *See also* Commerce; Connecticut; Jealousy of Trade; Massachusetts; New Jersey; Pennsylvania
Tradition, 52–54
Trinity Church, 39

INDEX

Tryon County (New York), 184
Two Acts, 91
Tyburn Riots, 65
Tye, John, 24, 34–38

United Irishmen, 92
United States. *See* Constitution, United States
Upholsterers, 59–60

Van Rensselaer, Stephen, 182–90
Van Winkle, Rip, 14
Varick, Mayor, 86
Vermont, 14, 125
Virginia, 51

Waddell, William, 32
Walker, David, 39
War of 1812, 108
Washington, George, 61, 89, 155
West Indies, 116, 122–24, 140
Westerlo, Eliardus, 184

Westminster (England), 75, 81
Whigs: American, 55; British, 92
Whiskey Rebellion, 89
Whitecuff, Benjamin, 32
Wilentz, Sean, 49
Wilkes, John, 81
Williams, John, 120
Wilson, Peter, 185
Winne, William, 177
Witherspoon, John, 184–85, 188
Women, 65–69, 100
Wood, Gordon S., 152

Yates, Abraham, 151–68, 176
Yates, Abraham, Jr., 176, 178, 180
Yates, family, 176–78, 187–88, 189–90
Yates, Peter W., 176, 180, 185, 186, 190
Yates, Robert, 176
Yorke, Henry, 88–89
Yorktown, 38
Young, Alfred, 49